THE MORAL REJECTION OF NUCLEAR DETERRENCE

The Contemporary Peace Witness
of Churches in Eastern and Western Europe
With Insights for U.S. Churches

Edited
and with an introduction
by James E. Will

Produced with the assistance of a grant from The Ford Foundation.

ISBN 0-377-99163-5

Editorial Offices: 475 Riverside Drive, Room 772,
New York, NY 10115
Distribution Offices: P.O. Box 37844, Cincinnati, OH 45237
Copyright © 1985 Friendship Press, Inc.
Printed in the United States of America

PROJECT PEACEMAKERS
745 WESTMINSTER AVE.
WINNIPEG, MANITOBA
R3G 1A5 (204) 775-8178

CONTENTS

Introduction: The Churches' Influence on Disarmament Decisions in East and West   1
By James E. Will

I. The Churches in the Netherlands and Nuclear Disarmament   23
By Philip P. Everts and Laurens J. Hogebrink

II. The Churches and the Debate on Nuclear Weapons and Disarmament in the Federal Republic of Germany   89
By Wolfgang Huber

III. Peace Witness and Service in the Federation of Protestant Churches in the German Democratic Republic   119
By Christa Lewek

IV. The Political Efficacy of the Church's Responsibility for Peace in the German Democratic Republic — 149
By Günter Krusche

V. What the Church in Poland Did for Peace, 1980–1983 — 179
By Joachim Kondziela

VI. Structural and Functional Possibilities for the Churches to Influence Disarmament Issues in Poland — 201
By Janusz Symonides

VII. Insights for the Churches — 223
By James E. Will

To all

those historically unnamed peacemakers in
Christian congregations throughout the world,
who are eternally named the "children of God;"

and particularly to

Herman Will, brother in Christ, who for
thirty-seven years helped guide the United
Methodist Church in its witness for peace.

The Churches' Influence on Disarmament Decisions in East and West

INTRODUCTION

by James E. Will

I. PURPOSE OF THE PROJECT

The Church as Emerging Ecumenical, Transnational Actor for Peace

The church's witness for peace is so clearly called for in Scripture, grounded in tradition and necessary in a nuclear age that it is hardly any longer in dispute. It shall not be debated in this study. What is at issue everywhere are the means appropriate to the church's witness, and the long-range strategies and short-term tactics the church should use.

To speak of "the church" in the singular, however, is an abstraction that obscures many dimensions of the problem. We must speak about "churches": congregations focused on spiritual ministries to persons, families and local communities; denominations maintaining ministries of evangelism, education, health care, etc.; national churches and councils of churches oriented to the "common good" of nation-states; and the ecumenical church as a conciliar reality focused in the World Council of Churches, the Vatican and the Ecumenical Patriarchate. The missional priorities and institutional needs of these various dimensions of the churches are not, and probably cannot be, the same. Yet the Gospel of Jesus the Christ that these churches proclaim requires each and all to witness to him as "our peace" who has made us one by breaking down the dividing walls of hostility. (Ephesians 2:14)

It appears, however, that the peace we seek in congregations, segregated by race and stratified by class and gender, is often in tension with the peace with justice sought in the national common good; and that the "peace through strength" that protects the national common good is in great tension with the international peace sought by the ecumenical church. This study is aimed especially at helping resolve this second tension.

The Vatican of the Roman Catholic Church and the Ecumenical Patriarchate of the Eastern Orthodox Churches have a history sufficiently long to remember periods in western medieval Christendom and eastern Byzantium when the church took responsibility for "universal" peace amid national struggles. Since the emergence of sovereign nation states in modern Europe, however, this function has largely atrophied. The autocephalous patriarchates of Orthodox churches are now very national indeed, and the Vatican diplomacy regulated by concordats with nation-states is clearly accommodated to their governments' understanding of their sovereignty.

Protestant churches in Western Europe and the United States do not even have the memory of the church having taken responsibility for universal peace, except as it is returned to them through ecumenical conciliarity in the World Council of Churches. The national character of the European Lutheran and Reformed churches after the Reformation left them only the possibility of seeking the national common good; and the denominational character of the free churches in the United States militated against even that. Since no U.S. denomination is sufficiently representative of the nation as a whole, the definition and protection of the national common good has been largely left to the "civil religion" articulated by political leaders with fragments of the Judeo-Christian heritage. For many decades, U.S. denominations oriented themselves almost exclusively toward resourcing the local needs of their congregations.

The devastation of two world wars, however, convinced the national churches of Europe and many of the denominations in the USA that the churches must again take responsibility for world peace. The Stockholm Conference of 1925 and the Oxford Conference of 1937 had begun to recover the ecumenical responsibility of the churches for international affairs, but World War II blocked the creation of any structures for ongoing work. Following the horror of that conflict, the churches moved quickly in a conference in Cambridge in 1946 to plan for what became the Commission of the Churches on International Affairs (CCIA) when the World Council of Churches was created in 1948. More than 300 churches around the world now share almost 40 years of experience in dealing with issues of international peace, human rights, and justice.

Whatever else has been accomplished in these four decades of ecumenical work—and it has been considerable—the problem of the universal and the particular has been concretely re-established in the life of the churches. Striving for some "universal" peace and/or justice becomes formal and empty when disengaged from the very concrete political, economic and social dynamics of particular congregations in nations having a social history uniquely their own. The recent criticism of ecumenical work for peace with justice in the *Reader's Digest* and the television program "Sixty Minutes" reveals how easily the universal may be interpreted as alien and even dangerous to the national common good.

This problem is exacerbated for U.S. and European churches by the ideological divisions and bloc politics that have emerged since World War II. Many of the justice issues are confounded by the differences between churches in the northern hemisphere from churches in the southern hemisphere emerging from a missionary movement unfortunately correlated with centuries of European colonialism. The more formidable problem for this study, however, is the East-West division between communist and capitalist ideologies institutionalized in the bloc politics of the North Atlantic Treaty Organization (NATO) and Warsaw Pact (WPO) alliances.

World military spending will exceed $1 trillion in 1985, according to the U.S. Arms Control and Disarmament Agency; the NATO and WPO countries between them account for about 75 percent of that world total. With $750 billion of military commitment to "peace through strength" strategies, it is obvious that no government on either side of this terrible division is about to allow its national policy easily to be affected by the peace perspectives of the ecumenical church. The two sides make it clear to anyone with sufficient temerity to address the issue, that defense and foreign policy are the prerogative of sovereign governments which alone have sufficient "intelligence" and diplomatic experience to make wise judgments.

The fact remains, however, that the ecumenical church constitutes an alternative international network with its own intelligence gathered from congregations in every village, city and nation, interpreted from a perspective on creation and redemption oriented to the universal common good, of worldwide *shalom*. The Sixth Assembly of the World Council of Churches, meeting in Vancouver in 1983, appealed to all churches to:

> a. challenge military and militaristic policies that lead to disastrous distortions of foreign policy;
>
> b. counter the trend to characterize those of other nations and ideologies as the "enemy" through the promotion of hatred and prejudice;
>
> c. assist in demythologizing current doctrines of national security and elaborate new concepts of security based on justice and the rights of the peoples.

Speaking more specifically to the nuclear arms race that is the subject of this study, the delegates from 300 churches went on to say:

We call upon the churches, especially those in Europe, both East and West, and in North America, to redouble their efforts to convince their governments to reach a negotiated settlement and to turn away now, before it is too late, from plans to deploy additional or new nuclear weapons in Europe, and to begin immediately to reduce and then eliminate altogether present nuclear forces.[1]

Almost every major denomination in the USA has also officially spoken to this issue in the last several years. The Fellowship of Reconciliation published the statements of twenty-five U.S. denominations in 1983.[2] Not all are as specific on the issue of nuclear weapons as the statement adopted by the United Methodist General Conference in 1980 and reaffirmed in 1984, but it may be taken as one representative statement:

We believe war is incompatible with the teachings and example of Christ. We therefore reject war as an instrument of national policy and insist that the first moral duty of all nations is to resolve by peaceful means every dispute that arises between or among them; that human values must outweigh military claims as governments determine their priorities; that the militarization of society must be challenged and stopped; that the manufacture, sale and deployment of armaments must be reduced and controlled; and [speaking specifically to our issue] *that the production, possession, or use of nuclear weapons be condemned.* (Emphasis added)

The Quest for Authenticity in Peace Witness and Action

Because peace work inevitably involves a political dimension, as the above statements already indicate, it is crucial that the churches continue to clarify the grounding of their political perspectives in the Gospel. This is relatively easy when the churches articulate only their ultimate vision of *shalom*, but becomes increasingly difficult as they apply their vision to alternative policies of national security and even to specific weapons systems. There usually has been little concern as long as the churches at least tacitly support the national security policies of their governments and the weapons systems judged necessary to implement them.[3] But a "hermeneutic of suspicion" has grown in the churches since World War II, which submits the ideologies and civil religions of national cultures to more careful theological scrutiny. The churches are increasingly unwilling to give even tacit consent to national policies appearing to endanger the basic ecological, economic and political foundations of the universal common good.

The most influential recent instance of this kind of deliberation in the U.S. was the Roman Catholic bishops' pastoral letter on "The Challenge of Peace" of May 3, 1983.[4] Basing their discussion largely on the theological and moral principles of Vatican Council II's pastoral constitution on "The Church in the Modern World" (*Gaudium et spes*), the bishops condemned counter-population warfare as murder; concluded, contrary to NATO policy, that the first use of nuclear weapons cannot be morally justified; and placed strict conditions on the moral acceptance of a policy of nuclear deterrence. As former national security advisor McGeorge Bundy commented, the moral conditions specified are more important than the conditional acceptance of deterrence, because they force a public debate of the very foundations of American security policy. Officials of the government of the USA took this debate sufficiently seriously to engage in the bishops' discussion between the second and third drafts of this important document. Though this led to the inclusion of the government's views on U.S. targeting policy, U.S. security officials did not change the bishops' minds about advocating a "halt to" testing, production and deployment of new nuclear weapons systems, nor their condemnation of NATO's "first use" nuclear policy.

The bishops used moral principles derived from a theology of peace and "just war" criteria to assess policy options. Their doing so aroused such concern in the apparently more conservative West German and French episcopates that the Vatican convened a meeting in January 1983 which led the U.S.

bishops to specify the levels of moral authority of their various teachings: The moral principle that prohibits counter-population warfare is judged absolute (Par. 148). Their condemnation of resorting to nuclear weapons to counter a conventional attack as "morally unjustifiable" (Par. 153), however, is classified as a prudential judgment that "allows for different opinions" (Footnote 69 attached to Par. 153) and recognizes that time must be allowed for the "development of an adequate alternative defense posture" (Par. 156). Thus the bishops recognize the ambiguities of applying Christian moral principles to specific policy options while courageously entering into the moral assessment of crucial national policies.

The issue of grounding political perspectives in the Gospel may be even more important for churches in Eastern European states with communist governments. Though these Eastern countries have a separation of church and state similar to the USA, there is little political tolerance for the kind of pluralism found in Western societies. All social structures except the church are subordinated to the state's ideological power. The only contrary ideology tolerated is the church's, because it is recognized as a transnational theology that has deeply permeated their national cultures for centuries. The 1983 "pilgrimage" of Pope John Paul II to Poland and the 1983 national celebration of the five hundredth anniversary of Luther's birth in the German Democratic Republic are indications of this historical reality.

This reduction of ideological pluralism to only two possibilities both enhances and endangers the churches' sociopolitical influence. The church alone provides the social space for articulating a moral critique of national policy, but it is necessary that such a critique be clearly based in a "universal" Christian theology. The churches may not practice a national counter-politics, but may and do articulate the implications of an ecumenical counter-ideology/theology. As we shall see later, this is why it is so crucially important for the church in East Germany to base its peace witness and action on the ecumenical moral principles of the World Council of Churches,[5] and for the church in Poland to base itself on the universal teachings of the Vatican.[6] Only then is any opposition to national military policies clearly a universal implication of Christian faith, not anti-communist national politics.

This need for clear theological grounding of the churches' peace witness also explains why the opposition to nuclear weapons in Europe, and perhaps especially in East Germany, is beginning to be discussed in terms of *status confessionis*.[7] This Latin phrase, still strange to American ears, means the act of witnessing to the Gospel in an extraordinary situation which sets the integrity of the Gospel itself at stake. It entered recent ecumenical discussion in the World Alliance of Reformed Churches and the Lutheran World Federation in relation to the churches' witness against apartheid in South Africa. Some have begun to use this concept to urge that the issue of nuclear weapons is of sufficient gravity for the Christian conscience to require resistance as an act of faith both to their use and their possession, even if only for "deterrence." Whatever our theological judgment on this issue, it underlines the importance for many European Christians of grounding their opposition to the nuclear arms race theologically.

All churches willing to take democratic responsibility for helping shape national policies on peace face the dilemma posed for them by their states' "peace through strength" policies. Every sovereign government clearly bears responsibility for national defense. The right of defense against aggression is recognized in the moral teachings of almost every church. The tension in this dilemma was defined twenty years ago by Reinhold Niebuhr's critique of John XXIII's *Pacem in terris* for failing to understand that in a world of nation-states it is impossible to realize the balance between national and international values that John XXIII sought.[8] The present almost anarchic character of international law, exacerbated by East-West bloc politics, gives substance to Niebuhr's judgment and reveals the reason why the churches have been so slow to press their resistance to the policy of nuclear deterrence.

Though this dilemma persists, the nuclear arms race has now reached such absolutely dangerous proportions as to shift the weight of its "horns." The necessity of national defense in an anarchic world no longer can be given moral precedence over the necessity to preserve the very possibility of human culture in so terribly endangered a world. "Just war" criteria refined over centuries by the church—especially the criteria of proportionality and discrimination—limit the violence any state may morally intend to use to protect national values. In simplest terms, no government defense policy or action that destroys more than it saves may be morally supported by the churches. Forty years into the nuclear era, most churches are convinced that "peace through nuclear strength" is no longer a morally supportable defense policy.

The churches increasingly recognize that the mass bombings of London, Coventry, Hamburg, Dresden, Tokyo, Hiroshima and Nagasaki during World War II inaugurated an age of "total war." The limits on conventional war laid down, for instance, in the Hague Conventions of 1907 were violated in a way that continues to lead toward complete brutality. The weapons of mass destruction now implementing national defense policies constitute so criminal a threat to innocent populations that a war to safeguard justice fought with them is simply no longer possible. Preparations for a possible war to protect Western democracy or Eastern socialism using such weapons turns whole populations toward the moral acceptance of mass murder. Thus the churches increasingly recognize that to be pastorally responsible for the care of souls in such a situation requires resolute political action. They grasp the horns of this dilemma as they begin to teach more clearly that no national defense policy in a nuclear age may be built on even the threat to use weapons of indiscriminate mass destruction.

To oppose national policies established for thirty years sets the churches on a collision course with the ideological and religious justifications for nuclear deterrence now politically accepted in East and West: the enemy images promulgated by religious anti-communism in the West and ideological class-enmity in the East. In both cases, the churches open themselves to charges of being idealistically "soft" in their assessment of the enemy and a dangerously manipulable "fifth column" within their own societies. It becomes increasingly crucial for the churches, then, not only to be able to differentiate their ideologies ever more clearly from national ideologies and civil religions, but also to articulate similar policy proposals in both East and West arrived at by ecumenical consensus.

Ecumenical consensus, however, cannot mean absolute similarity of church witness and action in such disparate societies. The relatively small size of the Netherlands, for instance, makes modes of witness and action feasible there that are simply impossible and perhaps unwise in much larger and militarily more powerful societies like West Germany or the USA. The national character of the Polish Roman Catholic Church provides possibilities that denominations in the pluralistic ethos of the USA cannot hope to imitate. The affinity between much in American civil religion and American churches is so different from the tension between East German churches and some of Marxist ideology that the social possibilities and limits of one are not transferable to the other. Thus we should not expect or even want entirely parallel national efforts from the churches as they seek to resolve this common international threat. What we can look for, and may indeed increasingly see, however, are highly analogous modes of witness and action by churches in these very different societies.

This study therefore has been carried out by colleagues in five nation-states with the following shared purposes:

1. To test whether the churches' influence for arms control and disarmament is in any ways reciprocal in both East and West;
2. To examine the authenticity of the churches' positions on disarmament in relation to the national policies of their governments;
3. To compare the possibilities for social/political influence for disarmament of churches in societies with diverse social, economic and political systems;

4. To elucidate the ecumenical/international relations of the churches as they learn from and support each other's disarmament efforts; and,
5. To share this research with U.S. churches to strengthen their peace witness in ecumenical solidarity; and perhaps to extend this research in a second phase to churches in the USA and even the USSR.

II. METHODOLOGICAL ISSUES

The Variety of Ecclesial and Political Traditions

Analysis of the churches' witness and action for peace and nuclear disarmament in five different societies confronts several difficult methodological issues. The first of these arises out of the variety of ecclesial and political traditions in these five nation-states. We noted near the conclusion of the last section that we cannot expect "absolute similarity of church witness and action in such disparate societies." We cannot make one-to-one comparisons of U.S. denominations in a free church tradition with national churches, some of which were state churches, in both the Roman Catholic and Reformation traditions.

These issues usually are dealt with under the category of church-state relations. They have become so important in our contemporary, highly dynamic world that the World Council of Churches brought fifty representatives from various countries on every continent together in a colloquium in 1976 to study them. They published their report with reflections on various situations as Faith and Order Paper No. 85: *Church and State: Opening a New Ecumenical Discussion.*[9] This careful study developed many insights, but it is remarkable that at no point in its 180 pages is there any discussion of the church-state problematic as it relates to the churches' witness and action for peace and disarmament.

What is recognized throughout this WCC study is that traditional answers are proving increasingly inadequate, not least because the new realities created by the ecumenical movement require every church now to take other churches into account as church-state relations are defined. The universality of the church has been translated in our twentieth century from a faith reality into a historical reality. Churches now must find ways and means of taking their obligations to the international community just as seriously as they take their obligations to the particular states in which they live and bear witness.[10]

Addressing this thorny issue of the universal mission of the church and church-state relations in their report, the WCC colloquium noted:

> There is in the world today a strong tension, often a conflict between universal and particular perspectives. In the course of the last centuries and decades, the world has been drawn more and more by scientific, technological, economic and political developments into one system. . . . It is becoming less and less possible to respond both to God's promise and the power which threaten the future on less than an international scale. . .
>
> Though drawn into one system, the world is as sharply, if not more sharply, divided than ever before. . . . There is not yet genuine interdependence among the nations. Their relations are distorted by political and ideological domination, economic exploitation, racial discrimination, etc.[11]

Our study of the churches' peace witness and action addresses some of the political and ideological issues only pointed to in this earlier study that make difficult the churches achieving a universal witness in their various national contexts. Yet it is not only issues that divide our world which complicate the churches' universal witness, but the continuing formative power of different ecclesiologies in the confessional traditions that shape church-state relations in the various nations. The WCC Consultation clarified these confessional factors by elaborating the following categories:

1. *The collaborative relationship of Church and state:*[12] The Roman Catholic tradition (represented in our study principally by

Poland) "... sees Church and state, ideally speaking, as two *societates perfectae*. The first is eternal, the latter temporal. They do not stand in opposition, but overlap each other.... Fundamentally, this view enables a collaborative relationship of Church and state. The Church, on the one hand, keeps in mind that it is responsible for the common good of all.... The state, on the other hand, accepts this service and provides the Church with the freedom to exercise its religion in all its dimensions."

2. *The complementary relationship* of Church and state:[13] The Lutheran tradition (represented in our study principally by the two German states) "has evolved in contrast both to the Catholic model of cooperation and the Anabaptist emphasis on protest.... The model of the two kingdoms or realms intends to distinguish between the two powers by which God both conserves the world and evangelizes it by his word of grace. To achieve this, God uses two authorities: the state is endowed with the authority to order the world and may, in pursuit of this, use force. The Church has the mandate to preach and enact the Gospel but without force."

3. *The inspirational and transforming* relationship of Church and state:[14] The Reformed Tradition (represented in our study principally by the Netherlands, and powerful in the briefer tradition of the WCC through the theology of Karl Barth) "sees Church and state ... as two more or less concentric spheres. Both spheres are subject to the kingship of Christ over all creation. Both are called to move ahead toward the realization of his kingdom.... The Church has the inspirational and transforming task to remind the state that it is not autonomous. It, too, has a share in the advancement of the kingdom. There is here the constant tension of the eschatological dimension inspiring and penetrating the ordering of human affairs. There exists the danger that the possible worldly manifestation of the eschatological hope is betrayed for the sake of a false utopianism. On the other hand, there is the danger of losing sight of the eschatological transcendence for the sake of some immediate goals."

Though not everything may be explained by these traditional confessional differences, readers of the following chapters who have them in mind will be better enabled to interpret some of the differences in the peace and disarmament work of the churches. The fact that the *churches in the Netherlands have been more directly politically active than the others to transform* their government's military policies becomes more understandable. The relatively greater concern of the *German churches to ground their peace witness theologically* and to characterize it primarily as witness rather than political action is likewise illumined. The stance of the *Polish Roman Catholic church* as it *"collaborates"* with a communist state to seek Poland's national common good, while communicating to their government the Vatican's concern to set the national common good within a framework of the international common good, should also be more readily understood.

These traditional confessional differences, however, must also be seen in their relation to the various juridical understandings of church-state relations. The WCC study differentiates these with the following categories:[15]

1. *The secularist state:* where public affairs are dominated by a secularist ideology actively promoted by the state; and where the churches' participation in public life may be tolerated or not.
2. *The neutral state:* in which the state seeks to be neutral with respect to the validity of religious ideas and practices. Historically this takes three forms: a) where Christian predominance is assumed; b) where predominance of a non-Christian religion is assumed; or c) where a multiplicity of religions is assumed, none of which is predominant.
3. *The "Christian" state:* where a Christian church is established or recognized by the state as a "folk" church.

These categories are helpful for our study if their abstract nature is remembered. All states have a long history and are in dynamic development, so they must be more concretely understood in terms of their transitions from one of these forms to another. It is obvious that the USA is in transition from category 2a toward 2c, as the Supreme Court continues to interpret our constitution. The Netherlands, Germany and Poland all have once been in category 3 with national and state churches, though none any longer completely are. Poland and the German Democratic Republic are now in category 1, with strong tendencies toward 2a because both still clearly have a national "folk" church. The Netherlands and the Federal Republic of Germany are now clearly in 2a, though some characteristics of the "folk" church continue to characterize especially the Evangelical Church of Germany, and to a lesser extent, the Netherlands Reformed church.

The basic difference between all U.S. denominations and the churches of the Netherlands, both Germanies and Poland is that all of these European societies have had, and perhaps except for the Netherlands, continue to have a national folk church. This is less true for the Federal Republic of Germany because of the relatively equal size of the formerly established Evangelical Church and the Roman Catholic Church, although here the tax structure of the state continues to support these major churches through the church tax. Even though there is no church tax in the German Democratic Republic or Poland, it is clear that the regional Evangelical churches organized in their increasingly effective *Bund* (Federation) remain in many ways a national folk church in the GDR, and that this is overwhelmingly the case for the Roman Catholic Church in Poland, which incorporates more than 90 percent of the Polish people in its membership.

The continuing influence of these European juridical traditions means that the churches in the Netherlands, the Germanies and Poland have a long history of direct involvement in the public policies of their states. It thus remains more "natural" for them to have a sense of responsibility for public policy than it is for the churches in the USA. The fact that these national folk churches now exist in secularist or neutral states also means that they now have greater opportunity to distance themselves from what was once their greater ideological dependence on their governments.

The denominationally pluralist character of U.S. religious life in a juridically "neutral" state throughout our history has meant that no one church could ever be a national church for our people, despite the predominance of Christianity in U.S. society. This situation inevitably gave rise to a powerful "civil religion." Professor Sydney Mead wrote in his essay, "The Nation with the Soul of a Church," that "in a very real sense the nation for many Americans came to occupy the place in their lives that traditionally has been occupied by the church."[16] When the churches of the USA have sought ecumenically through the National Council of Churches, in relation with the World Council of Churches, to define positions in public policy concerning national security and disarmament, they often have found themselves in strong tension with the more nationalist dimensions of the civil religion articulated by national political leaders. The fact that President Ronald Reagan, as President Nixon before him, refuses even to meet with the leaders of the U.S. National Council of Churches of Christ to discuss policy issues is a dramatic case in point.

Understanding these church-state relational differences enables more adequate interpretation of the varying modes of church witness and action for peace and disarmament in the five societies studied in this project. One cannot expect identical actions from churches that traditionally have understood the church-state relation as collaborative, complementary or transforming. Nor can one expect the same kind of socio-political influence from free churches in a neutral state as from national churches in a secularist state. Yet all of these church-state traditions are in the process of being altered in our twentieth century by the emergence of ecumenical church structures and relations in a world that internationally is increasingly one system. The crucial consequence for this study is to learn how to affirm the authenticity of the differentiated peace work and witness of them all, while remaining critically open to learnings that may enhance the ecumenically related work of each.

Difficulties in Assessing Socio-Political Influence

Professor Wolfgang Huber, one of the contributors to this study, earlier wrote the paper for the WCC colloquium on church and state in the Federal Republic of Germany. Commenting on what has been learned from the history of the German church's transition from an established national church to an autonomous church in a neutral state, he wrote:

> We can then conclude that the development of an independent church order which has as criterion the commission to preach the Gospel depends on there being a certain distance between the Church and the State. . . . This development has another side to it: the opportunities for the Church to influence public life diminish.[17]

Thinking further about what his church had learned from the Barmen Declaration of 1934 as it responded to the challenge of national socialism, he also wrote:

> The Church which submits itself to the sovereignty of Christ cannot, at the same time, be subject to the sovereignty of the state but must resist every total claim to power on the part of the state. Even the Church's public action is determined by the sovereignty of Christ: its criterion for state action is the duty of the state to strive for peace and justice.[18]

These reflections from the West German context of this study define an issue crucial for the whole study: How do churches, whose independence of, and separation from, the state diminish their opportunity to influence public policy, nevertheless affect state action for peace and justice in a discernible, if not measurable, way?

Dr. Philip Everts, another contributor to this study, from his vantage point as director of the Institute for International Studies of Leiden University, has reflected and written extensively on methodological issues in assessing the churches' influence on foreign policy.[19] He has noted that, though "influence" is a core concept in political science, it lacks agreed definition and can seldom be measured precisely, or even observed empirically in less precise ways. Yet no one doubts that "influence" exists as an ability to affect or change the likelihood of particular decisions or events. Influence may be seen as a continuum reaching from a pole of force and coercion to a pole of argument and persuasion. When seen on such a continuum, it becomes obvious that churches with little access to direct political power or economic sanctions in secularist or neutral states must find their influence largely near the pole of moral persuasion.

All governments, however, are subject to many internal and external influences. Since the real world is no laboratory, how is one to separate out the persuasive power of the church in affecting any governmental policy or behavior? The obvious answer of asking the decision-makers themselves runs into their general tendency not to admit any changes in policy and their general reluctance to admit having been influenced by certain persons, groups or ideas. Political leaders, that is, are concerned to project their integrity and independence. Though some will admit, or even proclaim, the basic influence of their religious faith on their political ethic, the separation of church and state in a religiously pluralistic society makes them very reluctant to admit the influence of any particular church or churches on any specific decision.

Dr. Everts thus suggests that if there is a consistent deviation from earlier declared goals of the government, there is a strong indication of the probability of external influence; and if there is congruence between these deviations in policy and the persuasive positions of others, say churches, then there is some basis for the hypothesis of influence. Even this, however, may not be taken for granted.

Because it is so difficult to establish or measure the exercise of influence directly, one can also look at the degree to which a number of conditions that *prima facie* appear to have an impact on the ability to exercise influence are fulfilled. Some of these conditions are:

1. The character and size of the group's support of the positions they advocate, both in terms of numbers of persons and their perceived depth of commitment.

2. The legitimacy and respectability of the group, in terms of moral authority, expertise and social prestige.
3. The degree of access of the group to decision-makers, either directly or indirectly through intermediaries and/or public opinion.
4. The amount of resources of organizational experience in, and financial support for, the group.
5. The availability of action strategies to mobilize people and sustain influence.
6. The timing on the public agenda, so as to be neither too early nor too late in the policy-making process.

Readers of this study will do well to keep these "conditions for public influence" in mind as they read the reports and analyses of our European authors, as well as when they reflect about the influence of U.S. churches. Some, notably the churches in the Netherlands, are in a position to point to some "consistent deviations" from their government's earlier declared goals as a basis for the hypothesis of church influence. Most, however, are not able to point to such deviations. All give important insights into how their churches meet these conditions for influence. The evidence is inadequate, however, to make judgments about the degree of influence the various churches have had on security and disarmament policies. What is clear is that the possibilities for such influence exist in all of these societies, and the churches are increasingly diligent in making use of these possibilities.

Research by Participant Observers

The last methodological issue to be noted is that the research for and writing of this study was done in each case by "participant observers." All of the authors are active leaders in the churches' peace witness in their societies, except Professor Symonides of Poland; and even he, from his position as director of the Polish Institute of International Affairs, strongly supports the churches' peace witness and is deeply involved in education for peace through UNESCO and in his own society. All of our authors, however, are also carefully trained scientifically to weigh evidence and objectively report their findings. Five have been, and four are, university or seminary professors; one is a university institute director; and three have responsible leadership positions in their churches or church-related agencies.

Such direct participation in the churches' peace witness guarantees strong motivation for carrying through a study of the churches' influence on disarmament, as well as access to important data. What we have then is an action-reflection methodology that approximates the praxis method of liberation theology and ethics. The question of necessary objectivity, however, inevitably arises. Adequate response to this question involves the insight that it is doubtful that we ever enhance our objectivity by reducing our participation in the social processes we are seeking to understand. The usual result of such abstraction is only a dulling of our sensitivities to many of the dimensions of the living matrix in which we have our being. Karl Mannheim, author of the classic study on ideology, supports this perspective:

> Man [sic] attains objectivity and acquires a self with reference to his conception of the world not by giving up his will to action and holding his evaluation in abeyance, but in confronting and examining himself. The criterion of such self-illumination is that not only the object but we ourselves fall squarely into our field of vision. We become visible to ourselves, not just vaguely as a knowing subject as such but in a certain role hitherto hidden from us, in a situation hitherto impenetrable to us, and with motivations of which we have not hitherto been aware. In such moments the inner connections between our role, our motivations, and our type and manner of experiencing the world suddenly dawns upon us.[20]

The self-awareness of our authors and of ourselves is a better guarantor of objectivity than actionless neutrality on the crucial issues being investigated in this study.

None of us, nevertheless, may be judges in our own case. Thus this study also has engaged an outside expert, Dr. Christoph Bertram, political editor of the important West German newspaper *Die Zeit* and former director of the International Institute for Strategic Studies in London, to review all of the essays. The authors alone take responsibility for the final form of their chapters.

NOTES

1. The World Council of Churches Sixth Assembly, 24 July–10 August, 1983, Vancouver B.C., Canada, Statement on "Peace and Justice," pars. 12 and 16.
2. John Donaghy, ed., *To Proclaim Peace: Religious Communities Speak Out on the Arms Race*, Nyack, N.Y.: Fellowship Publications, 1983; the United Methodist statement taken from its "Social Principles" is on p. 46.
3. See, for instance, the judgment of the Central Committee of German Catholics quoted in Huber, pp. 106, 107.
4. The National Conference of Catholic Bishops, *The Challenge of Peace: God's Promise and Our Response*, Washington, D.C.: U.S. Catholic Conference, 1983.
5. Cf. the essays of Günter Krusche and Christa Lewek.
6. Cf. the essay by Joachim Kondziela.
7. See the discussion by Günter Krusche on pp. 152, 154–157 and 159; and cf. Wolfgang Huber, pp. 103, 104.
8. Cited by Bryan Hehir in "The Relationship of an Ethic of War and a Theology of Peace," a paper read to the Society of Christian Ethics, January 20, 1984, Philadelphia, Pa.
9. *Church and State: Opening a New Ecumenical Discussion*, Faith and Order Paper No. 85, Geneva: World Council of Churches, 1978.
10. *Ibid.*, p. 13.
11. *Ibid.*, p. 161.
12. *Ibid.*, p. 169.
13. *Ibid.*, p. 170.
14. *Ibid.*, p. 171.
15. *Ibid.*, pp. 172–3.
16. Prof. Mead's essay is published among other places in *American Civil Religion*, eds. Richey and Jones, N.Y.: Harper and Row, 1974, p. 45–75; the sentence quoted is on p. 65.
17. *Church and State*, op. cit., p. 117. Cf. also his analysis in his paper for this study, pp. 91–93.

18. *Ibid.*, p. 119.
19. Philip P. Everts, *Public Opinion, the Churches and Foreign Policy: Studies of Domestic Factors in the Making of Dutch Foreign Policy*, Leiden: Institute for International Studies, 1983.
20. Karl Mannheim, *Ideology and Utopia*, tr. Wirth and Shils, N.Y.: Harcourt, Brace and World, Inc., 1936, p. 47.

The Churches in the Netherlands and Nuclear Disarmament

by Philip P. Everts and Laurens J. Hogebrink

I. INTRODUCTION

It is often assumed that the mass movement against nuclear weapons in Western Europe—also known as the "new peace movement"—began early in 1980 as a response to NATO's decision of December 1979 to deploy a new generation of U.S. nuclear missiles in Western Europe. That assumption is just as much a mistake as the belief that this new movement disappeared after the first new missiles were deployed toward the end of 1983. In fact, the new peace movement was there long before it appeared on the covers of international news magazines. Its concerns were, and are, broader than one particular weapons system, and its effects—as far as can be foreseen at the time of writing—more long-lasting. While supporters of the NATO decision of 1979 were celebrating the first deployments as their victory, opposition was growing at a more rapid rate than before.[1]

Dr. Philip Everts is Director of the Institute for International Studies, Leiden University, The Netherlands. The Reverend Laurens Hogebrink is Director of the Office of Church and Society, The Netherlands Reformed Church.

The churches in the Netherlands have played a major role in the new movement since its inception. In some respects, its roots are in the earlier wave of concern in the churches about nuclear weapons in the fifties and early sixties. The year 1977 marked the beginning of this new period of involvement and action. It was the year the Interchurch Peace Council (IKV) launched its long-term campaign with the slogan "Free the world of nuclear weapons and let it begin in the Netherlands". The aim of this campaign was to bring about a process of mutual disarmament through a series of unilateral or independent first steps, starting with removal of all nuclear weapons and nuclear weapons facilities from Dutch territory and the Dutch armed forces. It was also the year in which the trend in the nuclear arms race towards nuclear war-fighting postures was dramatized by the proposed introduction of ERRB weapons (commonly called the neutron bomb). Public opposition in the Netherlands was so strong that parliament and, at a later stage, the government itself felt the need to say "no" to the introduction of the new weapon system. Also, 1977 was the year in which NATO decided to establish its "Long-Term Defense Program," with the NATO decision of December 12, 1979 to deploy intermediate-range U.S. missiles in Europe as one of its indirect outcomes.

It is therefore evident that the common perception that it was the NATO decision which triggered the new peace movement in Europe is wrong. In the Netherlands—and in our opinion, also in most other Western European countries—it was almost the other way around: the already emerging new peace movement turned this NATO decision into the crisis it has become.

Whatever the further developments in the "Euromissile crisis" may be, one long-term effect seems certain: public acceptance of nuclear deterrence as a morally tolerable and politically credible instrument to preserve peace has greatly diminished. The main contribution of the churches in Western Europe to this "crisis of faith" in nuclear deterrence has been to give respectability to these reemerging doubts.

In the Netherlands, the groups mobilizing support against nuclear weapons were remarkably successful. For the first time an ad hoc coalition came about on the political level, reaching from the radical peace movement on the left into the moderate center parties. Its influence has forced the government not only to reject the introduction of the neutron bomb, but also to delay a final decision for more than five years on the deployment of cruise missiles in the Netherlands. The desirability and possibility of reducing the participation of the Netherlands in a defense strategy based on nuclear weapons has also become a topic of serious debate. While not yet strong enough to force through a new security policy, the opposition to established policies seems sufficiently strong to prevent certain actions. These developments gained some international notoriety, either as a subject for worry or as a source of hope. The fearful coined the term "Hollanditis" or "the Dutch disease," which was portrayed as a contagious infection spreading from the Netherlands to other countries of Western and even Eastern Europe.[2]

While it is true that the new antinuclear movement emerged in the Netherlands somewhat earlier than in most other countries, this does not warrant treating the Netherlands as the source of the "epidemic." If there are certain conditions in the Netherlands which have allowed a relatively stronger impact of the peace movement on political decision-making (compared to other European countries) they should be looked for in the strategy of the peace movement itself, the nature of its support (particularly from among the churches) and the relative accessibility and openness of the Dutch political system.

II. THE POLITICAL SITUATION IN THE NETHERLANDS

Like many other societies, Dutch society is undergoing major structural changes, such as technological developments, drastic increases in the scale of social organization and increased possibilities of individualization. This has led to politicization and polarization, to a sharpening of the distinction between progressive and conservative forces. Together with secularization these developments have led to a rapid decline of the confessional vote in the political center, from some fifty percent to less than thirty percent in thirty years. New political parties have come into being and "critical" groups have developed within the older established parties.

Despite an ongoing process of secularization which shows no signs of subsiding, a large majority of the Dutch (61 percent, according to one survey in 1981) still consider themselves to be "believers in the Christian sense." Taking church membership as a criterion, the figure is somewhat higher. Three major denominations exist in the Netherlands: the Roman Catholics, estimated at 38 percent of the population (5.6 million members); and two Protestant denominations, the Netherlands Reformed Church (*Nederlandse Hervormde Kerk*), once the established church and now estimated at 22 percent (2.7 million members), and the Reformed Churches in the Netherlands (*Gereformeerde Kerken*), which are generally more orthodox, at 7 percent (870,000 members). Together with the members of a number of much smaller denominations the total figure for church membership would be about 72 percent.[3] This, however, does not tell us much about the real significance of the religious factor.

Religiosity has become more a matter of personal choice. Church attendance is declining (some 40 percent of the Hervormden, 50 percent of the Roman Catholic and 75 percent of the Gereformeerden are regular churchgoers). Until quite recently church membership was a rather good predictor for political attitudes and behavior. Members of the Gereformeerde Kerken, for instance, could be expected to have rather conservative political views and vote for one of the Protestant political parties. Roman Catholics would be members of a Catholic trade union and vote for the Catholic People's Party, etc. But even in the heyday of this system there were exceptions. Members of the Hervormde Kerk could show either liberal or orthodox religious views; they might or might not vote for a religious political party.[4] As late as 1954 the bishops found it necessary to forbid Roman Catholics to vote for the Socialist party—so it appeared that many of them did.

The gradual breakdown of this system in Dutch society should be noted. Under this system each of the major social groupings—Protestants and Roman Catholics, socialists and liberals—had been living as more or less separate entities with little contact among them. Each had its own political party, trade union, schools, sporting clubs and the like. National social unity was maintained through the "depoliticization" of controversial issues and by skillful maneuvering by the political leadership of the various pillars which ruled the country through carefully balanced coalitions. Due to increased social mobility, the emergence of new middle classes and the process of deconfessionalization, this system started to crumble in the sixties. New coalitions across the old dividing lines became possible. Within the churches a strong ecumenical current made itself felt. Organizations like IKV could come into being as a consequence of this process. In the course of the sixties, the political passivity of the earlier postwar years was replaced by political activism in many spheres, including the realm of foreign policy and international affairs.

The established political parties showed themselves increasingly incapable of coping with newly emerging issues which cut across traditional ideological divisions. The political system was faced with many new demands, often voiced by pressure groups, or *actiegroepen*, as they are called in the Netherlands, representing specific interests or groups of concerned citizens. These new forms of political debate and activity developed largely outside the framework of the traditional political parties, which consequently had great difficulty in turning the diverse demands from society into coherent and consistent political programs. The relative failure of the political parties is one reason why the churches have come to play a major role in the debates over international politics, such as nuclear weapons, development cooperation, and human rights policies. The new peace movement which emerged toward the end of the seventies is a good example of this development.

The Dutch multiparty system has always been characterized by two cleavages: one between left and right, the other between parties with a religious basis and those which reject the notion that common religious views should lead to a common political approach. Going from left to right, there are three small leftist parties: the Communist Party, the Pacifist Socialists and the Radical Party (the closest equivalent to the German Greens). Together they account for some 6 percent of the votes. Left of center we find the PvdA (Social Democrats, some 30 percent) and the much smaller D '66 (left liberals). The center is occupied by the CDA (Christian Democrats, also supported by some 30 percent). On their right we find the VVD (liberal conservatives, 25 percent) and on the far right we find four other parties (accounting for another 6 percent), three of which are religious.

Due to its complicated multiparty system, coalition cabinets are always necessary in the Netherlands and the negotiations for a new cabinet are usually lengthy and acrimonious. Because neither the left nor the right is strong enough to rule by itself, the centrist Christian Democrats have been a necessary partner in all postwar cabinets. Presently a CDA/VVD coalition is in power. While this makes the prospects for a defense policy oriented to NATO policies somewhat better, it would be premature to say, for instance, that deployment of the new cruise missiles is a foregone conclusion. The left wing of the Christian Democrats in parliament plays a crucial role in such decisions. What these M.P.'s will do when they are faced with a true conflict between loyalty to party and loyalty to their own views under pressures from the churches remains to be seen.

III. THE INTERCHURCH PEACE COUNCIL AND ITS CAMPAIGN AGAINST NUCLEAR WEAPONS

Historical Background

The Dutch Interchurch Peace Council (*Interkerkelijk Vredesberaad*, IKV) is often referred to in the international media as one of the strongest forces in the new European peace movement. Although it is difficult, if not impossible, to measure power and influence exactly, there is general agreement that IKV is indeed an influential factor in Dutch society. While it is certainly not the only way through which the churches manifest their concern for peace, it represents their clearest commitment to this goal.

The peace movement in the Netherlands has a long and venerable tradition. We can distinguish here between socialist/communist, liberal and anarchist peace traditions. Christian pacifism, of course, represents the fourth major tradition. Each of these kinds of groups has been active in the past and, with the exception of the liberal tradition, they can still be found in one form or another. Despite organizational and political setbacks, the peace movement has never disappeared totally, even when it has been submerged from time to time by other tendencies and concerns. Its history, however, is characterized by a cyclical pattern, with periods of growth and influence being followed by decline and decay.[5] The cycles in the Netherlands follow patterns similar to those in other European countries, with some important exceptions. The movement prospered around the turn of the century and in the twenties and the thirties. World War I and the rise of fascism provided temporary but severe setbacks. After World War II it took the movement some time to recover, until it reached major proportions again during the late fifties and early sixties.

In the West, the prevailing cold war climate, however,

severely hampered the possibilities of growth. People concerned about the dangers of nuclear weapons were generally considered to be either "fellow travelers" or, at best, misguided idealists. The impact of the peace movement, thus, did not reach very far beyond its traditional recruiting ground: the communist-oriented and independent left and those who reject arms on primarily moral grounds. In the sixties, paradoxically, it was not the prospect of war, but the success of the movement (the conclusion of the 1963 test ban treaty and the improvement of the international climate after the Cuban missile crisis) which contributed to its decline. Besides, it was not primarily the abstract threat of nuclear war which mobilized people during the sixties and early seventies, but the very concrete killings in Vietnam. In 1976, one of us wrote an article titled "The Protest Against the Bomb has Evaporated," stating that few seemed to worry about nuclear weapons anymore, and concluding that it would be difficult to focus interest and activity again on this issue. Although this conclusion was shared by many at the time, it turned out to be very wrong. From 1977 onward, a new wave of primarily antinuclear protest set in and reached proportions which had never been seen before.

The Founding of IKV

There always have been small groups of Christians, both within the historic peace churches and the larger churches, who were committed to pacifism in a more or less pure form. Church and Peace (*Kerk en Vrede*), one of the founding members of the International Fellowship of Reconciliation, has been active in the Netherlands since 1924. Pax Christi, the Roman Catholic peace movement founded to bring about Franco-German reconciliation, has been active since 1948. Pacifists within the churches, pressing the churches to reconsider the validity of old positions in view of the advent of nuclear weapons, initially met with relatively little response. A breakthrough occurred in 1962, however, when the Synod of the Netherlands Reformed Church issued a lengthy but clear "no, without any yes" against nuclear weapons. It was the outcome of a debate that had lasted for more than ten years. This unequivocal rejection of nuclear deterrence was the base on which IKV was built.

Another equally important factor in the creation of IKV was the papal encyclical *Pacem in terris* (1963). The Dutch branch of Pax Christi called for an ecumenical effort to set up new peace work in the churches. The two major Protestant churches and the Roman Catholic Church, followed shortly afterwards by six smaller denominations, decided in 1966 to set up the Interchurch Peace Council (IKV), and charged it with the following tasks:

(a) to continue collective reflection on the problems of war and peace;
(b) to further discussion on these problems among the members of the churches;
(c) to voice the concern of the churches on these matters in society at large; and
(d) to propose suitable models of political action.

Thus, reflection and action, conscientization and mobilization at the grass roots, as well as political pressure at the top of society, have been part of its comprehensive mandate from the beginning.

Since it has a social force comparable to a political party or a trade union, it often surprises people that, formally, IKV has only twenty-five members. They are the representatives of nine Dutch churches, including the two major Protestant churches and the Roman Catholic Church in the Netherlands.

IKV has a rather loose and informal structure: the churches gave IKV their mandate and pay for its activities (together with donations from individuals) as an official ecumenical body; but IKV could not—and still cannot—bind the participating churches by its pronouncements or actions. Tensions and mutual recriminations were a logical consequence of this structure. Despite occasional efforts either to break the ties between the churches and IKV or silence the movement by withdrawing financial and moral support, the basic structure has remained unchanged and both sides seem to have profited from this arrangement.

The major activity of IKV in the beginning was the annual peace week, in which local churches and groups in all cities, towns and villages participated. The peace week was essentially a tool for education and consciousness-raising, mustering local church support for special activities, such as the World Council of Churches' Program to Combat Racism.

In the peace week of September 1977, IKV launched its long-term campaign against nuclear weapons under the slogan "Help rid the world of nuclear weapons and let it begin in the Netherlands." It was realized that such a political campaign needed visibility throughout the year and organizational muscle. Thus many actions have been organized since, often together with other peace groups, political parties, and (more recently) the largest trade union federation. More than 400 local IKV "core" groups have been formed, most of them church-related, which are committed to the goal of the campaign.

There were two major motives for the IKV campaign when it started in 1977. The first was pastoral. IKV considered it pastorally irresponsible to continue calling people to be concerned about the arms race while providing no opportunity for concrete action. The time had come to develop a new concrete proposal and to organize power behind this proposal.[6]

The second motive grew out of developments in the arms race itself, which was entering a new phase that would make the immediate future very much unlike the past 35 years. The major new factors were seen to be:

1. *the end of "pure" deterrence* and the trend toward postures and strategies of "limited" nuclear war-fighting;
2. *the end of arms control* as a potential force in stopping destabilizing weapon developments, and its new role in "controlling" public protest against the arms race rather than the arms race itself;

3. *the end of non-proliferation* (especially after the oil crisis of 1973) and therefore the approaching end of nuclear deterrence as a bipolar system; and
4. *the failure of détente* to translate the process or stabilization of Europe (the Helsinki Agreements of 1975) into disarmament steps.

In retrospect, these factors are the same as those motivating other major campaigns in Western Europe.[7]

If the term "Hollanditis" has any relevance, it lies only in the fact that the Dutch were the first to get organized, making use of the infrastructure of local groups that had organized their peace weeks. IKV concluded that the time had come for the churches to reject not only the *use* but also the *possession* of nuclear weapons. If the churches want to be effective peacemakers, they must go beyond voicing their moral concern in an abstract fashion and involve themselves in the political struggle. At the same time they must avoid even the impression of exercising moral pressure on the believers by making a distinction between "good" and "bad" Christians.

IKV also concluded that total unilateral disarmament was neither morally advisable nor politically feasible. Such a step would be destabilizing, making a dangerous system still more dangerous. It would also fail to take seriously the real or perceived security needs of people and, apart from the ethical aspect of such negligence, this would certainly not help achieve the political majority needed for new initiatives. Finally, too radical a departure from established policies would almost certainly imply that the Netherlands should leave NATO, and although expectations as to the influence which the Netherlands might have in NATO were never very high, leaving the alliance would rob the Netherlands of the little direct influence on international politics it has.

A middle course therefore had to be devised. Stimulated by the ideas developed by C.E. Osgood and others[8] about gradual and reciprocal initiatives in disarmament, the concept of independent first initiatives was taken up and developed into the proposal to remove all nuclear weapons from the Dutch armed forces and Dutch territory. This step, it was argued, would be small enough in purely military terms not to upset the military balance, and potentially capable of enlisting domestic majority support. Politically, however, it could have a major international impact in signalling to others a fundamental rejection of the system of nuclear deterrence. It was perhaps the minimum needed for international efficacy, and at the same time the maximum for which domestic support could be generated. The proposal developed by IKV was also in line with the requirement of the gradualist strategy that the first steps should be unambiguous and large enough to stand out against the general "noise" of international intercourse. It should not be possible to "explain away" such steps as intended to reach other goals, such as saving costs or improving one's military position. A continuing commitment to NATO would help make clear that the Netherlands does not wish to opt out by making itself a less likely target in case of war. IKV did not wish the Netherlands to cleanse its hands of a collective responsibility.

Although it was thought preferable that a strategy of unilateral initiatives be carried out by the alliance(s) as a whole, it was also thought possible that countries might decide for themselves what suitable first steps might be taken. They need not be the same for each country, nor need they be in the nuclear field. For the Netherlands, denuclearization seemed an obvious choice. For the Federal Republic of Germany, that would clearly be too big a step; it might be better, for instance, for Bonn as a first step to withdraw its consent to the NATO decision of 1979 to deploy cruise and Pershing missiles. Although the arguments in favor of denuclearization and the proposal itself were already developed in 1972, the formal decision of IKV to begin this campaign was not made until 1977. It was thought at that time that the campaign might have to last up to ten years.

IV. EVENTS SINCE 1977

The Neutron Bomb Affair

Shortly after IKV had decided to initiate its campaign for the removal of nuclear weapons, it was forced to pay attention to two issues of concrete and more immediate concern. One of these was the proposed introduction of the so-called neutron bomb.[9] In the summer of 1977, an American journalist discovered the funds for neutron weapons in the U.S. Department of Energy budget. This development dramatized the trends toward nuclear war-fighting and "limited nuclear war" (which to European ears sounds like "limited to Europe"). A small group, mostly related to the very small Communist Party in the Netherlands, began a campaign to "Stop the N-bomb," which gained a much larger response than initiatives from this sector of Dutch society usually get. The "Stop the N-Bomb" initiative coincided with the launching of the IKV campaign and for many of the newly formed local IKV core groups, the logical first activity was to help in collecting signatures against the N-bomb. In April 1978, more than a million signatures—from a population of 14 million—were offered to Parliament. The churches spoke out against the N-bomb, and soon there were local "Stop the N-Bomb" groups in villages where there was no Communist Party involvement whatsoever. In March 1978, fifty thousand people participated in a mass demonstration against the N-bomb.

On February 3, 1978, the Christian Democrats were the first large faction in parliament to come out against the N-Bomb. Their support was essential for the government to survive in Parliament. Although, for internal political reasons, no clear-cut motion expressing the majority view was adopted in Parliament, the government was left with little room to maneuver. Defense Minister R. Kruisinga resigned over this issue, referring explicitly to the critical role of the churches. In 1982, the government formally rejected the introduction of this weapon system.

The neutron bomb affair showed three things. First, that it was possible to generate massive popular support for opposition to nuclear weapons. Second, in order to have political impact, such popular protest needed to build a coalition with the "center" in Dutch politics, which is always the Christian Democrats. Third, the churches and church organizations were not necessarily less credible as sources of information about nuclear weapons than the government.

This third factor, based on the quality in general of publications by IKV and Pax Christi, was dramatized in the peace week of 1978. IKV revealed that the common perception that President Carter had deferred the production of the neutron bomb was wrong. In fact, he had only deferred a decision about the enhanced radiation (e.r.) components. IKV announced that production of these components would start in October 1978. Three times the Dutch government officially denied the accuracy of the IKV reports, and three times IKV came up with new evidence. Just after the Dutch prime minister had released his third denial, President Carter announced on April 7 that production of certain key elements of the e.r. feature would start.[10] In the parliamentary debate that followed, members of Parliament asked why a church organization had been aware of the facts while the government had not. The campaign against the neutron bomb certainly prepared the ground for the fiercer struggle against the next modernization round.

The Euromissiles Crisis

The actions against the neutron bomb set the stage for the second effort, one year later, when it became known that NATO wanted to introduce a new generation of intermediate-range nuclear weapons, allegedly to counterbalance the emerging Soviet superiority in this category. For all participants it was really a second round. The peace movement wanted to succeed again and the governments wanted to prevent a recurrence of the debacle of the neutron bomb affair. To show the Soviet Union that NATO was still capable of making unanimous decisions became an important, if not the most important, element in the decisionmaking process. This made the cooperation of the Netherlands essential.

The extensive educational work done by the churches and their peace movement in the preceding years now seems to have paid off. The concrete nature of both the neutron bomb and the modernization issues helped the peace movement mobilize and make manifest the latent opposition against nuclear weapons. People's opinions as such did not seem to have changed much—at least this is what public opinion data of the period suggest[11]—but their intensity probably increased, so many people were now willing to act on their convictions. In contrast to the early sixties, the peace movement was now also able to break out of the boundaries of that earlier period. Although at the time of this writing it is too early to come to a final judgment on the success or failure of the opposition in terms of deployment of the new missiles, the perseverance of the peace movement and the stubbornness of the NATO governments caused a deep crisis in NATO.

The Euromissile crisis requires lengthier consideration, both because it lies at the heart of the current debate in Europe and because there are so many wrong perceptions and so much official propaganda on both sides of the Iron Curtain.

On December 12, 1979, NATO made its decision to deploy a new generation of U.S. missiles in Western Europe. This decision became known as the "double track" decision: to deploy 572 Pershing II and ground-launched cruise missiles, and to offer negotiation. In the view of the peace movement, however, the second track (negotiations) was never intended as an alternative for the first track (deployment). Both tracks were running to the same station: deployment. This was not a conclusion reached later; it has been IKV's public position since 1979.[12]

The main original *military* reason for the NATO decision

was not the growing offensive potential of the Soviet Union, but its growing defensive potential—in particular, air defense. NATO said: our aging aircraft are losing their capability to penetrate, so the new program is just a "modernization" of this aging capability. A Dutch peace researcher commented: "That is like I modernize my bicycle by buying a car." The deployment of the Soviet SS-20 missile as the main argument was a latecomer. In 1977, the Soviet Union started its long-expected replacement of its almost 20-year-old SS-4 and SS-5 missiles targeted at Western Europe. But NATO had been expecting a replacement of these aging missiles for 10 years.[13]

More important than the military rationale for the NATO decision was its *political/psychological* rationale.[14] NATO needed to show firmness and cohesion after the conflicts between President Carter and West German Chancellor Helmut Schmidt about the neutron bomb. Ironically, it was arms control (SALT II) which provided the main impetus for the new round in Europe. The USA and the USSR planned further to codify strategic parity in the SALT II treaty; conservative Europeans feared that the Carter administration was not taking European security interests fully into account. They were most afraid that the possible transfer to the European allies of cruise missile technology (which looked like a cheap alternative for expensive aircraft) would be negotiated away.

Chancellor Schmidt then gave a major address in London in October 1977, which is often cited as the moment when "Europe" asked for new missiles. But Schmidt did not ask for new missiles; he merely pointed out that the existing military disparity (both nuclear and conventional) at the European level was getting more politically significant because in the SALT II process the two superpowers were codifying parity. Chancellor Schmidt pleaded for dealing with the European problem more seriously in the talks on mutual balanced forces reduction. The response to this public questioning of the American strategic guarantees for Europe was new missiles.

But did the people and parliaments of Western Europe want new missiles? Out of the five NATO countries where the new missiles were to be deployed, only the Netherlands had discussed this question in Parliament prior to the NATO decision; and its parliament had said "no" on December 6, 1979. This breakthrough followed months of very intensive discussion at many levels in Dutch society. There had been countless parish evenings in the churches. Bishops and synods had spoken out against the decision. Many local IKV groups had invited politicians to discuss the matter. There had been vigils, marches and picket lines. So the decision by the Dutch parliament was the culmination of an unprecedented social process in the direction of this "no."

This process was certainly deeper in the Netherlands than in the surrounding countries, although in West Germany some of the same concern had become visible. In England and Italy, the matter was discussed at the political level only after the NATO decision, when it was too late. In Belgium, the government informed Parliament on the day of the decision itself, when the ministers were already on their way to the NATO meeting.

That the Dutch government survived the parliamentary debate one week after the NATO decision was a miracle; rather, it was one of the blackest pages in Dutch parliamentary history. The key votes were, as usual, with the Christian Democrats. Their leader, Ruud Lubbers (presently prime minister), said at the end of the debate that his parliamentary group could not take responsibility for the NATO decision; then his group voted unanimously against a motion by the opposition expressing just that. This debate was broadcast live on television and went on all day and part of the night. One Christian Democrat (presently undersecretary of defense) later publicly admitted "we have clouded this issue in fog."[15]

There had been crises in NATO previously, but such crises were usually confined to the elite. They certainly were never broadcast live on TV. After December 1979, the "new peace movement" in Western Europe broke through as a mass movement. But it was not created by the NATO decision. Nor was it a product of the Reagan administration's loose talk about "limited nuclear war" in Europe. Rather, it was the already emerging peace movement which turned the

NATO decision into a crisis and created the atmosphere in which the loose talk of the new Reagan administration could stir so much controversy.

The Battle for Public Opinion

The fall of 1981 showed the strength of the appeal of the "new peace movement." Millions took part in the largest series of anti-nuclear demonstrations in European history, culminating in the four hundred thousand who marched in Amsterdam on November 21. By that time, NATO had already changed its arguments. The need to penetrate Soviet air defense was no longer stressed. The need to counter the SS-20 had faded into the shadow. The emphasis now was on arms control. Originally in NATO's double track decision, the negotiation track was added to the deployment track to sell deployment to public opinion; but now this was reversed. Deployment was called necessary for the success of the negotiations. The result, of course, would be the same: deployment. But how would social sectors sensitive to the call for negotiations, such as the churches, respond?

The Geneva talks proved to be the perfect disciplining instrument for most of the media and politicians. They failed to see that the *content* of the NATO negotiation framework represented an even tougher approach than the deployment track. NATO's negotiation track ironically pursued precisely the kind of separate Euro-strategic balance which many proponents of the deployment track opposed. The key phrase in the NATO approach was the demand of *equality* in *land-based* intermediate range missiles *between the USA and the Soviet Union*. In other words: a Euro-strategic balance.[16] The word "equality" applied to this category of weapons only, made clear that deployment of some new missiles was considered unavoidable. For NATO was calling for "equality" in the only category of missiles in Europe in which the Soviet Union had enjoyed a virtual monopoly for more than 15 years.[17]

In November 1981, the battle for public opinion in Europe really started. President Reagan scored a first victory on November 18 when he announced his "zero option" as an opening bid. This sounded like a concession, but in fact it was a hardening of NATO's negotiation position. It was the toughest stand possible. Zero deployment of the 572 new U.S. missiles was thought possible only if the Soviet side dismantled all Soviet SS-4, SS-5 and SS-20 missiles.

A NATO Assembly report published by the U.S. Senate described this "zero option" accurately just prior to Reagan's formal proposal: "The objective of recognizing the 'zero option' as a desirable but implausible goal is to place the responsibility for NATO modernization on the Soviet Union."[18] However once the offer was made, most European political leaders only heard the word "zero," and publicly celebrated it as a victory of their own policies.

The Geneva negotiations functioned from then on as an arena for the propaganda war. In December 1982, First Secretary Andropov responded in kind with what he called "a really honest zero option": no new U.S. missiles, no Soviet missiles to counter them, "only" 162 SS-20's to counter the British and French missiles. That also sounded simple and attractive, and this time a part of the European peace movement was impressed as well. However, it too was clearly devised to be unacceptable, because making such an explicit political link between Soviet and French-British forces meant that Western European security would be uncoupled from the U.S.

The constants in all negotiation proposals by the U.S. were: to guarantee deployment of a new generation of missiles (the numbers were negotiable), and to preserve the unity of NATO. The constants in all Soviet proposals were: to prevent the deployment of U.S. missiles in Europe (the numbers of Soviet missiles to remain were negotiable), and to weaken the link between Western Europe and the U.S.[19]

As a disciplining instrument to keep the allies in line, the Geneva talks were clearly a success. From November 1981 on, Western European politics was virtually paralysed. No independent initiatives could be undertaken, no criticism could be voiced because doing so would undermine the U.S. negotiating position.

When politics is paralyzed by arms control as the new label of the arms race, it is important that the churches not be caught in the same paralysis. How did this disciplining function of "Geneva" work in the churches? In the Federal Republic of Germany, the memorandum (*Denkschrift*) of the Evangelical Church on "The Preservation, Promotion and Renewal of Peace" (1981) combined a theological affirmation of "hope" with putting all its political hope on the current arms control negotiations, without analyzing what was actually going on in Geneva. The debate in February 1983 in the Church of England over the report "The Church and the Bomb" provided another example. The Archbishop of Canterbury warned against unilateral measures, arguing that "the kind of action being advocated will actually undermine the negotiations now in progress in Geneva."

In the Dutch churches, such tendencies were largely avoided, probably due in large part to the continuous strong effort by IKV to publish its critical analyses of the Geneva negotiations in sympathetic media. The Christian Democrats in Parliament, however, continued to make their final decision about deployment dependent on the outcome of the Geneva talks—even after the Geneva talks had ended in failure!

V. NEW DEVELOPMENTS IN SOCIETY

The Formation of a New Coalition

Among the developments in Dutch society, two seem to be particularly relevant in explaining the growing influence of the church-sponsored peace movement.

First, an informal coalition came about, stretching politically from the far left to parts of the political center. It brought together people who were against all armaments, nuclear pacifists and those who in principle accepted the concept of nuclear deterrence but had become increasingly critical of specific developments in the area of armaments and deterrence doctrines. Later, this coalition solidified into a more formal structure which undertook a number of collective activities, the *Overlegorgaan Kernbewapening*. It included the political parties of the left plus the Christian Democratic party, most of the peace organizations, the Central Federation of Trade Unions (FNV) and the soldiers' trade union (VVDM). The church-related peace movement played a vital role in bringing and keeping this coalition together, acting as a link between the two wings.

This linkage was not always easy. IKV, for instance, was strongly criticized by the left for its efforts, both in 1981 and in 1983, to arrange a compromise which would enable the Christian Democrats to participate in the mass demonstrations. Many (including parts of the IKV) thought the price for this cooperation—a watering down of the demands—was too high. Yet the importance of such a broad, if at times somewhat shaky, coalition cannot be overestimated.

Many groups in the traditional peace movement can be characterized as "prophetic minorities" whose concerns are not primarily to exercise direct political influence on government policy, but rather to give witness to the possibility of alternative and nonviolent forms of social organization and personal lifestyle. In contrast, groups like IKV and Pax Christi are oriented primarily toward exercising political influence through gaining maximum possible support. They are "coalition type" organizations.[20] They are oriented toward the parliamentary political process, and thus seek support of parts of the political center, where power resides. This political aspect of their work, especially their striving for the mobilization of power, has been criticized by those within the churches who believe the churches should not seek to exercise power in this way. Others have attacked the movement for its alleged neoclericalist tendencies.

The Long March through the Institutions

The second important development, closely related to the first, is the relative success of the "long march through the institutions." Many groups and institutions which would not normally consider themselves political institutions have become committed in recent years to working against further escalation of the arms race. The peace movement has thus gained a better and perhaps more permanent base of institutional support, which precludes an early decline.

The fact that Parliament did not maintain its rejection of the NATO modernization decision of 1979, and allowed the government to subscribe to NATO's decision—albeit with the proviso that the Dutch would delay a decision on deployment of the new missiles until the end of 1981—was a blow for the peace movement. Yet the delay also provided time to broaden the base of the opposition. This took the form of support from all kinds of institutions.

Groups of concerned military officers started to discuss their problems of conscience with respect to nuclear weapons. The soldiers' trade union (VVDM) promised legal support to members who refused to do guard duty at nuclear storage sites. A remarkable development was the renewed activity among many of the women's organizations (*Vrouwen voor Vrede*), including some of the more conservative groups. The Central Federation of Trade Unions (FNV) struggled with the problem that many members find employment in the arms industry and question the possibilities of conversion in a period of economic recession. Nevertheless the federation decided to sponsor the mass demonstration of October 1983. Groups of physicians also organized themselves—following similar initiatives in other countries—and pointed to the impossibility of providing medical treatment in case of a nuclear war; some of them also refused to register in a government scheme for emergency situations.

The physicians' action helped to focus the debate on yet another aspect of the deterrence system: the preparations for civil defense. This was particularly important since civil defense is a matter for the local authorities. Hence it was possible for many to address the issue of nuclear weapons at the local level to negate the claim that effective protection against nuclear attack is a real possibility. Other efforts at the local level included the more symbolic decision to declare one's village or city a local nuclear-free zone. Many local authorities accepted resolutions of this kind.

No Breakthrough at the Political Level

Although there were major successes in mobilizing public opinion and gaining the support of important institutions, the peace organizations, in their own eyes, failed to bring about a decisive breakthrough at the political level. This became apparent in the national parliamentary elections of 1981 and 1982. There was success in making the problem of nuclear weapons a major issue in the election campaign, but this was due less to the political parties themselves than to the strong pressures "from below" engendered by the peace movement. Apart from the small parties on the left which supported the claims of the peace movement, the two largest political parties, PvdA (the Social Democrats) and CDA (the Christian Democrats), were reluctant to make this issue an election theme. They are so heavily divided internally that a focus on the nuclear weapons issue would bring this division into the open.

IKV concentrated its efforts in 1981 on the PvdA. Its party congress in 1979 had adopted a resolution supporting the IKV campaign slogan. In the end, however, the party bowed to the pressure of the party leader and settled for a compromise refusing the complete denuclearization of the Netherlands but emphasizing an unconditional "no" to the new missiles. This was one of a list of six "essential points" which had to be part of the governing program of any new coalition in which the PvdA would take part.

The CDA was also internally divided and the influence of its left wing was not strong enough to overcome the position of the party leadership, including its leader, Andries Van Agt, who as prime minister had committed himself firmly to the NATO double track decision. The result was a compromise formula that allowed widely diverging interpretations. The elections brought gains to the far left and some losses to the PvdA, but apart from that there was little evidence that the nuclear weapons issue had played a major role in determining voting behavior. After long and difficult negotiations, a coalition between PvdA, CDA and the left liberals of D '66 was concluded, which could only "agree to disagree" on the deployment of the cruise missiles in the Netherlands.

Further postponement of a decision beyond the promised date of 1981 was to be expected. There were now two "veto groups"—one on the left of opponents to the new missiles, and one on the right that did not wish to deviate from the NATO path. Paralysis of the government and a decision to defer further decisionmaking on deployment of the cruise missiles, due for December 1981, was the result. Meanwhile, the Netherlands had seen the largest demonstration ever held since 1945.

IKV played a key role in the series of mass demonstrations held in most European capitals in the fall of 1981.[21] Together with two German church-related organizations, it took the initiative for the first demonstration, in Bonn, which drew two hundred fifty thousand participants.[22] IKV took a central role in the demonstration in Amsterdam (its secretary, Mient Jan Faber, was the chairman of its organizing committee), and as a result the participation of four hundred thousand and their completely peaceful behaviour were seen in the media as mainly the success of IKV. This was inaccurate because in fact it had been the work of a broad coalition of peace groups and political parties. For about one-third of the demonstrators it was the first time in their lives that they had taken part in such activity.

The government did not fall over the cruise missile issue, however, but over disagreement on socio-economic issues. This made new elections in 1982 a necessity. A renewal of the CDA/VVD coalition would make eventual deployment a more likely prospect. The polls predicted a victory for them at the elections. Prime Minister Van Agt began to press for a final decision in 1983, thus making the prospect of a new PvdA/CDA coalition more difficult. In the elections, the PvdA dropped five of its six "essential points" but stuck to its unconditional "no" on the modernization issue. The CDA, on the other hand, was as divided as before and could only decide "to do nothing which might hinder the negotiations in Geneva."

Unlike 1981, the peace organizations now tried to force the issue by presenting the voters with a pamphlet in which they advised "to vote against nuclear weapons." In practice this meant an appeal to vote for one of the parties on the left. This was clearly a breach of the taboo in Dutch political culture on "party political" activities by nonpolitical groups like the churches. The action backfired. Many church leaders criticized it. The CDA also rejected this form of pressure and accused IKV and Pax Christi of exceeding their responsibility. The right claimed that "IKV had finally dropped its veil by siding openly with the left."

The elections brought considerable gains for the PvdA, but also a potential majority for a CDA/VVD coalition. The difference between CDA and PvdA on the nuclear weapons issue could not be bridged and thus a new center-right coalition was formed, which brought the danger of eventual deployment closer than ever before. The elections themselves could not be considered a vote of confidence on the nuclear weapons issue because, as public opinion data showed, this issue did not score high among the priority issues of the voters on the right, who had brought the new coalition into power (unlike the situation for leftist voters for whom the issue was important).

Although the government that came to power in 1982 continued to maintain that it reserved its final decision as to the deployment or nondeployment of the new missiles, its room to maneuver decreased as the negotiations in Geneva dragged on (in fact, could not succeed due to the negotiating positions on both sides) and the international preparations for deployment proceeded according to the original scheme. The first missiles were to be deployed in Great Britain, Italy and West Germany toward the end of 1983. After having announced in the summer of 1983 that the missiles intended for the Netherlands would eventually be deployed at the Woensdrecht air base, the only decisions which could still be postponed were those of building the required facilities and the actual deployment itself. The government announced that it would decide about the beginning of construction of the base and about deployment at the same time. These decisions would be part of a comprehensive policy paper on the Dutch nuclear tasks to be presented to Parliament in the fall of 1983.

As that moment came closer, pressures increased again. As part of another internationally planned and coordinated series of demonstrations, a new mass demonstration was held on October 29, 1983 in The Hague. Attended by five hundred fifty thousand people, it surpassed even the record set in Amsterdam in 1981. The government, however, did not show itself to be overly impressed. Indeed, the cutting edge of this means of communication seemed to have lost much of its initial sharpness and the government seemed to count on its own capability to muster the necessary parliamentary support, hoping that opposition would dwindle after such a decision and gambling that mass support for more radical forms of opposition would be small enough to handle without too much trouble.

However, the new policy paper remained locked up in a controversy between the Dutch minister of foreign affairs, who favored deployment of the cruise missiles, and the Dutch defense minister, who was still looking for ways to avoid deployment. The government announced that a final decision would be made at the latest in June 1984. The NATO deployment schedule did not allow for further delay.

The Netherlands Council of Churches now organized meetings with all political parties, asking them to say no to the cruise missiles. The coalition of peace movements, political parties and trade unions, which had been responsible for the big march of October 1983, organized a decentralized "action week" in May 1984. Highlights among the many local and regional activities were the "peace watches" in numerous churches. The only central national activity was a brief symbolic strike. The fact that it had been called for by the largest trade union federation was seen as more important than its (limited) success.

On June 1, 1984, Prime Minister Ruud Lubbers cut the Gordian knot in his government with a decision which seemed to give both sides what they wanted because it could be interpreted both ways. The Dutch proviso (since 1979) with regard to deployment of cruise missiles was ended. The Netherlands now declared itself ready to deploy. In case of an arms control agreement between the Soviet Union and the USA, the Netherlands would deploy the reasonable number of cruise missiles. In case of no agreement, all 48 cruise missiles would be deployed unless—and this was a completely new element—on November 1, 1985, the number of Soviet SS-20 missiles was not greater than on June 1, 1984. The decision about construction of the base was delayed by one and a half years to November 1, 1985, when the decision about deployment would also be made. The deployment date itself was delayed one and a half years, to 1988.

The Christian Democrats, in their reactions, welcomed the arms control intention of the decision; they emphasized the delay. The (conservative) liberal coalition partners emphasized that in principle, the decision was a deployment decision; they did not worry about the curious link to SS-20's, since at the time it was known that in the Soviet Union three new SS-20 bases were under construction. For the same reason the peace movement strongly criticized the decision, adding also that it was bizarre to put the final Dutch decision in the hands of Moscow. However, IKV and Pax Christi also welcomed the fact that the Netherlands had stepped out of the NATO schedule and especially that construction of the base had been delayed. Words would be easier to fight than concrete.

VI. THE ROLE OF THE CHURCHES IN THE NUCLEAR WEAPONS DEBATE

The Evolution of Church Thinking

We have been speaking of *the* churches until now in a fairly general and unspecified way. Churches can speak and act on problems of peace and disarmament in a variety of ways. Yet each church is faced with similar debates about the proper political role of the church as such and about the consequence for individual political behavior arising from a common faith. The existing differences run through each of the churches and not between them.

Most of the churches in the Netherlands (representing some 90 percent of Dutch Christians) cooperate in the Netherlands Council of Churches, which has included the Roman Catholic Church since 1968 and the Reformed Churches in the Netherlands, after this body joined the World Council of Churches, also in 1968. The Council of Churches regularly expresses itself on urgent social and political questions in the form of public statements, letters to the government or informal contacts. In the field of foreign and international policy, these are prepared in its Commission for International Affairs, which also maintains contacts with the CCIA of the World Council of Churches.

Formal Statements

The churches are involved in the political process in a variety of ways. The most evident and visible way—although perhaps not the most important—is through the adoption of more or less formal resolutions and statements. These statements, coming from the church leadership, synods, bishops and other authoritative bodies, or from committed or specialized groups within the churches, seek to contribute to opinion formation and policymaking on issues vital to society. The churches in the Netherlands have become increasingly vocal in recent years with respect to problems of war and peace in general and nuclear weapons in particular.

However, views are determined not only by substantive considerations, but also by judgments about which the churches can and should speak collectively. At stake is the question of the delimitation of responsibilities: between the churches and the political parties on the one hand, and between collective and individual responsibility on the other.

On the one side, we find the view that churches cannot confine themselves to general statements rejecting war, the system of nuclear deterrence or the arms race, but must indicate the political consequences to be drawn from these general statements. Not to deal with the concrete political situation in which particular decisions have to be taken, it is argued, makes such statements both pastorally and politically irrelevant. Also, polarization cannot be avoided.

The opposing view contends that taking a position on concrete political issues is justified only under extreme circumstances or when other institutions, such as political parties, have clearly failed in their task. Churches should sharpen the conscience of their members on political issues but not dictate to them what policy decisions they should make. Some fear political divisions within the churches.

Although different churches have different traditions in this respect, all are faced with this problem in one way or another. All must resolve the dilemma of either exceeding their responsibility by prescribing in great detail what responsible politicians should do, or failing their responsibility by being too fearful of speaking out. "The churches can better fail by speaking than by remaining silent," someone remarked recently.

A fateful role is played in this connection by the use of Max Weber's well-known distinction between *Gesinnungsethik* and *Verantwortungsethik*, between the ethics of pure conscience and the ethics of responsibility. It is often suggested thereby that the "idealistic" views voiced within the churches should be listened to, but that they cannot and should not guide the politicans in policy decisions where "realism" must be the guiding principle. But if the churches acquiesce in this division of labor whereby the *Gesinnungsethik* is their province and the *Verantwortungsethik* that of the responsible politicians, they provide the latter with an alibi to discount their views when it comes to making decisions in the field of armaments and security policy.

Despite these problems and the resulting confusion, we can point to a number of notable developments, though it may appear that there has been little change in church thinking on the matters at hand. It is true that the points of debate are still the same as ten, twenty or even a hundred years ago: the tensions between the demands of peace and those of justice; the acceptability of violence as a lesser evil; the role of violence in an international anarchic system; the desirability and necessity or the dangers and foolishness of unilateral steps toward disarmament; the role of Christians in politics, etc. If one compares the terms of the earlier with the present debates, it is often difficult to suppress a feeling of *déja vu*. But we should note that although changes do not appear in the logical structure of the debates or in the arguments and value judgments used per se, they do appear in the distribution of these arguments among the participants and the weight given to them. The shifts in these distributions are reflected in what appears as the prevailing view. This does not mean that there is unanimity among the members of the churches. Indeed, considerable opposition continues to exist among the "ordinary" church members, and in an organized form, too, against both the "political" nature of many of the statements and activities of the church leadership and the policy direction of these statements. We shall return later to a summary description of the most important recent church statements on the question of nuclear weapons.[23]

The Church Elite

A second way in which the churches can at least potentially have an impact on policymaking in the realm of security and disarmament is through the participation of some of their members and officials in the network that is usually called "the foreign policy elite." This is the top layer of public opinion, consisting of those who regularly express themselves on foreign policy and who do so usually in order to influence government policy.

The Netherlands is no exception to the rule that direct influence on policymaking in foreign affairs is restricted to a rather small group of people who, either on the basis of functional responsibility, personal expertise or authority based on other criteria, have a considerable impact on what "public opinion" is considered to be. This small group in the Netherlands includes church leaders, members of special committees such as the Commission for International Affairs of the Council of Churches and the spokespersons of the church-related peace movement. These people often have formal and informal contacts with policymakers, appear in hearings held by Parliament and participate in the ongoing public debate in general.

Earlier research has led to some remarkable conclusions concerning the attitudes of this church elite compared to other sections of the foreign policy elite.[24] It appears that their attitudes on a great number of questions can be characterized on the average as rather extreme compared to those of the other groups within the foreign policy elite. The rank orderings of the eight sub-elites which can be distinguished show a strong concordance for a great number of questions. That is, a group which tends to come out at one end of the scale on, for instance, the question of defense expenditures or support for NATO, also tends to come out at this end on other questions. Attitudes and opinions on different political issues cluster together and form a coherent "world view." The church elite are clustered together with the groups which we called "special interest groups" at one end of the scale, in contrast to top government officials and members of government advisory committees, who represent the established views on foreign policy, at the other end. The members of the business elite show themselves to be even *plus royaliste que le roi.*

This research also shows that the church elite occupy a

relatively marginal position in the communication network linking the various sub-elites. The more divergent the attitudes of a group are from those of the decision-makers, the more difficult it is for a group to get access to the decision-making center. The church elite has relatively little direct access and is therefore forced to make use of more indirect approaches. According to the data of the survey, they do so more often than other groups and they are accorded little influence on policymaking by the other members of the elite.

Another interesting finding was that the views of the members of the church elite get relatively little support from those members of the total elite who consider themselves to be active church members. Their support within the elite comes primarily from those who are *not* members of any church. It is clear from the available data from public opinion surveys that in this respect the situation at the elite level does not deviate from that existing in society at large.

The Individual Believers

A third way in which the churches can play a role in policymaking is more indirect: it is through the beliefs and political activities of their members. If the statements, resolutions or pastoral letters of the churches are to be politically effective, they must not only be inherently convincing, but should also reflect and be supported by their members' views. This is not to argue that the truth of a certain view is to be decided upon by majority vote, nor that there should never be a gap between leaders and led. Indeed, it is the responsibility of church leaders to inform and sharpen the conscience of their members, to say what needs to be said even if these ideas are rejected by many of their members. Difficulties arise, however, when the discrepancies become too glaring, because that gives politicians a political alibi not to take these statements seriously. They can argue that the leadership is only speaking for itself and they need not fear any electoral or other political sanctions.

There is more at stake, however. In matters of war and

peace, security and disarmament, it is not only expertise which counts. Perceptions, world images, personal dispositions and values also play a major role in the judgments of those who are considered (or call themselves) experts. When it comes to these elements, the lay person is in most respects as qualified to speak and share in decision-making as the experts. This, in our view, is even more true for the church as a community of believers. The leadership is not necessarily better informed or qualified to speak than the rank-and-file.

There is also a second reason for concern. The available evidence indicates that there is considerable opposition to the radical statements by the church leadership, to the activities of those in positions of authority and to the continuous support of the churches for organizations like the Interchurch Peace Council. Available data from public opinion surveys also indicates that there is relatively more support for these statements and activities outside than inside the churches, predominantly among the political left. For instance, among the church elite, 29 percent thought peace could be maintained without NATO, while this idea was shared in another poll by only 6 percent of the Hervormden, 7 percent of the Gereformeerden and 10 percent of Roman Catholics at the mass level. For those who were not church members, this was 21 percent. Forty-six percent of the church elite thought that national security could be realized without alliance with the U.S., while for the Gereformeerden, Hervormden and Roman Catholics, this was 20 percent, 23 percent and 20 percent, respectively.

To the question, "Should there be modern nuclear weapons in the Netherlands?" 61 percent of the nonbelievers said "no," while the percentage among the Gereformeerden was 37 percent, among the Hervormden, 46 percent, and among the Roman Catholics, 55 percent. To the question, "Do you agree with the slogan of IKV 'Free the world of nuclear weapons and let it begin with the Netherlands'?" 65 percent of the nonbelievers said that they did, but fewer of the church members showed agreement: 36 percent of the Gereformeerden, 47 percent of the Hervormden, and 49 percent of the Roman Catholics. This disparity is even more glaring when one looks not at all church members, but at those who are regular churchgoers. A preference for less expenditure for defense was found among 25 percent of the active Gereformeerden, 41 percent of the Hervormden and 42 percent of the Roman Catholics; while among the nonbelievers it was 53 percent. This view, in a somewhat differently-worded question, was shared by 44 percent of the church elite.[25]

All this points to the fact that the statements issued by the churches fail to convince many of their members, or are simply taken for granted and neglected (for reasons which need closer inspection), which reduces the political efficacy of such statements.

The discrepancy between the views of the leadership and those of many of the rank-and-file presents a number of difficulties also for the fourth way in which the churches can be involved in the political process: through their support for the church-sponsored peace movements.

The Church-Sponsored Peace Movements

We have already noted in several places the central role played in the nuclear weapons debate by the church-related peace organizations. This is true for society at large, but of course even more so for the churches themselves.

In the postwar period in the Netherlands, most church statements about "war and peace" came about through interaction with church-related peace movements. This was at the same time an interaction with actual political and military developments which were put before the churches through these movements.

In terms of membership, the church-related peace organizations are small compared to the denominations they address. Church and Peace, the Dutch branch of the International Fellowship of Reconciliation, has some two thousand members. Pax Christi Netherlands, the Roman Catholic lay organization (although chaired by one of the Dutch bishops), has some thirty thousand members. The Interchurch Peace

Council (IKV) is not a membership organization. It has formally only the twenty-five members who represent the nine participating churches. The number of people active in the local IKV groups is also comparatively small; there are about four hundred fifty local groups averaging ten to fifteen active members. IKV's mailing list for regular mailings is twenty thousand.

These groups derive a considerable part of their unmistakable influence and authority from the clear mandate and financial and other support given to them by the churches. These factors give legitimacy to the peace movement in the eyes of the general public. IKV, while acknowledging that it cannot in any way formally bind the churches, has always stressed that it is operating under the mandate given to it by the churches. Since coming under increasing criticism because of its more pronounced political position and its engagement in the political struggle, it has sought to retain its protection by the churches.

Despite the substantial support the peace organizations receive from outside, the churches remain both their main field of action and the source of their legitimation. But their freedom to maneuver and the authoritativeness of their statements are in practice limited by the existence of the strong divisions of opinion detailed previously. Any growth of church-based countermovements has a negative impact on their legitimacy, thus reducing their influence in society. This, of course, is what the countermovements seek.

This situation exposes the church leadership to strong cross pressures. From the side of the peace movement, they experience constant pressure to support the political consequences the peace movement has derived from the many strong words the churches have spoken on the arms problem, along with pressure to continue supporting and protecting them against unfair attacks in the political arena. The leadership is also under pressure from conservative groups who want the churches to return to a nonpolitical course and/or to cut their formal ties to the peace movement.

For the peace movement and the sympathetic church leadership, the strategic question remains: How can one be a vanguard that discovers new realities and new possibilities and yet not lose support from the main body from which it derives its legitimacy? If they are not successful in this, one has to conclude that the two ways in which churches and Christians influence policy and decisionmaking—the one direct, at the level where the decisions are made; the other indirect, through public opinion—do not necessarily lead in the same direction. That the influence of the churches on foreign policymaking is generally considered to be small comes as no surprise under these circumstances.

The recent statements of the Dutch churches against nuclear weapons, of course, represent a much wider constituency than the "formal" constituency of IKV and Pax Christi. At the same time they do not necessarily represent a majority view among church membership. Church members who disagree or even actively oppose these church statements think IKV and Pax Christi have disproportionate influence and seek to restore a certain "balance."

Several organizations have been established in recent years to achieve this goal: the *Interchurch Committee for Bilateral Disarmament* (ICTO) was founded in 1980 and has about fifty local chapters and five thousand members. It has not obtained an official status in the churches. Its views tend to be fully in line with those of NATO and the Dutch government. Within the Netherlands Reformed Church, the *Reformed Council for Peace Questions* (HBV) was established in 1981 as a private group concerned about peace issues and other areas of life (and theology!) as well. Still, IKV is their main target. In August 1982, HBV launched its own variant of the IKV slogan, "Help rid the churches of IKV and let it begin from the Netherlands Reformed Church." In the course of 1983 it changed its tone and asked for equal access to the congregations, to end "the monopoly position of IKV" (so far without much success). In other churches, similar groups have emerged.

The journal *Shalom* was published for the first time in 1979 by a group which, in American terminology, would be called "evangelical." It is the "alternative" peace journal made for the annual peace week in September. Like the IKV journal, it is printed in three hundred thousand copies but distributed free. The IKV "official" journal is not free. Many local congregations and parishes are caught in a dilemma: to distribute only one of the two, or both, or none? This question is one of the focal points of polarization in the local churches. *Shalom*, however, cannot be put in the same category of pro-NATO organizations as ICTO and HBV. Despite a strong and often unfair criticism of IKV's positions, there is a serious effort to have the dilemmas of the nuclear age discussed in the more orthodox sectors of church life where IKV has little influence. Its success, however, in getting the discussion off the ground in those sectors, is questionable. *Shalom* increasingly regrets being used as a weapon by ICTO in local polarization and has become critical of the position ICTO takes in support of official nuclear weapons policy.

Moments of Conflict and Decision in Church and Society

IKV launched its campaign against nuclear weapons in 1977 on its own initiative. The churches were not yet asked to support the IKV proposal. They were asked, like society at large, to discuss the IKV proposal for unilateral removal of nuclear weapons from the Netherlands as a first step and to weigh its merits. Pax Christi's chairman, Bishop Ernst, said at that time that he would support the proposal unless somebody could come up with a better proposal. This was also the position of IKV itself.

In the parishes and congregations, concern about the nuclear arms race had been growing rapidly. Thus many in the churches were ready to consider alternatives to the system of nuclear deterrence. The first two years of the IKV campaign created surprisingly little polarization. Polarization started in the autumn of 1979 as a consequence of IKV's growing effectiveness in Dutch politics. The nuclear arms race rapidly became a main issue in Dutch politics. Churches speaking out on this matter became front page news. Once moral concern about nuclear weapons began to have political impact, polarization became unavoidable.

The first concrete issue had been the neutron bomb. On February 8, 1978, in a letter to the government, the Netherlands Council of Churches expressed its "no to the neutron bomb and any further development and expansion of nuclear weaponry." Although the NCC was unlikely to support the unilateral disarmament step IKV had been proposing since 1977, it clearly opposed any further escalatory steps in the nuclear arms race. Most leading bodies of the member churches, including the Roman Catholic bishops, subsequently endorsed this position and informed both the government and their own parishes of this decision.

The big question was what the passage about "any further development and expansion of nuclear weaponry" would mean once the 1979 NATO decision was made. Would they stand by this "no" in a situation which was politically much more controversial than the N-bomb affair? Although the Commission on International Affairs of the Netherlands Council of Churches was divided, the council itself did refer to its February 1978 position in a letter to the government on November 16, 1979. A delegation of the council had previously explained its "no" in private talks with the government and with members of Parliament. Most of the member churches followed by the council's position, though not all of them in an equally convincing way.

Polarization in society now emerged. When the council's chairman, Professor Berkhof, addressed a large demonstration and appealed to the Christian Democrats "to take the 'C' in their name seriously," the editor of an influential Catholic weekly called him "Ayatollah Berkhof." The leader of the Christian Democrats, Ruud Lubbers, spoke of "clericalism." For the churches to express moral concern was acceptable, but linking this concern to concrete developments and drawing political conclusions went too far.

The Churches in the Netherlands 61

In February 1980, IKV asked its member churches directly—not through the NCC—to express their opinion about the IKV proposal for unilateral steps. The proposal had now been discussed for more than two years. Meanwhile, tension had been growing due to the NATO decision of December 1979 and the outcome of the ensuing parliamentary debates. Many church members saw the IKV as having almost toppled the Dutch government and its popular prime minister, Andries van Agt. Polarization in the churches thus focused on IKV. So IKV asked the churches if they wanted to follow it in the direction it was going. This led to a series of bilateral meetings with all member churches.

In 1981, the relation between IKV and the churches again became tense. IKV played a major role in organizing the demonstration of four hundred thousand in Amsterdam on November 21. The weeks before this march were characterized by conflicts with the Christian Democratic Party, which wanted to speak at the rally without supporting the organizing committee's platform of demands. Conflict between IKV and the Christian Democrats, as always, led to criticism from the congregations to church leaders about the formal ties between the churches and IKV.

The churches had been asked by IKV officially to support the march and call upon their members to participate, but none except the Quakers explicitly did so. Instead, the Netherlands Council of Churches organized a national worship service on the evening before the demonstration, saying that this service should neither be seen as an alternative for the demonstration nor as supporting it. It was a relief for IKV that on the occasion itself the liturgy explicitly dealt with the strain in relations between the churches and IKV in a positive way.

In the summer of 1981, a smear campaign was started against IKV by the right-wing press and some high officials, including NATO's General Secretary Joseph Luns, accusing IKV of being under Soviet influence. The campaign stopped only after the Dutch minister of interior affairs declared in

Parliament that there was no evidence whatsoever, "neither hard or soft," to support this charge.[26] The churches fully backed their IKV in rejecting this charge.

In 1982 the conflict arose over the election folder issued by a large number of peace movements advising voting for the left (see p. 47). It had been IKV's policy *not* to give such advice, but when something went wrong in the presentation, IKV got the full blame. Many Christian Democrats were furious.

Groups like ICTO and HBV tried to seize the opportunity to strengthen their position. Various churches discussed how to respond to their request for official recognition and/or how to deal with the polarization at the local level. The synod of the Netherlands Reformed Church (*Nederlandse Hervormde Kerk*) in November 1983 decided against recognition of ICTO and HBV, but it was clear in the debate that this could not be read as a vote of confidence in IKV. However, when the synod of the Reformed Churches in the Netherlands (*Gereformeerde Kerken*), where ICTO support was strongest, took a similar decision in March 1984, it became clear that this challenge to IKV's formal relation to the churches at the national level had failed. In November 1984 when the synod of the Hervormde Kerk finally had a long debate about IKV itself, a proposal for continuing its ties with IKV found the support of the large majority.

In 1983, the question arose anew what the position of the churches would be with regard to the (second) national demonstration on October 29. The Christian Democrats, after almost agreeing to join the organizing committee, finally decided again not to join, which once again precipitated a conflict with IKV. Nevertheless this time, the Netherlands Council of Churches officially supported the demonstration, an indication that the churches and their peace movements had come closer again.

Like two years before, the sheer success of the demonstration made the preceding conflicts fade away—for a while. But when this demonstration appeared to have no political impact as the government continued to move toward a deployment decision, the next conflict erupted. IKV proposed a blockade-like demonstration, clearly limited to the goal of enforcing a new parliamentary debate, as a logical next step. Though several church officials who had endorsed the "Covenant for Life, Justice and Peace" at the World Council of Churches Assembly in Vancouver in August 1983 were prepared to participate, several other church leaders protested. They argued that such a step was theologically beyond the scope of the church. They were clearly worried that their constituency would not accept an endorsement and they feared the consequences for the official link between their churches and IKV.

IKV listened to their warnings. IKV had always been reluctant to take the step to civil disobedience because it feared marginalization. Although not ruling out such actions, it now clearly defined its own limits: no action should call into question the legitimacy of the Dutch system of parliamentary democracy. The final decision also with regard to missile deployment should rest with Parliament, not with demonstrations.

This political orientation, which is also characteristic of Pax Christi, created a conflict with more radical segments of IKV's constituency who wanted to move to tax resistance and other symbolic forms of civil disobedience. IKV has tried to involve the churches in this debate, but so far without much success.

At the moment of this writing, there is tension within the Dutch peace movement (not only IKV and Pax Christi) about the extent to which a peace movement must "play the political game." IKV is often accused of being too closely involved in the political process and suspected of being susceptible to compromise. IKV's response to this is that it is not selling out its ideals when it tries to realize them. So the debate about civil disobedience and the limits to actions is at the same time a debate about the identity of the movement as an actor in politics.

For the period until November 1985 a massive petition drive is now planned as an action which virtually all movements can support, although not all are equally enthusiastic. The action is not supported, however, by a new organization of activists who want to move to civil disobedience.

IKV and Pax Christi are eager to prepare actions for beyond November as well, focused on the political parties, because they think that the national elections of May 1986 will be decisive for the deployment issue. However, it is likely that if the government and Parliament finally decide in favor of deployment of cruise missiles, many spontaneous protests will erupt in Dutch society. Conservative forces will then blame IKV regardless of what IKV's own position is. Such a conflict in society will then once again take the form of a conflict within the churches.

VII. STATEMENTS BY THE CHURCHES

The Netherlands Reformed Church (Hervormde Kerk)

Key sections in the Pastoral Letter to the Congregations issued by the General Synod of the Netherlands Reformed Church in November 1980 show its clear support for the IKV proposal[27]:

> The experience of the last eighteen years has shown us how the possession of these weapons can sweep us along in their accelerated build-up and sophistication and in the development of a strategy of "limited" nuclear warfare. So first of all, we must repeat our "no" of 1962 and then in all clarity state that this "no" also holds without qualification for the possession of all nuclear weapons. However, this repetition and clarification of our 1962 standpoint will not suffice. We also have to consider where we ourselves have fallen short. And we must dare to take another road. . . . Of course we continue to hope for steps toward bilateral and multilateral disarmament. But at the same time we consider it necessary to plead for an approach in which negotiation goes hand in hand with steps which are already clearly set upon the road of disarmament. Since it has turned out to be

impossible to reach multilateral decisions leading toward such steps, they should be taken unilaterally. They should not only point out the direction to be taken; they should also testify to a readiness to take that road ourselves. We consider (and this concerns our responsibility in our own society) that the denuclearization of the Netherlands would be such an unambiguous step. We call for your support for this proposal.

This call by the synod of the Netherlands Reformed Church stirred considerable controversy. After discussing an initial discussion report in the synod, it was sent to all local parishes; after intergrating the comments received, the pastoral letter was adopted thirty-nine votes to thirteen. In drafting these documents, the synod had engaged in extensive consultation with politicians and with military and civilian experts. In the course of preparing its pastoral letter, the synod twice experienced an unusual direct effort to intervene in the debate by two consecutive ministers of defense, both members of the Hervormde Kerk.[28] Through one of the delegates they criticized the drafts and accused the authors of being biased and misrepresenting the facts. In both cases, the advice was ignored.

Following the advice of the two defense ministers would have meant ignoring more than a quarter-century of the synod's own history. In 1962, as a result of a twelve-year-long process of reflection in the synod and following a pastoral letter of 1952, an extensive report was adopted which unequivocally condemned nuclear arms and expressed a "no without any yes" against such arms. Christians should, it was said, not participate in their use even if the government required them to do so. Consequently, the church was accused of undermining NATO strategy, and rightly so, since in order to make NATO's deterrence credible the possible use of nuclear weapons cannot be excluded.

This 1962 report, however, left some doubt as to the synod's position on the *possession* of nuclear arms as part of the West's deterrent. In spite of the fact that the synod had called its "no" a "no without any yes," it had not spoken as unequivocally about the possession of these weapons as it had about their *use*. The reason was a practical one: nuclear weapons could not simply be done away with in one stroke; to abolish them would require a whole process. But this distinction between the use and the possession of nuclear weapons took on its own life. In practice, it diminished the impact of the 1962 report. Many in the church argued, in accordance with the logic of deterrence, that the only way to prevent the use of nuclear weapons was by possessing them.

Nevertheless, by formulating its "no" as a "no without any yes," the synod had said the basic thing. At the time, the Netherlands Reformed Church was the only large "established" church in the West to take this radical a position. Having said the basic thing in 1962, the pastoral letter of 1980 was, from a formal point of view, little more than an update. Still, there were several differences that make it likely to have a more lasting impact than its 1962 predecessor.

First, the distinction between use and possession is clearly overcome. It is explicitly said that the "no without any yes" applies equally to both the use and the possession of nuclear weapons. By adding the specific proposal of denuclearization of the Netherlands as a unilateral first step, the synod did not stay in the sphere of general moral condemnations but moved to the sphere of concrete political proposals.

Second, the new position taken by the synod was the result of a process of unprecedented involvement on the part of the local congregations. The discussion report was sent to all fifteen hundred congregations in September 1979. It was discussed at literally thousands of parish evenings and other meetings. More than seven hundred written responses were received by the synod; some were thirty to forty pages long. A majority supported the general tendency in the discussion report, which condemned the very possession of nuclear arms and not only their use. This response also contained questions and criticism which the synod took into account in its pastoral letter of November 1980, and in twenty-five pages of "considerations" added to it.[29] This process of consultation involved many church people for whom the issue was new, whose interest was likely to become more permanent. The broadness of the discussion process also ensured a higher degree of acceptance in the congregations of what the synod itself said.

Third, unlike 1962, the 1979 report and the 1980 pastoral letter reflected as well as strengthened a rapidly growing movement against the nuclear arms race. For this same reason they were strongly criticized by many leading politicians. The fact that the IKV itself was not mentioned in the pastoral letter was a gesture to those synod delegates who agreed with its proposal but did not want to be associated with IKV and its controversial image.

The political concreteness of the position taken by the synod immediately resulted in a new round of discussions in many local parishes, where it proved to be important to make clear to church members who disagreed and sometimes felt left out, that the synod's statement aimed at communication, not at excommunication. Dissenters were not regarded as second-rate church members.

Fourth, the discussion report and the pastoral letter had some impact on other churches both at home and abroad. In the Netherlands, several other churches referred their congregations to the discussion report as they started their own rounds of discussion. The report by Pax Christi based itself on the Reformed report.

Internationally, the synod formally presented its pastoral letter to a number of sister churches and to the WCC. This gave impulse to a new initiative by the British Council of Churches. In Belgium, the Protestant churches developed a discussion report which clearly drew on the Dutch one.

The report had special influence in the two Germanies. In the Federal Republic, the German edition of the Discussion Report meant welcome support for its rapidly growing peace movement. It came out prior to the peace *Denkschrift* of the Evangelical Church of Germany (EKD). The two reports were very different: the Dutch took a clear position on the problem of nuclear weapons; the Germans sought a compromise. The former chose sides with the peace movement; the latter virtually ignored it. The one spoke out on the most pressing political issues; the other avoided them. When the moderature of the German Reformed Federation challenged the EKD by a far-reaching *status confessionis* position, it based itself on the Netherlands Reformed Church.

In the German Democratic Republic, the text of the pastoral letter was distributed to all regional churches (*Landeskirchen*) and a number of local parishes. An encouraging response came from the Ad Hoc group on Disarmament of the Theological Study Department of the Federation of Evangelical Churches in the GDR. Quoting the pastoral letter extensively, it issued a statement proposing that the GDR should unilaterally abolish its nuclear weapons systems. This statement was supported by a study congress on church and society in Brandenburg in April 1981. The GDR delegation to the 1983 WCC Assembly in Vancouver also gave strong impetus to the World Council's rejection of the spirit and logic of deterrence (which in fact was the same position the Netherlands Reformed Church had taken since 1962).

Immediately after the pastoral letter was issued in November 1980, strong criticism came from two strong "modality organizations" in the Reformed church, which together perhaps represent a majority of church members. HBV (the Reformed Council for Peace Questions) was also created, focusing its influence on members of the Hervormde church. In response to this criticism the moderature of the synod organized meetings with representatives of trade unions and employers' organizations, organizations of military personnel, politicians, and civil servants from the defense sector. Unfortunately, it was not always clear in these discussions to what extent the political significance of the synod's position was recognized by synod members themselves. It was again stressed in these discussions that the pastoral letter was intended "to communicate" and not "to excommunicate." However, by stressing almost exclusively the discussion character, it looked less like a position—or it looked as if the Reformed church took its positions only for the sake of its own education. Of course it was both: it was a position for which the synod would stand *and* there was continuing freedom to discuss it.

In March 1982, a proposal virtually to recognize ICTO lost in the synod by a surprisingly narrow margin. A commission was set up for discussion with ICTO and HBV. In November 1983, the synod agreed to this commission's conclusion that formal recognition of ICTO and HBV be rejected. In March 1984, amid growing tension about the forthcoming government decision about cruise missile deployment, the leadership of the synod added this issue to the synod agenda. Again it became a full debate which led the synod to reconfirm its support for withdrawing all nuclear weapons from the Netherlands and its opposition to admitting new ones, emphasizing that this witness clearly applied to the current deployment of cruise missiles. The votes were thirty-nine in favor and fifteen against. One reason for this rather sudden debate was a surprising development one week earlier in the synod of the other Reformed church, the Gereformeerde Kerken. This church, usually considered more conservative and certainly more reluctant to enter pressing political controversies with concrete statements of its own, had made front page news by saying "no" to cruise missile deployment in clear and strong language.

The Reformed Churches in the Netherlands (Gereformeerde Kerken)

This church had commissioned a study committee to make a discussion report, but the committee was badly divided. When a draft was finally presented to the synod, it was rejected; the committee had to rewrite it. While the conflict was locked up in this study committee for several years, polarization at the local level went on unrestrained. It became worse than in any other church. Supporters of IKV and ICTO fought bitter battles at parish evenings through open letters, advertisements, etc. The Gereformeerde Kerken is smaller than the Hervormde Kerk but its members tend to be more involved in church life. Here one still sees a social difference: the Hervormde church is the former state church; the Gereformeerde church split away from it one century ago as part of a social and theological emancipation process from below. Support for ICTO is stronger in this church than in any other church.

Therefore it came as a complete surprise, causing considerable confusion among politicians, when in March 1984 the synod of the Gereformeerde Kerken declared that "all trust in weapons of mass destruction and threatening populations with them is contrary to a life following Christ." This categorical condemnation of nuclear deterrence was a milestone in a church which heretofore had spoken only in general terms about nuclear weapons as evil but had left political interpretation to its members. The synod now explicitly called upon the government and Parliament to decide against deployment of cruise missiles. Finally, the synod also rejected a special relation with ICTO. The votes were 50 in favor and 18 against. It was front page news in most Dutch newspapers.

Criticism focused on the synod's "no" to the cruise missiles so shortly before the government's decision. The leaders of the Christian Democratic Party strongly criticized what they called the synod's interference in politics. The party chairman is a member of the church, as is the current defense minister. His response was more nuanced, however, questioning thepolitical wisdom of the statement, but also calling it a "contribution" which touches upon a string in himself. Some members of Parliament said that although they agreed with the synod's position, they thought it went beyond the competence of the church to say these things. The chairman of ICTO said the synod's call was "a stab in the back of Parliament."

The new clear "no" to nuclear deterrence had been preceded by almost two decades of internal conflicts and vain efforts to find compromises. In 1957, the synod had seen no reason to address the government on the issue of nuclear weapons. In 1967, the issue could no longer be avoided. Some now even wanted to go further than the position of the Hervormde Kerk in 1962. Others were strongly opposed to any statement challenging the country's defense policy.

For a long time the synod repeatedly appointed new study commissions. A proposal to say that a war with nuclear, bacteriological and chemical weapons is a sin against God was rejected in the synod of 1969–70. In 1978, the synod, while again deciding to study the matter, stated that: "Weapons and methods of mass destruction, and the arms race, are contradicting God's plan of salvation for this world, and are therefore evil." Though church members making conscientious decisions could count on pastoral support, this statement about the demonic character of weapons of mass destruction did not prescribe or proscribe any political decisions. However, the synod offically endorsed the Netherlands Council of Churches' opposition to the N-bomb and against further modernization. This position was repeated in 1979 with regard to the NATO modernization plan.

In the period 1980–83, most of the attention of the synod went to a new study report, which was not accepted, and to conflicts about its relation with IKV and ICTO. In the meantime, no discussion on the issue of the nuclear arms race itself was organized. In November 1982, the synod finally called for local "platforms" to discuss the matter, informing its local churches through a brief "pastoral letter" that dealt more with internal polarization in the church than the dangers of the nuclear arms race. Nevertheless, in almost half of the Gereformeerde local churches, discussions were started which showed the degree of internal dissension. Immediately after the synod itself suddenly cut the Gordian knot of 1984, ICTO spokespersons claimed that 75 percent of the membership of the Gereformeerde Kerken supported its position and that many would suspend their financial contributions to the church. ICTO would seek a revocation of the synod's statements. Indeed, the synod received some 140 formal requests from local churches to this end. In October 1984, the synod decided to postpone their discussion until 1985. Polarization seemed far from over.

The Roman Catholic Church in the Netherlands

A prominent role in stimulating discussions within the Roman Catholic Church in the Netherlands has always been played by the Dutch branch of Pax Christi. It was Pax Christi that took the initiative to organize the peace work of the churches on an ecumenical basis in the framework of IKV. In their early years, IKV and Pax Christi were seen as twins.

Pax Christi is both part of IKV and a member organization of its own. However, since the beginning of the IKV campaign in 1977, IKV has become dominant in the perception of most people. It took Pax Christi until February 1980 before it wholeheartedly endorsed the IKV campaign and decided to give it top priority in its own work.

Pax Christi's influence within the Roman Catholic Church has varied, even in the period that it carried much prestige because Cardinal Alfrink was its chairman. A pastoral letter in 1969 from the bishops about the question of war and peace meant clear support for Pax Christi. But when in 1976 the Dutch bishops issued an episcopal statement on the arms race and disarmament, Pax Christi was hardly involved in its formulation. In this statement, the bishops described three views which were to be considered legitimate: a) pacifism, b) partial pacifism (e.g. nuclear pacifism), and c) the view of those who "reject modern weapons on moral grounds, because of their massive destructive powers, but who are also morally convinced that these weapons cannot be unilaterally abolished overnight because doing so would increase the chances of war, threaten freedom, and give room for the possibilities for new injustices." The bishops seemed to want to give all three views an equal chance.

The reactions showed that politicians with very divergent views from far left to right all found support for their own points of view in the statement. Pax Christi was unhappy; IKV less so. The statement called the system of nuclear deterrence a serious moral problem but did not condemn it. It did condemn striving for a "first strike capability," though did not plead for a "no first use" declaration. On the other hand, the statement said that unilateral steps "should not be excluded." Two criteria were formulated: such steps should be "compatible with an allowed and effective protection of one's own security," and they "should contain an invitation for a positive response, which is necessary for real disarmament."

At first, Pax Christi also was hesitant about the IKV campaign. A main impulse influencing Roman Catholic thinking in the Netherlands came from abroad: the increasingly critical position of the bishops in the U.S., who in their pastoral letter, "To live in Jesus Christ" (late 1976), went much further than the Dutch bishops in condemning nuclear deterrence.

On February 14, 1978 the Dutch bishops wrote a letter to the Dutch government opposing the neutron bomb and endorsing the position of the NCC. On December 6, 1979, they wrote a letter to parliament opposing the NATO modernization decision. In February 1980 the national board of Pax Christi finally endorsed the IKV campaign and decided to give it full priority. The bishops asked Pax Christi to advise them on the IKV proposal because in February 1980, IKV put a number of questions before all participating churches. In October 1980, Pax Christi published its advice: a report of some 70 pages about the IKV proposal with ethical, scientific, political and pastoral considerations. Pax Christi advised the bishops:

1) to reject both the use and possession of nuclear weapons and so to contribute to the further development in this direction of the Roman Catholic Church as a whole;
2) to stress the need for new roads toward disarmament;
3) to plead for unilateral steps toward bilateral disarmament and to help develop moral norms for responsible steps on this road;
4) to stress again its earlier "no" to any modernization;
5) to support the IKV proposal; and

6) to support and protect the work of church-related peace movements, such as IKV and Pax Christi.

At that time, polarization in the Dutch Roman Catholic Church was much less than in the Protestant churches. No lay organization was formed, as in the Protestant churches, to counter the influence of Pax Christi and IKV. One explanation may be that conservative Catholics were confident that the bishops, and certainly the Vatican, would simply not allow radical positions. It is well-known that a small group of archconservative Dutch Catholics, including NATO secretary general Joseph Luns, was listened to carefully in Rome. Rome was replacing progressive bishops with conservative ones. But as to the short-term effects, these conservative forces may have been somewhat too confident.

In December 1980, the bishops decided to have a consultation round on the Pax Christi report. The main question the bishops put before the Roman Catholic Church province was: "Are you in principle in favor of a unilateral step under the double condition we have formulated in our statement of 1976?" Because of the ambivalent language, this question caused some confusion.

The consultation round was organized differently in different dioceses. In some, all parishes were approached; in others, not. Nevertheless, it turned out to be an intensive process of discussion and conscientization. Especially the "alternative structure" in the Roman Catholic Church of many religious orders and congregations became very much involved.

It is estimated that forty thousand persons participated in the discussions. There were more than 2,200 reactions: 1,180 from individuals, 1,037 from groups and institutions. The individual reactions were split: half in favor and half against unilateral steps. A majority of the group and institutional reactions were in favor of unilateral steps. After intensive discussion in closed sessions, the bishops published in June 1983 their pastoral letter on "Peace and Justice," containing a much stronger condemnation of nuclear weapons than before and repeating their opposition to the new missiles. The bishops declared themselves against any use of nuclear weapons, including for political pressure. The possession of nuclear weapons in their intention to "deter" could only be accepted on a temporary basis as a step or phase in the process of disarmament.

Again, many different sectors in Dutch society welcomed the letter as support for their own views. But this time, the peace movement had more reason to do so than the government, which could only quote the positive remarks of the bishops about the Geneva talks as support for government policy.

One conclusion was clear: the Dutch church province had been set in motion at all levels. After the pastoral letter was published, Pax Christi organized a new discussion round to keep the process going. The huge demonstration on October 29, 1983 was addressed by Bishop Ernst as chairman of Pax Christi. The day before, more than 4,800 members of religious orders and congregations had placed page-long advertisements in the newspapers to express their solidarity with the demonstration.

Early in 1984, however, the bishops seemed to waver. After a meeting with the Christian Democrats, the newly-appointed Archbishop Simonis said that the bishops had pressed for diminishing the role of nuclear weapons, but if a politician conscientiously came to the conclusion that deploying cruise missiles could contribute to this goal, he could respect this. The also newly-appointed Bishop Bär, who shortly before he became auxiliary bishop had written an article in the official *NATO Review*[30] critical of the antinuclear tendencies in the church, addressed an ICTO meeting in March. He criticized pacifism, unilateral steps and concrete statements, and supported NATO and ICTO. He emphasized that (critical) statements by the Netherlands Council of Churches had no authority.

The conditions formulated by the Dutch bishops in their June 1983 pastoral letter for their temporary tolerance of nuclear deterrence virtually amounted to a rejection of nuclear deterrence. But given these later statements by individual bishops, it could easily turn out to be a slippery position, not necessarily providing the firm ground to oppose new developments at the moments when its opposition would really count. Much will depend on Pax Christi's ability to keep up the momentum.

Other Churches

Since the launching of the IKV campaign in 1977, the development in the positions of the three large Dutch churches has been in the direction from "rather moderate" to "more radical" and from "rather general" to "more concrete." More precisely, the movement was from conditioned tolerance of nuclear deterrence toward categorical rejection, and from general expressions of concern to concrete proposals for a way out. The point of departure of the churches was not the same, but the direction was identical. The same tendency has become visible in the ecumenical movement, resulting in the position of the 1983 WCC Assembly in Vancouver. A brief survey of developments in the smaller churches in the Netherlands shows basically the same pattern.

The three churches discussed so far together account for more than two-thirds of the Dutch population. All other churches combined account for only six to seven percent. However, positions taken by the smaller churches on nuclear weapons tend to get more attention than their numbers would seem to warrant; their views are very much seen as part of a pattern, and therefore of political relevance. This section will deal only with those churches which participate in the IKV and Netherlands Council of Churches. However, even small (mainly orthodox Protestant) churches which refuse to take part in such ecumenical cooperation have not been left untouched by the nuclear weapons debate. In September 1983, fourteen ministers of the Christian Reformed Church (a church with 75,000 members and some 150 ministers) caused much stir by supporting an appeal against deployment of cruise missiles.

The *Remonstrant Brotherhood* traditionally plays a vanguard role on social-political issues, despite its rather elitist and often conservative constituency. In 1957, it condemned the use of nuclear energy for purposes of destruction, but the Brotherhood Council was unable to formulate a new position following the 1962 "no without any yes" of the Netherlands Reformed Church. However in 1979, the discussion report of the Netherland Reformed Church was sent to all local Remonstrant congregations asking them to respond. In June 1980, a new "no" to nuclear deterrence was expressed. A special council meeting was held in December 1980 to discuss the IKV proposal. It called for "unilateral steps" without specifically endorsing the IKV proposal. The IKV was invited to present regular progress reports on its work in order to strengthen the link between the churches and IKV.

The *Evangelical Lutheran Church* is traditionally reluctant to speak on social-political affairs. It was one of the few member churches of the Council of Churches not to endorse the Councils's "no" of 1978 to the neutron bomb and any further modernization. The synod's argument was that it could not judge the merits of the neutron bomb in NATO's strategy of "flexible response." However, the issue remained on the agenda. In 1979, the IKV campaign was supported (including financial support) although the IKV proposal was not endorsed as such. In 1980, a discussion round was started in the local congregations. In May 1981, the synod expressed explicitly that the IKV was "its" peace organization. Two years later, in May 1983, a motion to cut the links with IKV lost in the synod.

The *Mennonite Brotherhood* gives priority to personal witness above official positions. Nevertheless, it supported the statement of the Council of Churches in 1978, calling also for further discussion and study in light of Mennonite tradition. In 1979, the Brotherhood's council endorsed the IKV campaign and appealed to the government not to agree with the NATO decision. In 1980, a discussion round was started, trying to revive the tradition of the Brotherhood as a "historic peace church." Although a significant minority of the church members proved to be against the Brotherhood's official participation in IKV, the link with IKV was reconfirmed by a strong majority in the Brotherhood's council in May 1983.

The *Old Catholic Church* is reluctant to make concrete statements. It did not endorse the Council of Churches' position of February 1978. Instead, a study committee was set up, which produced a discussion report about the IKV campaign. In November 1982, a proposal to endorse the IKV campaign in general terms was withdrawn because it proved to be too divisive. Instead, appreciation was expressed for IKV's work of conscientization.

The *Moravian Church* supported the Council of Churches' position of 1978 and immediately informed its sister churches in other NATO countries. The reaction from the Moravian church in the U.S. was especially discouraging, warning its Dutch sister church against "communist" ties. The parishes in Surinam also were informed, where membership is much larger than in the Netherlands. In 1982, a liturgy was created for a special Peace Sunday.

The *Society of Friends (Quakers)* endorsed the IKV campaign already in February 1978. In November 1979, it called upon Parliament not to agree to the NATO modernization. A study report was made, and in May 1983, the Quakers spoke out clearly against the NATO modernization.

VIII. PUBLIC OPINION AND THE ROLE OF THE CHURCHES

We are faced with a discrepancy between public opinion at the mass level and at the level of the active and interested public as it takes an organized form in the statement and activities of important institutions like the trade unions and the churches. Although public opinion polls continuously show considerable opposition to the new missiles (two out of three reject deployment on a simple yes/no question, while 40 percent can be considered to be unconditionally opposed) even among liberals and Christian Democrats, these feelings so far have not had a major impact on the distribution of political power at the level of Parliament and government, because parliamentary elections are decided on other issues. Public opinion polls, while showing strong disaffection in general with the system of nuclear deterrence and the deployment of (new) nuclear weapons (including majorities for the unilateral removal of nuclear weapons from the Netherlands), also show strong support for membership in NATO and the need to maintain military equilibrium between East and West. They also show more signs of continuity than change. What has happened, however, is that the intensity of the feelings of a considerable segment of the public have increased to the level that these people are willing to act upon their beliefs. But this is not true for all. Indeed, important groups are either uninterested or cling to traditional views of security. Others are undecided and wavering between traditional views and those expressed by the churches and propagated by the peace movement. They are found primarily among those church members who still vote for the Christian Democratic Party. While as many as 40 percent of these oppose deployment of the new missiles, others are wavering or would be prepared to accept, in the end, a deployment decision. Further discussions are clearly necessary.

At first sight it would seem that the churches are eminently suited to play a role in this and to help build bridges between the "center" and the "periphery" of society, between those supporting the peace movement and its ideas and the supporters of "peace through strength." They provide the platform where the necessary dialogues may take place. For the churches themselves, the urgent question poses itself: Why do the church statements fail to convince so many of their members?

IX. THE NEED FOR POSITIVE ALTERNATIVES

Nuclear deterrence is going through a "crisis of faith" in Europe. Whatever the impact of the Dutch churches on immediate issues like the deployment of cruise missiles, one long-term effect is likely to be their great contribution to this "crisis of faith." The social base for NATO's and the Warsaw Pact's deterrence strategies as credible ways of securing peace is eroding. This means at the same time that a potential social base for political alternatives is growing. The response of NATO to this "crisis of faith" has been a great effort to "restore faith" by massive public relations campaigns, by strategic adjustments, by calling for conventional arms improvements, etc.

This places the churches in a dilemma. On the one hand, their deep concern allows no restoration of "faith" in nuclear deterrence by these simple mechanisms. The only acceptable response is a search for real alternatives.[31] On the other hand, to challenge and resist those official efforts to "restore faith" requires a degree of expertise not always available in the churches; when it is available, churches may be reluctant to use it. Nevertheless, the development from "general" to "concrete" and from "moderate" to "more radical" cannot stop at this point. The "no" to nuclear deterrence will have to be translated gradually into a "yes" to certain alternatives. In this respect, the churches have only just begun the discussion and much work remains to be done.

It is true that the concept of unilateral initiatives has been endorsed cautiously, in some form or another, by most churches. The churches have been less creative, however, when it comes to converting notions like reconciliation, the breaking down of false enemy images, the creation of international trust and the management of antagonistic relationships into concrete political programs. Thinking about alternative and less violent systems of security has also lagged behind. New ideas about overcoming the bloc divisions in Europe are urgently needed.

This paucity of new ideas is deplorable because in our experience, the willingness of many people to reject our present system of security as immoral and leading to a dead end is hampered by the lack of convincing answers to their pressing questions. These include the very topics mentioned above: "Can we trust our opponents?", "How can we create trust?", "Does the striving for peace at all costs not detract from obligations to defend justice?", "Are there viable alternatives to the current military defense system?" These are hard questions. Emotions as well as rational arguments play a part here. It is clearly not sufficient merely to call for trust, to point out that security is a matter of weighing risks, that a risk-free system seems an impossibility and that Christians are called to risk even their lives. Doctors may know what it takes to cure a disease, but if the patient is not willing to take the prescription this knowledge is of no avail.[32]

Regardless of how the "Euromissiles crisis" will end, a political discussion about the future of Europe is urgently needed. This will necessarily have to be a discussion in which the countries of Eastern Europe are included. In fact, the discussion about the future of Europe has been the context of IKV's work since it was founded. The basis for IKV's campaign against nuclear weapons was already laid in 1972 with a position paper on "The Future of Europe" and in 1984, IKV and Pax Christi again published a report about political alternatives in Europe to avoid their anti-missiles actions being isolated from the general political context.[33]

In this connection, the evolving dialogue with the Federation of Evangelical Churches in the GDR is particularly important. This church is one of the rare instances in both East and West where the ethical and theological "no" to nuclear deterrence has been linked to the search for political alternatives, using the concept of "common security" of the Palme Report.[34] In many churches, this discussion has hardly been started. There is still a tendency to discuss nuclear weapons in moral terms, abstracting them from social, cultural and political reality as if they were a completely separate entity.

For prophetic minorities within the churches and in the peace movement, the matter may be more simple. Some of them take the view—if they think about ways of convincing others at all— that it is of primary importance to build "an alternative society" ("within this world, but not of it") and to give witness through one's personal commitment to a nonviolent lifestyle. Dramatic acts and unorthodox forms of communication such as acts of civil disobedience may indeed help to communicate intensity of feelings and grievances, as we know from the history of social movements. The limitations of this approach are, however, also well-known.

The enormous energy raised in recent years has increased the expectation that real changes may be possible and the arms spiral may be reversed. But if those now mobilized are not to fall back out of despair to fruitless radicalism or renewed apathy, successes are necessary. This requires consolidation of the gains made in the centers of our societies. This is all the more true if we agree with W.A. Williams that the opportunities for real change depend "on the extent to which calm and confident and enlightened conservatives can see and bring themselves to act upon the validity of a radical analysis."[35]

There is some evidence that some conservatives in positions of power in our societies are getting nervous. They no longer defend "established truths" about peace and security with the same amount of self-confidence. We see a real reversal of roles, where those who used to be the accusers now have to defend themselves. Such a loss of confidence among the established elites may be a precondition of change, but may also lead to a hardening of positions in which those in command no longer listen to the signals from their environment.

Indeed, the criticism of the doctrine of deterrence is based in part on the well-known phenomenon that under conditions of threat, people may just as well refuse to give in as bow to pressures. The same phenomenon may apply to traditional elites coming under increasing pressure within their societies. It seems a proper task of the churches, therefore, not to abandon their fundamental rejection of the system of deterrence or their demands for disarmament, but to combine them with a serious effort to restore the communication and dialogue necessary for a new consensus to arise. Polarization is often healthy and unavoidable, but only as a first step. Under conditions of threat people may change their behavior, but not their minds.

X. THE NEED TO ESTABLISH A NEW CONSENSUS

We have pointed out that there are still very different views or even contradictory interests within the churches which stand in need of reconciliation. We can distinguish at least four concrete areas where the need to establish a new consensus is evident.

(1) The churches are faced with the task of coping with the reality that very different views on how to reach peace and security exist in their midst, and therefore of witnessing to their own beliefs while assisting the necessary social process of founding a new consensus. The church cannot decide the truth or falsity of certain views about reality by a majority vote. To be a community of believers, however, we must do more than just take each other seriously. Compromises are always compromising, and their necessity for getting anything done may stand in the way of a commitment to truth and faith. But the degree to which conscientious commitment should outweigh the striving for consensus, even at the cost of a certain ambiguity, must always remain an arguable point.

(2) The churches—at least in the Netherlands—are faced with the need to overcome the gap between their leadership and the rank-and-file. If the latter are reluctant to follow their leaders' political conclusions, this may well be caused by their overwhelming feeling of powerlessness. When people feel powerless, they are inclined to make the best of it by rationalizing a more positive view of the status quo. Conservatism is a useful protection against insecurity. This problem does not pose itself in the same way for the leadership, because they are not powerless; thus the gap between the demands of "idealism" and "reality" is less self-evident for them. To restore the people's confidence that they do matter and that politics is not decided "over their heads" may be the most effective way to narrow the present gap in attitudes. This is also pastorally relevant.

(3) A third area is the relationship between the churches and their peace movement. While the latter is threatened by self-righteousness, an absolutist view of its own proposals and a lack of patience, the former is faced with the danger of complacency and an unacceptable reluctance to disturb the peace of mind of their members. A certain ambivalence or even love-hate relationship between the churches and their peace movement is probably unavoidable. Psychologically and sociologically they are different types of organizations. Yet one cannot live without the other. The churches will not take their role as peacemakers seriously without the continuous prodding of the peace movement, despite its often clumsy behavior. But the peace movement cannot do without the churches either, not only because they provide the essential assets of legitimacy and respectability, but also because they remind the peace movement that a vanguard only does useful work if it does not lose contact with the main body. When both see each other as "them" and "us," something is definitely wrong.

(4) Finally, both the churches and the peace movement must deal with the fundamental and complicated question of the proper role of the churches vis-à-vis other institutions in society, especially the political parties. While many in the churches (especially in the leadership) accept a clear collective political responsibility of the churches as such (if only because this legitimizes their own political role), others reject this involvement. Some reject it because of its alleged divisive nature or its direction ("no politics in the church," meaning today "no leftist politics in the church"); others, because of the impossibility of reaching such forms of unanimity and concreteness that the statements by the churches may be relevant to politicians who have to make decisions here and now.

In summary, what we are arguing is not that the churches should come to a different assessment of the nuclear predicament, nor that they should lessen their engagement in the concrete political struggle into which they have been drawn under the prodding of the peace movement. What needed to be said has been said. The ensuing polarization was both healthy and unavoidable. Polarization is not always to be deplored, but neither is it the final answer. What needs to be done now is both to consolidate the positions gained by maintaining and strengthening the newly-won support, and also to make a more serious effort to build bridges for those who have remained unconvinced or wavering in their attitudes. For this, new questions and new answers should be formulated, as well as new forms of communication sought. Otherwise the changes necessary on the governmental level will never be obtained.

One advantage of moving toward clearer political statements in the future could be more clarity about the very nature of church statements on political issues. The more clearly political a statement is, the easier it should be to discuss it, precisely because it is political. This should certainly be so in nonpolitical bodies like the churches. In practice, the opposite is often the case, which in the Dutch situation may very well be due to lack of experience in how to be the church in the context of a secular, pluriform society and a parliamentary democracy.

NOTES

1. Early in 1984, membership of CND (Campaign for Nuclear Disarmament) in Britain was growing, with 1,000 new members a week. And in February 1984, polls in the Netherlands showed that opposition to deployment of cruise missiles had grown significantly among voters of the ruling government coalition (according to one poll, opposition among voters of the key Christian Democratic party had increased from 40 percent in October to 51 percent).
2. Walter Laqueur, " 'Hollanditis': A New Stage in European Neutralism," *Commentary* 72 (1981), pp. 19–27.
3. All figures are from 1981 or 1982, based on official census data.
4. G.A. Irwin, "Patterns of Voting Behavior in the Netherlands," in *The Economy and Politics of the Netherlands since 1945*, ed. R.T. Griffith, The Hague: Marinus Nijhoff, 1980, pp. 199–223.
5. The history and development of the peace movement in the Netherlands are discussed in Ph.P. Everts and G. Walraven, *Vredesbeweging* (The peace movement). Utrecht: Spectrum, 1984.
6. The IKV proposal is discussed in more detail in Ph.P. Everts and B.J.Th. ter Verr, "Unilateral Steps Toward a Disarmament Process: New Initiatives in the

Netherlands," in: *Nuclear War in Europe*, eds. G.M. LaRoque and H.W. Tromp, Groningen: Groningen University Press, 1982, pp. 193–227.
7. See, for instance, M. Lumsden, "Nuclear Weapons and the New Peace Movement", in *SIPRI Yearbook of World Armament and Disarmament*, 1983; B.J.Th. ter Veer, "New Peace Movement in Western Europe", *International Peace Research Newsletter*, 21 (1983), pp. 3, 10–17; and N. Young, "The Contemporary European Anti-Nuclear Movement: Experiments in the Mobilization of Public Power", *Peace and Change*, 11 (1983), pp. 1,1–16.
8. See, for instance, A. Etzioni, *The Hard Way to Peace*, New York: Collier Books, 1962; C.E. Osgood, *An Alternative to War or Surrender*, Urbana, Ill.: University of Illinois Press, 1962; and *Peace Research Reviews*, Vol. 8: issues 1 and 2 devoted to the writings of Etzioni, Osgood and others on unilateral initiatives.
9. For the history of the "Stop de N-bom" campaign, see P. Maessen, *Wie stopt de neutronenbom?*, Leiden: Institute for International Studies, 1979; and D. Whitman, *The Press and the Neutron Bomb*, Cambridge, Mass.: Center for Press, Politics and Public Policy, Kennedy School of Government, Harvard University, 1984.
10. The key sentence in Carter's Presidential Statement on Enhanced Radiation Warheads of April 7, 1978 was: "Accordingly, I have ordered the Defense Department to proceed with the modernization of the Lance missile nuclear warhead and the 8-inch weapon system, leaving open the option of installing the enhanced radiation elements. . ." The reports by IKV were based on, among other sources, *Hearings on H.R. 11036, DOE Authorization Legislation (National Security Programs) for FY 1979* by the Intelligence and Military Application of Nuclear Energy Subcommittee of the Committee on Armed Services, House of Representatives, February, March and April 1978.
11. R.C. Eichenberg, "The Myth of Hollanditis," *International Security* (1983), 2, pp. 143–159; Ph.P. Everts, *Public Opinion, the Churches and Foreign Policy, Studies of Domestic Factors in the Making of Dutch Foreign Policy*, Leiden: Institute for International Studies, University of Leiden, 1983; and Ph.P. Everts, "Public Opinion on Nuclear Weapons, Defence and Security: The Case of the Netherlands", to be published in *Public Opinion and Atlantic Defense*, eds. G. Flynn and H. Rattinger, for the Atlantic Institute, Paris (forthcoming).
12. Twice in the official communique of the special NATO meeting of December 12, 1979, the modernization decision and the arms control part were called "two parallel and complementary approaches". This was correct. The second track never provided an *alternative* to the first track.
13. For instance, pictures exist from before 1970 of a mobile SS-14 missile in the field, at the time assumed to be the successor of the SS-4 and SS-5. In 1965, a SS-15 missile was shown at Red Square, also thought to be their successor.
14. "Finally, while the military rationale, and particularly the threat of the SS-20, was used consistently to gain public support for LRTNF modernization, political and psychological factors provided the predominant criteria for the final proposal. Most officials conceded that the strictly military rationales—other than the renewal of old systems—were not convincing." *The Modernization of NATO's LRTNF*, Report prepared for the Subcommittee on Europe and the Middle East

of the Committee on Foreign Affairs, U.S. House of Representatives, by the Congressional Research Service, December 31, 1980, p. 33.
15. For a more detailed account, see Laurens Hogebrink, "The NATO TNF Debate in the Netherlands," *Disarmament Campaigns*, No. 1, February 1980.
16. The only flexibility in NATO's approach as described in the official communique of the NATO meeting of December 12, 1979 was to be found in the formula *"de jure* equality," apparently meaning that the U.S. would have the right to have equal numbers but could choose not to exercise this right. In later statements of the "principles" guiding the U.S. (and NATO's) negotiation position, this flexibility was lost; it was restored again by Reagan in September 1983: *"de jure"* now could apply to Asia, "equality" applied to Europe, thereby only underlining the desire for a separate Euro-strategic balance.
17. In 1963, after the Cuban missile crisis, U.S. land-based ballistic missiles were withdrawn from Turkey, Italy and the U.K. Their role was taken over by submarine based Polaris missiles, assigned to NATO. This sea-based force has been steadily modernized since. For instance, the MIRV technology was not introduced in the European theater by the Soviet SS-20 in 1977, but a few years earlier by the MIRVing of the U.S. Poseidon missiles assigned to SACEUR.
18. *Interim Report on Nuclear Weapons in Europe*, prepared by the North Atlantic Assembly's Special Committee on Nuclear Weapons in Europe. Report to the Committee on Foreign Relations, U.S. Senate, 1981, p. 24.
19. For a detailed overview of developments in Geneva and the response by the peace movement, see articles by Laurens Hogebrink in *Disarmament Campaigns*, Nos. 15 (Oct. 1982), 16 (Nov. 1982), 19 (Feb. 1983), 22 (May 1983), 24 (July/Aug. 1983) and 28 (Dec. 1983). The complete set can be obtained from the Department of Church and Society, Netherlands Reformed Church, Carnegielaan 9, The Hague, Netherlands.
20. See Everts and Walraven, op. cit., for a discussion of these concepts.
21. For a survey and background story, see Laurens Hogebrink, "Why They Marched," *Disarmament Campaigns*, No. 9, March 1982.
22. For the full story, see Volkmar Deile and Ulrich Frei, "Wie es zur Demonstration von 10.10.81 in Bonn kam," *Bonn 10.10.81*. ASF/AGF, Lamuv Verlag, 1981.
23. See for further information, Everts, *Public opinion* . . . , pp. 135–145.
24. P.R. Baehr et al., *Elite and Buitenlandse Politiek in Nederland* Elite and Foreign Policy in the Netherlands, The Hague: Staatsuitgeverij, 1978; and P.R. Baehr, "The Dutch Foreign Policy Elite: A descriptive study of perceptions and attitudes," *International Studies Quarterly* 24 (1980), 2, pp. 223–261.
25. See for the sources of these and other data Everts, *Public Opinion* . . . , pp. 154–177.
26. For a description, see Laurens Hogebrink, "Soft and Softer Evidence," *Disarmament Campaigns*, No. 9, March 1982.
27. *Kernbewapening*, Handreiking van de generale synode van de Nederlandse Hervormde Kerk voor een nieuw gesprek over het vraagstuk van de kernwapens, The Hague, 1979. The German translation has appeared as *Kirche und Kernbewaffnung*, Neukirchen-Vlyn, 1981.

28. The following section is partly based on Laurens Hogebrink, "A New Phase in the Nuclear Arms Debate? Comments on the Pastoral Letter of the Netherlands Reformed Church," *The Ecumenical Review*, July 1981. The same issue contains the English translation of the synod's "Pastoral Letter on Nuclear Weapons" of November 1980.
29. The pastoral letter itself is only four pages long. The "Considerations" have also been published in a German translation, *Wort an die Gemeinden zur Kernbewaffnung*, Brief, Erläuterung und Bericht, Neukirchen-Vlyn, 1982.
30. *NATO Review, February 1982*.
31. Cf. the article by Mient Jan Faber in *END Journal*, 1983, 6, and Laurens Hogebrink, *Prospects and priorities for the peace movements*, paper prepared for the SIPRI Workshop on Surprise Attack, December 1983.
32. Ph.P. Everts, "Friedensforschung, Friedensbewegung und die Kirchen—Einige Erfahrungen aus den Niederlanden," in *Friedensforschung, Kirche und kirchliche Friedensbewegungen*, H.M. Birckenbach (editor), Jahrbuch für Friedens- und Konflikt-Forschung, Vol. 10. Frankfurt: Haag u. Herchen, 1983, pp. 126–138.
33. *The Future of Europe: Armed Security or Political Peace*, discussion paper by IKV and Pax Christi, November 1984.
34. Cf. *Sicherheitspartnerschaft und Frieden in Europa. Aufgaben der deutschen Staaten, Verantwortung der deutschen Kirchen*, Theologischen Studienabteilung beim Bund des Evangelische Kirchen in der DDR, 1983.
35. W.A. Williams, *The Tragedy of American Diplomacy*, 19th pr., New York: Delta Books, 1962.

The Churches and the Debate on Nuclear Weapons and Disarmament in the Federal Republic of Germany

by Wolfgang Huber

I. THE SETTING

New Challenges in the Eighties

With the beginning of the eighties, a fresh and lively debate on peace, nuclear weapons and disarmament started both in Europe and in the United States. Seen from a Western European perspective, there were three main reasons for this new intensity.

In the seventies, an attempt was made to control East-West conflicts on the political level by the policy of *détente*. This policy diminished the danger of using the military arsenals both sides now possess. But *détente* did not touch the system of arms itself. Under the umbrella of *détente* and a parallel development-aid policy during the seventies, the arms race continued on both sides. New systems of weapons were produced. The expenditure for arms rose to an inconceivable height.

Professor Wolfgang Huber, Executive President of the *Kirchentag*, is Professor of Social Ethics at the University of Heidelberg, Federal Republic of Germany.

While the guiding concept of *détente* was to minimize conflict by seeking agreement on the level of interests, the guiding concept of military policy continued to increase the other's risk. The fact that the one approach contradicted the other came to light as soon as severe international conflicts shook the policy of *détente*. Can security be increased by imposing incalculable risk on the potential enemy? This logic proved to be a deception. In the case of crisis or, worse, warlike struggle, the other's risk inevitably turns against oneself. The shock to *détente* caused a growing number of people to realize that the concept of security by risk leads into a blind alley. In a world bristling with weapons we either have common security or none at all. The consequence of this realization was an increasing protest against politics linking ideological confrontation with military rearmament. Euromissiles become the symbol of this protest.

The doctrine behind military policies since the end of the fifties has been prevention of war by means of deterrence. Explosion of the means of destruction stored on the globe is to be avoided by threatening to explode them. This implies a twofold paradox.

First: deterrence is credible only when the threat implies the readiness to employ these means of mass destruction. However, there is no imaginable moral or political end which might possibly justify their use. The assumption that peace and liberty can be defended by mass destruction is ethically untenable. Will peace be protected durably by threatening something that is untenable? The system of deterrence entangles all in an endless ethical dilemma. Everyone concerned is supposed to credibly threaten to do what he cannot justify doing.

Second: In addition to the ethical self-contradiction of the system of deterrence, there is a technical one. The idea of mutual deterrence presupposes a stable balance between the opponents, including their second strike capability. The balance, however, is constantly jeopardized by technological innovation. At any time, one or the other side—NATO or the Warsaw Pact, the United States or the Soviet Union—can declare itself inferior in a certain aspect of armament, and thus obliged to "counter-arm" prior to any limit or decrease of arms. What is said to be a balance tends, in fact, to be a race. Under the guise of concern for stability a competition for superiority takes place. In order to stop this deadly race, the deceptive power of thinking in terms of "balance" must be broken.

Over the years, both sides in the arms race have shown now and again the readiness to secure their own sphere of political influence by military force. An increasing number of people understand this intervention policy to be one of the most dangerous elements in the contemporary international situation. The sense of danger sharpened when voices were heard from the U.S. administration suggesting a shift from "retaliation deterrence" to "warfare deterrence." This is the reason for the fear in Western Europe that American military policies might assume that nuclear war can be limited, waged and won. The shift to such a concept blurs the distinction between threatening with and employing nuclear weapons. There is no longer a clear-cut difference, but a gliding continuity. The ethical discussion hitherto had judged that whereas the use of nuclear weapons is unjustifiable, threatening with them is justifiable, since the end is the prevention of war. Today, however, this proves to be a rather doubtful argument. So there are both ethical and political reasons for the decision by the European peace movement to say "no without any yes" to nuclear weapons. Politically, the peace movement opposes the stationing of new middle-range nuclear missiles on European soil. Ethically, it affirms that both using and threatening to use nuclear weapons are to be rejected.

These factors challenge the churches to reconsider their peace ethics and political options with new intensity.

The Relationship of Church and State and the Church's Responsibility for Peace

The relations of the Christian churches in Germany to state and society are deeply affected by the confessional split between Protestant and Catholic. The policy in the post-Reformation era had sought to preserve the confessional homogeneity of the different German territories. However, the concept of the "one confession" state (*cuius regio eius religio*) could not be maintained. Since 1800 at least, confessional policy in Germany has had to deal with the parity of two large confessional churches, the Catholic Church and the Protestant *Landeskirchen* (regional Lutheran, United and Reformed churches). These two confessions include by far the majority of the population and therefore regard themselves as *Volkskirchen*, or "people's churches." The political turning points of 1918, 1933 and 1945 brought little change in this respect. Church membership has decreased for some decades. But still today, about 85 percent of the population in the Federal Republic of Germany belongs to one of the two main churches. At present, the Catholic Church is a little larger than the Protestant church, which had been the somewhat larger church during the first years after the war.

The leading bishops of the Protestant Landeskirchen used to be the reigning princes of the territory. Until 1918, these churches were especially near and loyal to the state. The Catholic Church tried to avoid the charge of ultramontanism (allegiance to the Pope "beyond the mountains") by a pronounced national-political loyalty. The alliance of "throne and altar" was strongly emphasized during the First World War. Even after 1918, some elements of this alliance remained. Both confessions were badly prepared by their traditions for their struggle with the National Socialist state. The struggle of the Confessing Church was supported merely by a small minority within German Protestantism. Only a few—Dietrich Bonhoeffer in particular—perceived the political-social dimension of the struggle against Nazism. Nevertheless, the Barmen Theological Declaration of 1934 formulated a rudimentary political ethics which obligated the church to take up its task of critical public responsibility.

After 1945, however, it was not so much the Confessing Church which set the pattern for the future as it was the exceptional situation of German postwar society. Decisions made under those exceptional circumstances still dominate, in essence, the relations between church and state. The churches after 1945 were the only social institutions which survived the Third Reich more or less intact. They could take up and continue their pre-Nazi traditions earlier and more easily than other sections of society. This made them "partners" of the state in building the new political and social order. They realized their public mandate (*Offentlichkeitsauftrag*) mainly by legitimating the new order. The churches, backed by their international and ecumenical contacts, soon established a system of social service (*diakonia*). Pastoral care and preaching provided important remedies for the emotional disturbance many had experienced at the end of the war and in the following years. The churches proved to be a place to find a new inner orientation after the seduction of National Socialism and its downfall.

This elevated state of the churches did not last long. In the sixties, the church was no longer the only organization still intact after the Third Reich; it was one among a number of associations in competition with each other. The church's preaching and pronouncements of social questions were no longer so powerful in offering comprehensive orientation. Instead of "words" spoken with authority, the churches began to issue *Denkschriften*, introducing arguments into public discussion. Legitimization by the churches for political and social rule receded. The pattern of "partnership" between church and state became less plausible. As yet, however, theology and the churches have scarcely begun to respond to this change. One of the most important aspects of the recent peace discussion in the churches is that it stimulates the quest for new clarity in ethical thinking and discernment of political responsibility.

Mainstream political ethics in German Protestantism traditionally gave priority to national allegiance over commitment to peace. Only after the Second World War, which Germany had initiated, was a thorough revision felt to be necessary. The first declarations by the church in the postwar years argued against any hope for a divided Germany in a further war and refused any idea of rearmament. In

April 1950, the Synod of the *Evangelische Kirche in Deutschland* (EKD), meeting in Berlin-Weissensee, issued a message on "What the Church Can Do for Peace." The covenant of peace between God and humanity in Christ, said the declaration, is the reason why Christians hope for peace even when an apparently imminent war arouses fear. To proclaim the peace of God is the service which the church owes the world. The ecumenical community of Christians in the world, the mutual connection between Christians in divided Germany and the refusal to obey the spirit of hate and enmity were declared to be the most important contributions of the church to peace. The message emphasized the correlation of peace and social justice and supported conscientious objectors to military service.

The unanimity expressed in the message from Berlin-Weissensee was soon a matter of the past. It was disrupted in the early fifties by the decisions to rearm the Federal Republic of Germany and the German Democratic Republic. A few years later, the issue of German participation in the production, testing and use of nuclear weapons came into view. In the face of this, ethical attitudes toward peace became deeply divided. Partisans of Karl Barth's theology, particularly Gustav Heinemann and Martin Niemöller, remembering Germany's guilt in the Second World War and the hope for a reunion of Germany, proposed an ethics based on the recognition of Christ's reign in all spheres of life and called on Germany to refrain from any military contribution. Others held that securing peace is a problem of secular reason that does not immediately concern Christian confession and obedience; they agreed that the rearmament of Germany was a political necessity. In the era of the cold war, anti-communism (which during National Socialism had made it easier for many Protestants and Catholics to accept that regime) proved once more to be one of the most important motivations for political decision by Christians and churches in the Federal Republic.

The controversy came to a peak in the dispute over nuclear

weapons. In the "Göttingen Declaration" of April 12, 1957, eighteen nuclear scientists refused any cooperation in the production or testing of such arms. The views represented within the Protestant church spanned from the conviction that it is a sin to produce means of mass destruction of whatever kind to the conviction that it can be a responsible action before God to defend one's society by using weapons of the same kind. The EKD Synod, meeting in Berlin-Spandau in 1958, took note of these divergent attitudes, and responded with the formula: "We remain together under the Gospel, and endeavor to overcome these opposing views."

In order at least to clarify if not overcome the contradiction, consultations were held which resulted in the "Heidelberg Theses" of April 28, 1959. Although not an official document of the church, they had a considerable influence on subsequent Protestant peace ethics. The theses explained that common ground for decisions on both sides was found in taking responsibility for worldwide peace, since peace is prerequisite for life in the technical era. Decisions to use or not to use these weapons may be seen as complementary. On the one hand, the church must recognize that the refusal to use arms is a Christian way of acting. On the other hand, the church must recognize also that under current circumstances the use of arms may *still* be a Christian way of acting (emphasis added).

These two judgments were seen as asymmetrical in time, because if peace is secured at all by nuclear weapons it cannot be secured in this way for long. In this interim period we must grasp the opportunity to achieve a worldwide peace which, instead of being secured by nuclear weapons, is guaranteed by an adequate political organization. The "still" in the Heidelberg thesis signalled that the one side of the complementarity is at best preliminary. When the Heidelberg thesis was shortened to the formula of "peace service with and without weapons," however, the complementarity came to be misunderstood as symmetrical in time. Much of the emphasis was also lost in this abbreviated formula that either of the decisions, whether for or against the use of weapons or military service, ought to be part of a responsible peace policy.

By far the most important among the memoranda published by the EKD since the early sixties is the 1965 *Denkschrift* on the situation of the expellees from the former German east and the relationship of the people of Germany to her eastern neighbors. Its theological focus is the concept of reconciliation. It encourages the integration of those who came from the east into the West German population. It pleads for recognition that the eastern areas are now part of the Polish state, hoping thus to open a way towards an understanding between the Federal Republic and Poland. Although this *Denkschrift* was heavily disputed, it has proved to be the most influential attempt at political *diakonia* in postwar Germany.

Studies were later issued on the peace service of Christians and on development aid from the churches. The ethical judgments expressed in them were also put into practice. It was decided that ministers and church staff should counsel and aid conscientious objectors, just as soldiers were by the military pastorate (which, however, is organized and financed by the state); that there should be continuous cooperation with the churches in the German Democratic Republic, Poland and other Eastern European countries; that the development aid projects of the EKD should be extended; that peace services formed within the churches should be supported; and that peace research (especially in the Protestant Institute for Interdisciplinary Research, Heidelberg) should be financed.

Until the early eighties, the consensus to support these projects was sustained because the opposite views were understood as having equal validity in the church. To support the deterrence policy and, consequently, the arms race, was regarded as just as legitimate as working to overcome the system of deterrence by a consistent disarmament policy. It is not surprising, therefore, that the influence of the Protestant church during that period on armament decisions in the Federal Republic of Germany remained marginal. Impulses for peace politics were effective, however, in other fields: in stimulating political reconciliation with Eastern European states, in advocating the right of conscientious objection to military service, and in pleading for the recognition of non-military peace service.

We can draw the following conclusion: when the debate on armament policies was resumed in 1979, the Protestant churches did not think of entering this debate by propagating certain positions. The peace initiatives did not come from the official institutions of the churches; they sprang up among the church members, and became points of crystallization for the emerging peace movement.

The Catholic Church in Germany is in a similar position. Most German Catholics have agreed with the changes in Catholic peace ethics intitiated by Pope John XXIII and the Second Vatican Council. Peace now is understood as the "universal common good." In present Catholic social teaching, peace and development are indissolubly connected. Recent teaching concerning the means of mass destruction has become more and more critical. The Second Vatican Council sharply repudiated any action of warfare which aims at indiscriminate destruction of whole cities or regions with their populations. These positions were affirmed in December 1975 by the general synod of the dioceses in the Federal Republic of Germany concerning the contribution of the Catholic Church to development and peace. Prevailing Catholic opinion sees these principles as the basis for an "interim ethics" which tolerates deterrence with nuclear weapons while declaring the use of such weapons to be morally unjustifiable. As long as this "interim ethics" does not state when the "interim" ends, it can support every increase in nuclear armament, provided they are interpreted as measures to prevent war in the deterrence system.

So we find a remarkable growth of peace-ethical consciousness and political co-responsibility in the churches in the Federal Republic of Germany since 1945. But the attitude of the churches was ambivalent about the arms race. No resolute intiatives for disarmament issued from the churches. They could not convince themselves to withdraw their legitimation of the deterrence system. We must examine whether any change has occurred in the years from 1980 to 1984.

II. PEACE-ETHICAL AND PEACE-POLITICAL OPTIONS IN THE EIGHTIES

Ecumenical Impulses

By the late seventies, the peace discussion in the Protestant churches of the Federal Republic had begun to focus on issues of military armament. This new emphasis had ecumenical roots. In 1975 the World Council of Churches had introduced a "Programme to Combat Militarism and the Arms Race" with an appeal to the churches: "The church should emphasize its willingness to live without the protection of arms, and should take significant initiatives to urge an effective disarmament. Churches and Christians, individually and corporately in all countries, should plead with their governments that national security be guaranteed without the use of weapons of mass destruction."

This suggestion was accepted by a group called "Living without Armament" (*Ohne Rüstung leben*) in 1977–78. Those who join the group bind themselves with the following promise: "I am ready to live without protection by military armament. I shall urge in our state the importance of developing peace politically without weapons." This attitude is considered to be an essential contribution of individual Christians and churches to overcome a situation of imminent military self-destruction. It is hoped that the symbolic act of publicly declaring oneself against protection by arms may initiate a learning process which, by making unilateral steps towards disarmament possible, can have political results.

Opposition was voiced immediately. In the summer of

1980 a working group (*Arbeitskreis*) called "Securing Peace" invited persons to sign the following declaration: "Every political organization has the duty to protect with all available strength the life of its citizens and their fundamental human rights. Such protection is needed not only internally against criminal activity, but also against external powers which endanger freedom and human rights. The directing principle must be the preservation and restitution of peace. Insofar as military security is necessary for peace, I say yes to it. Above all, I say yes to disarmament efforts on the basis of a balance of power." Comments accompanying the theses show, however, that the task of providing the state with means "to hinder actions of violence by individuals and by whole states" has precedence over the task of disarmament. So the result of this first ecumenical impetus to the recent peace discussion was that both of the polarized views came out in plain and public language.

A second ecumenical impulse had considerable consequence. Since 1972, peace groups had tried to organize annual peace weeks on the local level like those organized by the Dutch Interchurch Peace Council. In 1980, the peace group *Aktion Sühnezeichen/Friedensdienste* ("Signs of Reconciliation and Service for Peace") succeeded in having the peace week model propagated all over the Federal Republic of Germany. Following the Dutch example, and influenced by the NATO decision of December 1979, the peace weeks concentrated on the issues of nuclear weapons and disarmament. "Make peace without weapons" served as the basic formula. In 1980, peace weeks were held in about 120 places. The official Protestant Landeskirchen remained at a distance. But soon the process became so dynamic that in 1981, thirteen member churches of the EKD sent out the call to peace weeks on their own, and provided study material. In that year, between 3,500 and 4,000 peace weeks were held. They focused on the projected stationing of new American medium-range missiles in Western Europe.

In the summer of 1981 the new peace movement emerged. Its central concern was the protest against the new missiles.

Out of this concentration of a single topic grew both the strength and the weakness of the movement. Much of its high mobilizing power was certainly due to the opposition against this military-political decision and to the hope that this particular decision would be influenced by discussions and demonstations. But the interest was too largely concentrated on the military-political aspects of peace, and often only on a span of time which ended in the autumn of 1983.

The first major demonstration of the new peace movement took place in connection with the Protestant *Kirchentag* in Hamburg on June 20, 1981. It was also decided in Hamburg to call a general demonstration in Bonn on October 10, 1981. Two Protestant peace groups, *Aktion Sühnezeichen/Friedensdienste* and the *Aktionsgemeinschaft* called "Services for People," issued the call, thereby taking central responsibility for the course and action of the new peace movement in the Federal Republic of Germany. This decision met with some criticism from church officials and with defamation from some whose political interests were involved. Later developments proved the decision to have been right and necessary. Opinion polls now confirm that the majority of Protestant Christians agree with the support given to the peace movement by the Protestant church.

International ecumencial cooperation was also influential in the background of the actions in 1983. The first peak was the campaign of the peace movement at the Kirchentag in Hannover for a "Return to life—the time is ripe for a no without any yes to means of mass destruction." The second peak was reached with the action week from October 15 to 22, 1983, which heavily underscored the refusal of new nuclear weapons.

A good deal of the reflection in the peace movement focused on a political perspective which lost nothing of its urgency even after the start of the stationing of Pershing II and cruise missiles. These reflections were most clearly presented in the memorandum issued by the ecumenical *Arbeitskreis* on "Steps towards Disarmament." It argued that experience shows that arms control will at best result in a cooperative steering of the arms race. Up to now, it has achieved no effective limitation, let alone reduction of armament. Under these circumstances, the *Arbeitskreis* pleads for a political concept of disarmament based on the idea of gradual steps. The following four are advocated as unilateral steps that might begin a reciprocal process: renouncing any claims to new nuclear weapons; renouncing any first use of nuclear weapons; changing all conventional armaments into weapons which are useful only for defense; and prohibiting any export of arms outside of NATO.

Theological Controversies

As the political controversy became more vehement in the early eighties, the official church began to react. Compared with, for instance, the *aide-memoire* and the pastoral letter of the Dutch Reformed Church, EKD reactions look rather cautious. The EKD *Denkschrift* of 1981 on "Preserving, Promoting and Renewing Peace" was applauded mainly (not without reason) for maintaining a dialogue in spite of polarization, but it did so at the cost of adequate clarity.

The *Denkschrift*, however, does speak clearly in several respects: it is unambiguous in diagnosing the various points from which peace is threatened in the eighties. Those who had argued that anxiety for peace frightens people for no reason were not aided by the EKD. The *Denkschrift* is unambiguous also in stating that political commitment to peace belongs to Christians' essential duties. It is also clear, in the face of a growing predominance of military logic, that political ways to secure peace must be found. The *Denkschrift* proposes the building of an international peace order, intensified international cooperation, the shift to defensive armaments and determined efforts to bring about effective disarmament. It suggests the value of calculated unilateral steps in disarmament negotiations.

With regard to the conflict between those declaring themselves ready to "live without armaments" and those who think military arms indispensable for "securing peace," the

Denkschrift restated the formula of complementarity from the Heidelberg Theses of 1959. The church still recognizes that the refusal of arms is a Christian way of acting. Likewise, the church continues to consider support for securing peace in liberty by nuclear weapons still possible for Christians. The authors of the *Denkschrift* retain the clause with respect to time, arguing that a situation in which war is prevented by threatening indiscriminate destruction cannot last. This option is said to be "ethically justifiable only in circumstances where all political endeavors aim at diminishing the causes for war, establishing procedures for nonviolent control of conflicts, and taking effective steps to reduce the amount of armaments."

The *Denkschrift*, however, does not draw clear consequences from these conditions limiting assent to deterrence policy. It did not say what this means, for instance, for the very controversial issue of the stationing of new Euro-strategic weapons by the Warsaw Pact and NATO. Nevertheless, in giving only a strictly conditioned moral acceptance of deterrence policy, the Protestant church is now obligated to sue its proposed criteria to provide guidance for political decisions. Steps in this direction may be seen in the common study report on peace problems by the EKD and the Federation of Protestant Churches in the German Democratic Republic in August 1982, and the "Word" of the EKD Council in the autumn of 1983 on the peace discussion. These statements urged more strongly the stopping of the arms race with a "freeze," and supported more clearly unilateral calculated initiatives and defensive rearmament. But the political commitment to which the EKD obligated itself with the *Denkschrift* of 1981 demands yet more.

The cautious political positions of the EKD *Denkschrift* fit the rather noncommittal formulations of many of its theological statements. A clearer theological formulation was attempted by the moderature of the *Reformierter Bund* (the alliance of Reformed churches and parishes in the Federal Republic) in their declaration "Confessing Jesus Christ and the Responsibility of the Church for Peace" in the summer of 1982. They affirmed the theological necessity of stating explicitly that political peace is a matter of Christian confession. The declaration rightly stresses that "taking a position with regard to means of mass destruction is a matter of confessing or denying the Gospel." This statement is theologically correct because from a Christian perspective, no part of human life or activity may be regarded as having no relation to the confession of faith. Moreover, the obligation to confess will be stronger where the life and future of God's creation are in jeopardy. This is the reason why the declaration of the *Bund* insists that to produce, provide or use weapons of mass destruction is incompatible with the confession of Christian faith. By weapons of this sort, "humankind, loved by God and chosen as partner in God's covenant, can be destroyed and creation can be devastated." Thus the Christian confession implies saying an unconditionable no to nuclear weapons without any yes.

Since sober theological reflection shows that it can hardly be disputed that weapons of mass destruction require Christians' confession, it must have been political motives that moved some German church leaders to oppose it with what amounted to the assertion that it is unjustifiable "to declare political decisions, even if dealing with life and death, to be a matter of the church's confession." One must ask whether the churches' confession could ever be called for if this were not the case in matters of "life and death."

Yet it must be admitted that the term *status confessionis*, used in the declaration of the *Bund*, lent itself to contradiction. In the history of the Protestant churches, *status confessionis* (or case of confession) emerged as a concept at points where issues that had been left to individual discretion now needed to be answered unequivocally for the sake of the clarity and purity of the church's confession. The case at hand does not have this character, for Christians have always known that the will of God whom they confess prohibits war; the use of deadly power demonstrates human sinfulness. Nuclear weapons have put this confessional issue before Christians at least since August 6, 1945. Rather than speaking of a "case" of confession, we must carry out an overdue step in a "process of confessing." Christians and the church have to discover how to be obedient to the Word of God in this process. The Word is both gospel and law, both liberating promise and a call to responsibility. The church must confess not only its belief but also witness by faithful obedience. The task of confessing has utmost urgency when war and peace are concerned.

The proclamation of a *status confessionis* was also questioned in another way. It was asked whether such a declaration would not cause separation from those who judge the matter differently, or with a different emphasis. The answer must be that the process of confessing occurs in the heart of the church, not at the church's boundaries. A confessing church does not aim at excluding people, but aims to answer concretely in faith. When in the process of confessing, certain views appear to be incompatible with the Christian confession, the final judgment of human beings holding such views lies with God alone. Repudiative sentences in confessional texts expel false doctrines, not persons. To include the Christian's responsibility for peace in the church's confessing means to launch a *process* of intensive communication rather than of excommunication. There must be communication so that Christians may help each other find the one path of obedient discipleship today.

The controversy over *status confessionis* is not the only discussion within the Protestant churches in the FRG. It is remarkable that during the last two years nearly all of the Protestant Landeskirchen have dealt with the peace issue by synodal resolutions which claim to be binding in the church. They are passed by a body of representatives with strong democratic legitimation. In many cases, they were preceded by a long process of judgment formation on the grass-roots level. A notable consensus is documented in the synodal texts—though differences remain—which can be summarized in the following points:

First: Christians have to judge security politics by Biblical criteria. Consensus must be achieved on the question of whether threatening mutual destruction contradicts the spirit of Christ, as well as whether to introduce reconciliation and creative love of the enemy into the realm of political reason.

Second: The Heidelberg thesis of complementarity may be restated today, provided that narrow time limits are set. Though the churches accept the strategy of securing peace in freedom by possession of nuclear weapons as "still" possible for Christians to support, this may not be understood as a never-ending sanction. Only if an intensive policy of disarmament and *détente* is pursued, can the "still" remain valid.

Third: Christians must say "no" under all circumstances to the *use* of weapons of mass destruction. Their use destroys what is supposed to be defended. There is only disagreement on whether this "no" to their use does not necessarily imply, already today, a "no" to threatening their use in a strategy of deterrence.

Fourth: Even if this "no" in Christian faith is extended to the possession of the means of mass destruction, these weapons will not disappear. So peace confession impels Christians to participate in finding political ways of nonviolently securing peace. Many recent synodal declarations agree emphatically that "the system of nuclear deterrence must be unconditionally overcome" (EKD Synod, November 1983). It is a specific task of the church "to try to hinder, by all means, that we become accustomed to the situation of nuclear threat" (Synod of Nordelbien, September 17, 1983). This means continuous opposition to both the present state of armaments and the imminent increase of arms. The Synod of the Westphalian Landeskirche, for instance, explicitly stated: "We neither wish nor are able to acquiesce either in the fact that medium-range missiles are already stationed, nor in the plans for stationing new missiles in West and East" (November 11, 1983).

Thus the Protestant churches have now taken a clear and unequivocal position on the question of nuclear armaments which is unprecedented in earlier epochs of their history. They consider it their special task to help reorient public opinion. It is true that up to now, neither the activities of the peace movement nor the public statements of the churches could stop the stationing of new "Euromissiles" in Western Europe and the preparation for "counter-counter-armament" in Eastern Europe. Nevertheless, the churches and the peace movement may be credited for the fact that the spirit, logic and practice of deterrence have lost much of the unquestioning acceptance they had a few years ago. They have helped counteract the trend of getting used to the deterrence system.

The statements issued by the Roman Catholic Church in the FRG on nuclear arms are less clear than some of the Protestant declarations—and far less so than the pastoral letter of the Catholic Bishops' Conference in the United States. Still, here also a remarkable shift can be noticed. In the autumn of 1981, the Central Committee of the German Catholics (the alliance of Catholic lay organizations) published a statement in which the logic of deterrence was presented as the highest rule of political conduct. According to this declaration, the only possible way of preserving peace would be to keep or restore a military balance. The Soviet Union and the Warsaw Pact are presented as having disturbed, or even destroyed, this balance by their military and political actions, while NATO is seen as having pursued a strict and continuous policy of balance. On the basis of these presuppositions, the NATO decision of December 1979 is interpreted as unambiguously positive. All arguments against the decision are rejected as expressions of a "radical ethics of pure conscience." Consequently the peace movement is strongly condemned: "Where the fatal tendency to escape from history prevails, and is associated with political ignorance, a lack of ethical discernment and an unwillingness to engage in service for the common peace order, these minorities are able to win an influence reaching far beyond their importance."

Measured by this declaration, the "Word" of the German Bishops' Conference, "Justice Brings Peace," of April 1983, shows a considerable progress in Catholic thought and judgment. It is as impossible for the Catholic bishops as for the EKD to say a clear "no without any yes" to nuclear weapons (as the Dutch Reformed did). Military defense remains for them a possible peace policy because this follows from the nation's natural right to self-defense (compare article 51 of the Charter of the United Nations). The state has the concomitant duty to provide the necessary means to ward off any encroachment. Therefore the German bishops say that service at arms and the refusal of arms complement each other. But they make their provisional acceptance of nuclear deterrence dependent on three main criteria: the military potential which exists or is planned should make it "neither possible nor more probable" to wage war; the potential for deterrence must not exceed the limit of "sufficiency"; the arms should "barely suffice." Finally, all military measures taken must be compatible with arms control.

These criteria attempt to apply some basic elements of the traditional doctrine of "just war" to the new situation of a nuclear age. The Catholic bishops in the United States chose the same approach, but the conclusions they drew were much more concrete than those of the German bishops. The bishops in the United States rejected the first use of nuclear weapons in response to an attack with conventional arms; they raised serious objections to some concrete strategic aims set by military planning in the United States; they repudiated nuclear arms which can result in predominance or in the ability to wage war for a long time; thus they rejected expressly certain weapons systems (MX, Pershing II). Finally, they not only advocated disarmament in general, but demanded concrete disarmament measures (removal of short-range nuclear missiles, zones free of nuclear weapons).

So the churches in the Federal Republic of Germany, including the Catholic Church, took a course which has many ecumenical parallels in other countries. In the early eighties, the churches began to review critically their tacit or explicit acceptance of deterrence. A process of learning, largely initiated by the peace movement, is alive in the church. The peace movement has created mobility which remains a fact in spite of the failure to reach its short-range political goal. Accordingly, the church can and must be expected to seek still greater clarity about the question of the means of mass destruction.

Political Conflicts

What has been said in the preceding section on the consensus forming in the church does not mean that political discord disappeared from the churches. It is mainly divergence in political opinions that hinders a clearer testimony of the church concerning nuclear weapons. Five points of political controversy prominent in recent debates in the FRG will briefly be indicted:

First, the relationship between peace politics and military arms is controversial. It has been observed critically that during the phase of *détente* a clandestine militarization of political thinking occurred, unnoticed by many, which has resulted in an "affinity to war" not only among generals, but even among politicians. In order to counteract such militarization of political thinking, the EKD *Denkschrift* urgently pleaded for restoration of the priority of politics; measures for securing peace must be taken on the political and not on the military level.

The reproach of being restricted to military points of view was also directed at the peace movement. Trutz Rendtorff, chairman of the EKD Chamber for Public Responsibility, sharply and repeatedly argued that to discuss a "more" or "less" with respect to weapons is still no peace discussion. A movement concentrating on this point does not deserve the name of "peace" movement.

It certainly is true that the priority of political perspectives over military categories must be restored. But it must not be forgotten that we experienced a peace policy which failed to penetrate into the system of military arms. The task before us today is to find political instruments and develop political methods so that the deadly dynamics of the arms race can be interrupted and steps towards disarmament introduced. This cannot be achieved without concentrating on the problems of military armaments.

Nevertheless, the reproaches addressed to the Western European peace discussion of the past few years are worth considering. The new phase of the arms race has caused many people to be concerned only with the problems of East-West conflict and of an imminent war with nuclear weapons in Europe. They tend to lose sight of the increasing North-South conflict and the actual (instead of possible) victims of hunger in the Third World. The World Council of Churches, in its public statement "Peace and Justice" of August 1983 [see Appendix], affirmed that these two fields of contemporary Christian peace commitment can neither be isolated from nor be turned against each other.

The deepest political differences in West German church and society, to my mind, still consist in differing analyses of the threat to peace. On the one side, the danger of war is seen as rooted in the aggressiveness of Soviet communism; other the other side, the most serious threat is understood to be the antagonism of the systems and the claims to hegemony as such, in combination with the dynamics of military development. Some feel threatened most of all by the enemy, others most of all by enmity.

These opposing judgments are influenced by persistent patterns of attitudes, in part characteristic of the different generations. On the one hand, the traditional anti-communist attitudes are so deep-seated that a sober analysis and assessment seems impossible. On the other hand, the tendency prevails in sections of the peace movement not to bother about any analysis of Soviet power politics or assessment of Warsaw Pact arms. Although this may be understandable as a reaction to anti-communism, it is myopic nevertheless.

A fair evaluation of Soviet interests and politics, however, will not support the conclusion that present dangers to peace originate in the Soviet Union. Rather, it will support the greater probability of the judgment that it is the antagonism of interests, of claims to hegemony and of armament systems which endanger life on this planet. Consequently, it is not the destruction of communism that promises peace; the more plausible policy is to look for common security.

The formula of military balance often disguises the search for predominance. Those who locate the threat with the enemy rather than with the system of enmity ascribe a high priority to the concept of balance. They will accept, at the most, measures of arms control, but can never consent to effective disarmament. Those who see the threat rooted in antagonistic attitudes will be ready to take risks in the hope of diminishing the danger and will plead for unilateral calculated initiatives to launch a process of disarmament.

These opposites—rigid insistence on the concept of arms control and advocacy of a strategy of gradual disarmament—are central to the present political controversy. Opinions differ within the churches as much as in society as a whole. Yet the recent discussions have led to considerable shifts in opinion. In the summer of 1981, an opinion poll found 33 percent of the populaton of the Federal Republic of Germany in favor of unilateral disarmament initiatives; by the summer of 1983, 46 percent shared this opinion.

One of the most remarkable results of the recent peace discussion is the fresh attention given to basic problems of the nations' democratic order. On the one side, it is held that majority decisions in a democracy demand loyalty in each and every case. The fact that such decisions are legal is said to warrant their being legitimate. On the other side, it is pointed out that there are prerequisites for majority rule in a democracy. The legislator is bound above all to honor fundamental human rights which are not at his disposal. Thus the question arises: should a person who sees the threat of collective self-destruction in certain arms decisions maintain resistance after such decisions were made by parliamentary majority? Is he or she obliged to resort to actions of civil disobedience when nothing else will help? The problem of whether civil disobedience should be recognized in cases like this as an element of mature political culture has not yet been adequately discussed.

The opposing political views connected with the problem of military arms can be described in still another way. It is evident now that different sections of the population place different political priorities on the problems of peace and security policy. A majority of the population in the FRG in 1983 opposed the stationing of new American nuclear weapons on German soil. But this opposition did not decisively influence the outcome of the election for the Bundestag (parliament) in March 1983, where the problems of economic policy took precedence. Moreover, the Geneva negotiations on intermediate nuclear forces (INF) were not yet over. So the Social Democrats who, while Helmut Schmidt was chancellor, had supported the NATO decision of December 1979, could not articulate a clear opposition to the imminent stationing during the election campaign. The problem of stationing influenced the election results only in that, for the first time, the Greens won seats in the Bundestag. The peace discussion of the past few years has contributed considerably to a growing awareness of peace political problems, but as yet has had no essential effect on voting behavior and political practice.

III. PERSPECTIVES

The fact that the stationing of Pershing II and cruise missiles on West European soil has begun will not end the debate on peace politics, although it means a deep change. A new phase of the nuclear arms race has been initiated against the protest of major parts of the population, against opposition from the churches and against objections raised by many scientists. It has become clearer that in political as well as military and strategic respects, our time has the characteristics of a prewar period—that is, of a time when chances for the prevention of war are highly uncertain. The stationing of medium-range nuclear missiles (the warning time for which is extremely short) was said to make peace more secure; but now only a very few people, even among those who recommended their stationing, still seem to believe it. The more thoughtful fatalistically declare this step a necessary destabilization within the arms race. They speak with the same fatalism as the Russian commentators, who take the "counter-counter-armament" with longer-range tactical nuclear weapons in the German Democratic Republic and the Czechoslovakian Republic to be an unavoidable further destabilization. In this situation, any celebration of the beginning of the stationing as a victory is frivolous self-complacency. The truth is that all who are convinced that the arms race needs to be brought under control and decreased have suffered a severe defeat by the stationing. This is a defeat for large numbers of people who had pleaded to refrain from any stationing now. It is also a defeat for the official policy, which argued that the threat of stationing would serve as a bargaining chip for negotiations. Everyone involved in the recent debate has reason for gloom.

Everyone with a vivid sense of the present danger to peace must also realize that the concerns of many during the last years remain valid and cannot be abandoned. The hope of keeping and shaping peace and preventing war, even of overcoming the institution of war, must live and gain strength.

The present lull in the discussion on missiles invites recollection concerning the results of the preceding phase of the peace debate in the Federal Republic of Germany. Let me name five interrelated elements of such an evaluation:

1. The realization has grown that peace is the horizon for political responsibility today. Although the majority of the citizens of the Federal Republic place economic prosperity and growth (in order to overcome unemployment) higher than peace politics, there is nevertheless an increasing awareness that peace is in danger, and that a new peace policy is urgently needed. Many citizens fear the arms race, its getting out of control and an ensuing military confrontation of the superpowers in Europe more than they fear the expansionist ideology of the Soviet Union or their military superiority in certain aspects of armaments. The understanding is spreading that the crucial threat to us is enmity rather than some enemy, an enmity which consists in an explosive mixture of hegemonial conflict between two superpowers and an uncontrolled technological arms development.

2. Public opinion concerning peace politics has formed in the FRG since 1981, as in other European countries. A critical attitude towards a security policy based on nuclear arms gradually has won influence within all the major institutions of society; rather soon within the churches, hesitatingly within trade unions, and relatively late within the universities. Thus a public penetration of the system of management by experts has occurred, the consequences of which we cannot yet foresee. Both in environmental policy and in peace policy, it is clearer than ever that the opinions of official experts are not necessarily adequate and may be challenged. The new social movements, particularly ecological and peace movements, do their own research. Many discussions between generals (or other members of the armed forces) and security politicians on the one side, and people representing peace research and the peace movement on the other, may not be interpreted by the familiar polarities of experts versus amateurs, rational versus emotional, responsibility versus "pure conscience," though some keep using this pattern of interpretation. Only in a much more limited sense can management by experts still rely on the axiom that "he may rule who has the status of an expert." His propositions are more likely to be scrutinized. This is some progress, however, modest, toward democracy regaining lost ground.
3. The relation of politics and ethics has been raised anew. Until a few years ago, the central fields of modern politics—especially economics, finance and armaments—were said to be ethically neutral. No ethical categories could be applied to them; they followed their own laws. One of the key problems in the social controversies of recent years lies in the demand to measure political decisions by ethical criteria because they are not ethically neutral. "Innate laws" constitute no adequate platform for politics because any major political decision has consequences that are better or worse. Elements of a new political ethics seem to be emerging. The question of the consistency of ethical maxims arises. Are those which are valid in personal life not equally valid in public life?

The new ethics demands a turn toward the wholeness of life, following the guidance of love also in the field of politics. It looks for an economic policy in which nature, instead of being exploited, is preserved, thus yielding what human beings need to live. It is oriented to the task of peace, a peace surpassing the absence of war in one's own country, which means pursuing the happiness of all human life together. It contradicts the dominating ethos of a world of science-based technology, in which one must do all he/she is able to do, and pleads for a selective use of the scientific and technological means at one's disposal. It teaches honoring solidarity more than competition, and the other's dignity more than one's own rights, common peace more than heedless self-realization. Set within this scope, the peace discussion of the churches has covered wide ground.

4. Participation in the debate is wider than ever. The discussion takes place not merely between official church bodies and peace initiative groups, but has begun to include parishes, institutions, associations, district and regional synods. A process of taking mutual counsel (or a "conciliar" process, in the sense in which Bonhoeffer used the term when he suggested that an ecumenical peace council should be called) has been launched, opening communication between controversial positions while aiming at clear results. The results still lag behind the expectations of the peace movements; the German "people's churches" have not yet been transformed into "peace churches." When the stationing of missiles was under way, the churches' opposition was not clear enough to gain real influence. Nevertheless, important steps have been taken towards a decision as a church about weapons of mass destruction. Official statements issued by churches are more outspoken than they were a few years ago in disagreeing with the spirit, logic and practice of deterrence, while more clearly affirming a policy of common security, even including calculated unilateral initiatives. Much of this occurred when ecumenical impulses were taken up. Communication within the worldwide church (in matters of peace) has gained impetus.

Of highest importance, however, is that the theme of peace has entered with fresh intensity into the worship and spiritual life of Christian communities. The more recent bi-annual mass rallies of the churches—*Kirchentage*—have impressively symbolized the unity of spirituality and responsibility for peace. There are many who discover the unexpected relevance of biblical texts to life here and now. Most of all, the Sermon on the Mount, indicating the possibilities of nonviolence and inviting practice of love for the enemy, is winning influence in the orientation of life. "Silence for peace" is becoming a distinctive feature in many of our cities. Prayer services for peace and justice begin to be celebrated regularly in Christian parishes. The Eucharistic experience of the gift of peace is giving decisive support to many. The announcement of the peace of God is proving meaningful for daily life. Only when thus rooted in Christian communal life may the witness to peace by individual Christians and churches be credible. In this way the church may contribute to actual disarmament decisions, and—possibly—far beyond.

5. The expansion of the peace discussion in the churches has been paralleled in the political parties—especially in the Social Democrats and the Greens—and in the labor unions. This parallel expansion in other institutions provides a counterbalance to the decline in influence of the peace movement in public life since the fall of 1983. This decline was not as surprising as many have thought; indeed, it was in many ways predictable.

The peace movement during recent years took on the character of a single-issue campaign. Groups with different origins and orientations united into an action movement to oppose the stationing of Pershing II and cruise missiles. After the beginning of the missile stationing they faced the question of what long-range political goal might now orient the work of the peace movement. At the same time, there no longer was a clear short-term goal that could mobilize large numbers to participate in demonstrations. This placed in question the continuance of their previous basis for action. A lively discussion concerning the goals and forms of action of the peace movement was therefore ignited in the coordination committee of the peace movement. So one cannot expect, in the near future, public actions in the Federal Republic of Germany with the extent and intensity of those between 1981 and 1983.

This series of events repeats what has been a frequent history in the peace movement as well as other social movements. Such movements mobilize large numbers of people in their immediate spheres of influence only during periods that have a horizon of clearly contoured and limited conflicts. These phases are succeeded by periods in which this new level of consciousness is strengthened, new insights are won and long-term perspectives are developed. The experiences gained during the conflicts of the immediate past are now reflected upon; they can be acted upon in new conflict situations. There are many signs that the social basis for the peace movement in the Federal Republic of Germany has been expanded; a social consciousness has been created that will be aroused more quickly during the next conflict over peace and disarmament than was possible after the NATO decision of December 1979. And there is much reason to expect that such occasions will soon reappear.

SELECTED LITERATURE

Aktion Sühnezeichen/Friedensdienste (editor), *Christen im Streit um den Frieden: Beiträge zu einer neuen Friedensethik*, Freiburg: Dreisam-Verlag, 1982.

Franz Alt, *Frieden ist möglich:* Die Politik der Bergpredigt, München: Piper, 1983.

Günter Baadte, Armin Boyens, Ortwin Buchbender, *Frieden stiften: Die Christen zur Abrüstung*, Eine Dokumentation, München: Beck, 1984

Peter Bender, *Das Ende des ideologischen Zeitalters:* Die Europäisierung Europas, Berlin: Severin und Siedler, 1981.

Wilhelm Bittorf (editor), *Nachrüstung*, Reinbek: Rowohlt, 1982.

Wolfgang Däubler, *Stationierung und Grundgesetz*, Reinbek: Rowohlt 2nd edition, 1983.

Volkmar Deile (editor), *Zumutungen des Friedens:* Kurt Scharf zum 80. Geburtstag, Reinbek: Rowohlt, 1982.

Anselm Doering-Manteuffel, *Katholizismus und Wiederbewaffnung:* Die Haltung der deutschen Katholiken gegenüber der Wehrfrage 1948–1955, Mainz: Grünewald, 1981.

Erhard Eppler, *Die tödliche Utopie der Sicherheit*, Reinbek: Rowohlt, 1983.

Evangelische Kirche in Deutschland, Kirchenkanzlei (editor), *Die Denkschriften der EKD, Frieden, Versöhnung und Menschenrechte*, Gütersloh: Gütersloher Verlagshaus Gerd Mohn, 1978.

———*Frieden wahren, fördern und erneuern:* Eine Denkschrift der EKD, Gütersloh: Gütersloher Verlagshaus Gerd Mohn, 1981.

———*Kirche und Frieden:* Kundgebungen und Erklärungen aus den deutschen Kirchen und der Ökumene, Hannover: Kirchenkanzlei der EKD, 1982.

———Nordelbische Evangelisch-Lutherische Kirche, *Gottes Friede den Völkern:* Wissenschaftlicher Kongress, Kiel, Juni 1984 (Materialien).

Peter Glotz (editor), *Ziviler Ungehorsam im Rechtsstaat*, Frankfurt am Main: Suhrkamp, 1983.

Hirtenworte zu Kreig und Frieden. Die Texte der katholischen Bischöfe (. . .). Köln: Kiepenheuer & Witsch, 1983.

Klaus Horn/Eva Senghaas-Knobloch (editors), *Friedensbewegung-Persönliches und Politisches*, Frankfurt am Main: Fischer, 1983.

Günter Howe (editor), *Atomzeitalter, Krieg und Frieden*, Berlin: Ullstein, 1963.

Wolfgang Huber, *Der Streit um die Wahrheit und die Fähigkeit zum Frieden*, München: Kaiser, 1980.

———*Folgen christlicher Freiheit:* Ethik und Theorie der Kirche im Horizont der Barmer Theologischen Erklärung, Neurkirchen: Neukirchener Verlag, 1983.

———"Frieden," in: *Theologische Realenzyklopädie 11*, Berlin: de Gruyter, 1983, pp. 618–646.

Wolfgang Huber/Gerhard Liedke (editors), *Christentum und Militarismus*, Stuttgart: Klett/München: Kösel, 1974.

Wolfgang Huber/Johannes Schwerdtfeger (editors), *Kirche zwischen Kreig und Frieden:* Studien zur Geschichte des deutschen Protestantismus, Stuttgart: Klett, 1976.

Bertold Klappert/Ulrich Weidner (editors), *Schritte zum Frieden:* Theologische Texte zu Frieden und Abrüstung, Wupertal: Aussaat Verlag, 1983.

Christel Küpper/Franz Reiger (editors), *Atomwaffen und Gewissen:* Entscheidungshilfe für Christen, Freiburg:Herder, 1983.

Oskar Lafontaine, *Angst vor den Freunden*, Reinbek: Rowohlt, 1983.

Wolfgang Lienemann, *Kernwaffen und die Frage des gerechten Krieges als Problem ökumenischer Friedensethik*, Habilitationsschrift Heidelberg, 1983.

Bernhard Moltmann (editor), *Militarismus und Rüstung:* Beiträge zur ökumenischen Diskussion, Heidelberg: FEST, 1983.

Moderamen des Reformierten Bundes, *Das Bekenntnis zu Jesus Christus und die Friedensverantwortung der Kirche*, Gütersloh: Gütersloher Verlagshaus Gerd Mohn, 1982.

Der Palme-Bericht: Bericht der Unabhängigen Kommission für Abrüstung und Sicherheit—"Common Security," Berlin: Severin und Siedler, 1982.

Wolf Werner Rausch/Christian Walther (editors), *Evangelische Kirche in Deutschland und die Wiederaufrüstungsdiskussion in der Bundesrepublik 1950–1955*, Gütersloh: Gütersloher Verlagshaus Gerd Mohn, 1978.

Klaus von Schubert aus der Evangelischen Studiengemeinschaft (editor for the FEST on behalf of a study group), *Heidelberger Friedensmemorandum*, Reinbek: Rowohlt, 1983.

Sekretariat der Deutschen Bischofskonferenz (editor), *Dienst am Frieden:* Stellungnahmen der Päpste, des II. Vatikanischen Konzils und der Bischofssynode von 1963 bis 1980, Bonn: Deutsche Bischofskonferenz, 1980.

Friedhelm Solms, (editor), *Peace and Disarmament:* Documents of the World Council of Churches and the Roman Catholic Church, Geneva: World Council of Churches/Rome: Pontifical Commission "Iustitia et Pax," 1982.

Reiner Steinweg (editor), *Der gerechte Krieg: Christentum, Islam, Marxismus*, Frankfurt am Main: Suhrkamp, 1980.

———(editor), *Die neue Friedensbewegung:* Analysen aus der Friedensforschung, Frankfurt am Main: Suhrkamp, 1982.

Theodor Stohm/Bernhard Moltmann/Christoph Meier (editors), *Friede ist der "Weg zum Frieden":* Dienst der Versöhnung als Auftrag der christlichen Gemeinde, München: Kaiser, 1983 (Themen der Praktischen Theologie—Theologia Practica 1983/1-2).

Heinz Eduard Tödt, "Frieden," in: *Christlicher Glaube in moderner Gesellschaft*, vol. 13, Freiburg: Herder, 1981, pp. 79–119.

Johanna Vogel, *Kirche und Wiederbewaffnung:* Die Haltung der evangelischen Kirche in Deutschland in den Auseinandersetzungen um die Wiederbewaffnung der Bundesrepublik 1949–1956, Göttingen: Vandenhoeck & Ruprecht, 1978.

Karsten Voigt, *Wege zur Abrüstung*, Frankfurt am Main: Eichborn, 1981.

Christian Walther (editor), *Atomwaffen und Ethik:* Der deutsche Protestantismus und die atomare Aufrüstung 1954–1961, München: Kaiser, 1981.

Carl Friedrich von Weizsäcker, *Der bedrohte Friede*, München: Hanser, 1981.

Erwin Wilchkens (editor), *Christliche Ethik und Sicherheitspolitik*, Frankfurt am Main: Evangelisches Verlagswerk, 1982.

Rolf Wischnath (editor), *Frieden als Bekenntnisfrage:* Zur Auseinandersetzung um die Erklärung des Moderamens des Reformierten Bundes "Das Bekenntnis zu Jesus Christus und die Friedensverantwortung der Kirche," Gütersloh: Gütersloher Verlagshaus Gerd Mohn, 1984.

Peace Witness and Service in the Federation of Protestant Churches in the German Democratic Republic

by Christa Lewek

I. INTRODUCTION

The Federation of Protestant Churches in the German Democratic Republic understands itself as a community for witness and service in a socialist society. From its very beginning, it established a committee for "church and society," which was given the mission of investigating how to make Christian witness concrete within a changing world and society: witness for peace, witness for a just order and witness for the freedom of the human being to be truly a human being. Since then, this community of Protestant churches in the GDR has gradually moved a wholistic understanding of Christian peace responsibility into the center of Christian thought and action. In January 1980, in a time of extraordinary world tension—marked by the NATO decision in Brussels concerning the stationing of medium-range missiles in Europe, the Iran-Iraq conflict and the sending of Soviet troops

---

Oberkirchenrätin Christa Lewek is Secretary for Church and Society of The Federation of Protestant Churches, German Democratic Republic.

to Afghanistan—the federation issued a declaration in which it programmatically established the priority "that the work for peace no longer be understood by the churches as an occasional task, but rather that it be understood and practiced by the churches as one of the most important challenges to their witness and their service."

It was sharply and unambiguously affirmed in 1980 that "the peace responsibility of the church follows fundamentally and directly from the message of the Gospel." The statement defined the necessary consequence of the church's concrete contribution as making visible ways "which reveal the Gospel and which themselves often disappear in political action," namely:

—forgiveness, which makes possible one's own action and one's own first steps, even when they involve risk;

—the privilege of encouraging others, without concern for oneself, to exhibit freedom from prejudice, openness and temperance in negotiations and discussions;

—the admonition given in God's Word to see ourselves, the church and our own country critically; and

—the prayer that within and beyond our activity the final decision be left to God.

The motivation and the scope of reference of the Protestant churches' understanding of Christian peace witness and service in a socialist society are clearly stated here:

1. from the Gospel,
2. for the people, and
3. beyond the borders.

With this declaration in their baggage, representatives of the church federation traveled in January, 1980 to a conference in Budapest of the World Council of Churches with church leaders from socialist countries. There the profound value of such an approach for other churches as well was not only unanimously recognized, but experienced in practice. On the one hand, it was recognized that precisely in moments of heightened world tensions it is necessary for Christians to remain united in mutual trust, not allowing themselves to be divided by newly emerging cold war; on the other hand, the value was seen of articulating their common peace responsibility in the politics of their particular historical context. The closing communiqué, unanimously passed, stated it thus:

> In a situation in which relations between nations are tense or even blocked or broken off, we believe it is the task of the church to serve as an instrument for communication. [churches] are not to contribute to the escalation of polemics; rather, they are called to reestablish trust and mutual understanding, even when such actions are misunderstood. They should imaginatively explore new means of education for peace, means which lead to a deeper understanding and to a reestablishment of trust in the instruments and methods of a peaceful, political solution of conflicts. Furthermore, they should through their life and witness, their prayers and mutual intercession, drive out fear and work against attitudes of helplessness and resignation.

I. THE CHURCH IN A SOCIALIST SOCIETY

In order to understand the church's service in the GDR it is important to describe more exactly the situation of the church—our church—in a socialist society. The Federation of Protestant Churches in the GDR has defined itself programmatically as the church in socialism, *Kirche im Sozialismus*. It does not want to be a church superior to or subordinated to socialism, nor a church against or for socialism, nor by any means a socialist church. The church in socialism does not mean a closed, defensive system, nor a reservoir of opposition forces, nor some form of counter-culture. Bishop Albrecht Schönherr put it: "both total adaptation and total rejection of socialist society are out of the question."

The peace activities of the Protestant churches in the GDR are carried out within a very specific socio-political context in which the Communist Party (SED)—plays the determinant role. This means a domestic policy integrated by the party and an ideological peace policy that gives security priority in both domestic and foreign policies. Any political discourse and activity of the church, above all in the area of disarmament and the safeguarding of peace, is open to conflict. The church is easily suspected of interference in matters under state jurisdiction and competence, of questioning existing political power relations or of "neutralism." The church in the socialist society of the GDR, however, is not an integrated social organization under the leadership of the SED. It goes its way independently and has its autonomous place. Because the SED interprets the conflict between East and West as part of the class struggle, the churches in the GDR must always face the charge of taking sides (as in the question of their support for conscientious objection). The Communist Party insists one must take sides in the class struggle; there is no third position. The church must therefore always make clear that its position is not above the divisions in the world, but rather in the midst of its conflicts, among the human beings to whom it is sent. In these conflicts the church is neither judge, nor supporter of any one side. It is given the task of reconciliation. What does this mean?

As the church within socialism, churches in the GDR must seek and find specific means for this service, carefully investigating both its possibilities and attendant dangers, and acting accordingly. In our continuing dialogue with the National Council of Churches of Christ in the USA concerning questions of disarmament, we investigated the opportunities and obstacles in bringing the influence of both the NCCC and the Federation of Evangelical Churches in the GDR to bear on their respective social systems, and discovered the following:

> The participants have attempted to formulate what distinguishes the peace efforts of their respective churches.
>
> The social pluralism in the USA, on the one hand, makes the churches' voice in the *one* voice among many. On the other hand, it facilitates political effectiveness. Moreover, when churches in the USA speak with persons in various political areas, they very often encounter other Christians.
>
> In the GDR, political power is integrated in one single system. The voice of the churches is, as a non-integrated social force,

distinct. The churches speak and act autonomously and on their own responsibility. They can discuss political issues, support the interests of others and speak in their own behalf.

In the political system of the GDR there are only a few Christians in responsible positions, but the churches are able to address the state on the basis of its expressed desire for peace. The criteria for the political efficacy of the GDR churches' peace witness is developed above all out of theological-ethical reflection. Such reflection relates the theological knowledge of the churches to their analysis of the situation and options for political action so as to make theology fruitful for peace action. Herein lies the fundamental requirement for the autonomy of church peace work. Moreover, churches have direct political effect through consciousness-raising and education toward peace in Christian congregations and in individuals. (Third dialogue of the Federation of Evangelical Churches in the GDR with the National Council of Churches in the USA: Ferch/GDR, April, 1980—Collective Report)

The mandate of the hour for the churches in the GDR is to find, develop and translate into practice specific models and opportunities for Christian peace activity in their society. There is a great temptation to copy Western models of action, which are broadcast widely in our society to impress our people. This would be a failure in our duty, however. Banners carried in Western demonstrations saying such things as "Who's demonstrating in Red Square?" miss the point. They fail to mesh with our situation. The Federation of Protestant Churches has carefully analyzed the means, possibilities, opportunities and hindrances in order to become active in its own society, sometimes out of difficult experience. Accordingly, it attempts to fulfill its peace mission practically. Generally there is a tendency to move from demonstration to argumentation. Actions accompany and interpret this line.

The decisive world-political context in which the Federation of Protestant Churches in the GDR must fulfill its peacemaking mission in witness and service is the East-West conflict which divided the world after the Second World War. Our church lives and works in the German state which belongs to the military alliance of the Warsaw Treaty and the economic alliance of the Council for Mutual Economic Aid (COMECON). On the other side of the line that runs through the former German Reich lies the other German state, which is a member of NATO and the European Economic Community.

The existence of the churches in the GDR on the "seam" where these world systems confront each other is a particular challenge to their peacemaking commitment. Seams connecting fabrics of different textures are particularly fragile and vulnerable. They can rip if the thread is weak—or if the fabric is worn. On the occasion of the fortieth anniversary of the outbreak of the Second World War—September 1, 1979—Protestant churches in both German states developed a statement in which, from their respective current situations, they confessed a common guilt and responsibility: "Placed in different political, economic and military world systems, the Protestant churches in the two German states accept the mission of applying the Gospel in an autonomously truthful way, each in their area of responsibility. Today they raise their voices together in consciousness of their common concern and guilt. On the seam of two world systems they confess together their particular responsibility for peace."

Since the stationing of Pershing II and cruise missiles in the Federal Republic of Germany and the subsequent stationing of short-range missiles in the GDR, the situation has become even more aggravated, the challenge even greater. The government of the GDR speaks of the necessity of limiting the danger (*Schadensbegrenzüng*); asking for a coalition of reason, it offers a community of responsibility to the other German state. The church has entered this debate with the means available to it.

In the GDR the principle of separation of church and state prevails. "An excellent principle," as the secretary for church affairs of the GDR government once put it half-ironically, "It has only one flaw: we have only *one* human being." In him or her, the one individual, both citizen and member of the Christian church meet inseparably. In questions concerning human beings, the church is awarded a say in society; in the question of peace it is nothing short of commanded to do so.

Let us shift the focus concerning political consequences from the issues arising from the church in the GDR as a church in socialism to concern for human beings in their conflicts—for outer and inner peace belong together. If peace and reconciliation have priority for us, then our concern cannot be changing the power structures in Europe—rather, it must be a matter of making the prevailing ones capable of peace. The political function of the Christian peace witness in the GDR does not intend to be destabilizing. The alternative to destabilization, however, is not simple affirmation of the status quo; rather, it is above all a change in direction toward more real security and an increased capacity for peace. This means advocating foreign policy concepts which fit the realization that "more weapons do not create more security," which requires making room in one's own country for dialogue and participation.

This means looking beyond the limitations of the East-West conflict and creating as well the conditions for a just peace between North and South. The triad "peace-justice-reconciliation" is to be held together and developed in a continuous process.

III. THE PEACE SERVICE OF THE FEDERATION OF PROTESTANT CHURCHES

From the Gospel

"The peace mission of the Church follows fundamentally and directly from the message of the Gospel" (Declaration on the World Political Situation, 1980).

If we, as churches in the GDR, emphasize our autonomy in peace witness so strongly, this must not be misunderstood as distancing ourselves from other peace initiatives. It is an autonomy based on unmistakable and non-interchangeable motives—the Gospel impels us. These motives must be expressed in the nature of our peace activity. The decisive biblical "given" for practical action is the peace which God has made with us in Jesus Christ: "He is our peace."

That is to say, peace is first a blessing from God, given to us in Jesus Christ, although hints of it may already be found in the world. Peace is a promise from God still to be fulfilled, in the face of which all worldly realizations of peace remain temporary and incomplete. This tension between the "already" and the "not yet," however, does not allow Christians to assume the lethargic position of observers; rather, it mobilizes the hope and activity of Christian peace service. The message of reconciliation places Christians and churches in the service of building trust among nations.

The concept of "confidence building" (taken from the "confidence-building measures" of the Helsinki Final Act) has proven particularly inspiring for the ethics of peace during recent years in the Federation of Protestant Churches in the GDR. Public and concrete dedication to furthering the process of *détente* through the realization of the Helsinki Agreement, signed by thirty-five European and North American countries, is clearly based in the biblical concept of "trust" as understood in our evangelical tradition:

> Awakening trust belongs to God's peace-work in the man Jesus. In the growing anxiety which characterizes our world, Jesus is both the ultimate trust-awakener and one worthy of trust. By creating trust, he makes us worthy and capable of trust. In this way he brings peace to human beings and makes them capable of peace. Precisely in conflicts, antagonisms and divisions he builds bridges of trust. . . . The fact that he holds the invitation to trust open to all human beings, and promises his kingdom of peace to the world gives us again and again—in spite of all disappointing experiences—trust in our world and its future, and frees us to seek dialogue with our antagonists as well as seek their own political wisdom and responsibility, instead of writing them off and even demonizing them. The trust that

Peace Witness in the German Democratic Republic

comes from Jesus Christ is not an unworldly, beatific trust. It knows the risk and pain of shattered trust. It is sober work in the midst of the conflicts, suspicions and anxieties of our time. (Report of the Conference of Protestant Church Leaders to the Federation Synod, 1980)

In their theological endeavors, the churches in the GDR are much less concerned with legitimizing their peace service than with providing inspiration for it. Theologians seek to make the wealth of biblical peace testimony accessible: the Old Testament understanding of *shalom* or Jesus' proclamation of God's Kingdom, or increasingly, in recent times, the "higher wisdom" of the Sermon on the Mount. That which has been elaborated and described theologically in the Federation of Protestant Churches since 1982/3 as "renunciation of the spirit, logic and practice of deterrence" has its origin here and is developing its inspirational power in the direction of a political concept of "common security".

For the People

The peace service of the churches in the GDR relates to concrete human beings and takes place in concrete society.

We see opportunities for becoming effective in this way in three directions:

—In the direction of the individual. Here, the concern is enabling the faithful subjective answer of individuals to the challenge posed by their Christian congregations and the church as a whole.

—In the direction of church groups and congregations which creatively translate into action the ethical insights into peace of the churches. They are to be given encouragement and support.

—In the direction of political processes. This means the responsible and thoughtful support of promising political ideas, suggestions and ways to help overcome the deadly antagonism of the two systems and avert the danger of a threatening war.

A few activities and initiatives of the Protestant churches in the GDR which aim in these three directions may be cited.

Education toward Peace

First place in our consideration must be given to education toward peace as a deliberate process of changing consciousness. Christians everywhere are deeply affected by statements heard in current peace discussions that harshly predict that humanity, even the entire planet earth, will only survive if we are radically converted and radically alter our way of thinking. Such statements come from Christians and non-Christians alike: Albert Einstein, Carl Friedrich von Weizsäcker, and Grigorij Arbatow, among others. They point in the direction of a genuinely Christian task, the call to conversion, to change one's thinking.

The Federation of Protestant Churches in the GDR has taken up this task with great determination. At first, we encountered misunderstanding and mistrust among other peace forces in our society which saw here a kind of counter-program to the tendencies toward militarism in society so frequently challenged by the church. Since then, by way of intra-societal trust-building, a more correct evaluation of the church's intentions has developed, as well as certain kinds of cooperation between church and state in this area.

"Education toward peace as a life-long process" is a basic concept in the Framework for Peace Education which the Federation of Protestant Churches developed for congregations in 1980. This offered a framework for the various efforts and models in operation in our churches, within which particular projects and programs could be oriented.

"A life-long process" means that adults also must be learners today; indeed, adults' ability to learn has special importance for the education of the younger generation. This framework of the church defines the following tasks which peace education should accomplish among all age groups in the congregations:

   a) imparting knowledge,
   b) changing attitudes, and
   c) enabling action.

Peace Witness in the German Democratic Republic

Programs and activities oriented by this framework follow these three steps; as they do, it becomes clear that the middle step of changing attitudes is the real core of the work.

The world political and social situation at the beginning of the 80s, and the particular situation of Protestantism in the GDR as a "church in socialism," have been taken into consideration as we have defined and developed practical peace education for Christians and Christian congregations. Education toward peace must enable, encourage and guide Christians to:

1) Settle and overcome conflicts by means of dialogues of understanding and compromise;
2) Critically control and renounce violence (pressure, force, corporal punishment) in relations between human beings;
3) Be prepared to take the first step toward solution of a conflict;
4) Value trust and trust-building measures in coexistence;
5. Respect the convictions of those who think differently and work cooperatively with them;
6) Be sensitive to the suffering of others, expressed in clear signs and sacrifices; be capable of solidarity with and willingness to suffer for others;
7) Be independent in thought, feeling and judgment—that is, be mature;
8) Critically question convictions, value-judgments and attitudes which claim alone to be valid;
9) Express objectively and persuasively one's own opinion;
10) Overcome irrational ideas characterized by anxiety and feelings of threat, as well as enemy images and feelings of hatred;
11) Be willing to have one's own peace disturbed for the sake of peace—to the point of accepting personal disadvantage;
12) Perceive, consider and speak of global processes and problems, even when one as an individual "has nothing to do with it and can do nothing about it";
13) Accept joint responsibility for a healthy environment;

14) Be more sharply aware of the urgency of genuine steps toward disarmament and have an informed interest in contemporary political efforts toward disarmament;
15) Struggle for just economic relations between rich and poor countries; and
16) Critically disagree with exclusively militaristic images and concepts of security, including the personal decision concerning the question of military service.

This survey goes from individual interpersonal relations to the societal political dimensions of peace education. Using the model of a church conference, "What makes us secure?" the Protestant churches in the GDR attempted to relate experiences of security in interpersonal relations to the area of political peace education in a societal and worldwide framework. This provoked the question: What *really* makes peoples and states secure? The realization was then conveyed that security is above all a consequence of trust, openness and cooperation.

We have discovered that this concept of ensuring peace must overcome a variety of barriers among us. Just to name a few: dulling of the meaning of peace by its inflation; weariness of learning; feelings of powerlessness; lack of information; the lack of transparency of military-political constellations; among such a preponderance of words, lack of opportunities for action; and a lack of willingness to suffer.

On the other hand, there are genuine, specific starting points for a change of thinking in our part of the world. The following points deserve mention here:

1) *The experience of the horror of war.* For many—above all the older people—the experience of the Second World War is a lasting call to a change in thinking and to active efforts for peace. In the telling of one's own personal history, such experiences may be conveyed to younger persons to influence their attitudes toward peace and war.
2) *Sensitization to global human problems.* The confrontation with hard facts—for example, the arms race or the ever-growing misery in Third World countries—creates a critical consciousness of problems of peace and justice which can find an ap-

propriate translation in the area of peace education in individual congregations.
3) *Opportunities for action in one's immediate sphere.* The frequently deplored lack of clarity in political events on the global level leads to the search for meaningful tasks in the more immediate area of personal peace responsibility. Parents often discover practical opportunities for peace education for the first time in the education of their children.
4) *Rejection of tendencies toward militarization.* Experiencing the extension of military language and behavior into what are civilian social areas (for example, military education and training in secondary education) became for many dismayed persons the trigger to awaken their concern for other means to secure peace in an atomic age. They seek answers in peace education for their often onerous experiences, and thus search for alternative ways to secure peace.
5) *The example of the historical peace churches.* The discovery of the heritage of the historic peace churches has made many Christians in our country sensitive to the failure of their own churches on the peace issue, creating an attitude of penitence. For this reason, the search for the responsibilities the church has for the service of peace goes on anew.

The fundamental idea behind education toward peace—the alteration of the ways of thinking of Protestant Christians in the GDR—is that it must come from below, from the congregations. For only from a conscious foundation in the congregations whose members are active in the life of the society, can a powerfully effective influence on society be established that reaches to direct dialogue between church leaders and the government. Speaking just from above can only promote a passive attitude and hinder creativity and activity on a broad plane.

The new requirement of military instruction in the ninth and tenth grades of the general schools presented a special challenge to the GDR Protestant churches' understanding of their responsibility to educate for peace. The Ministry of Education issued a directive in January 1978 that announced the beginning of this program for the school year starting in

September 1978. The Federation of Protestant Churches responded to this situation by:
1. entering into intensive negotiations with the government of the GDR;
2. speaking concretely and publicly to the congregations through a message to be read in all churches; and
3. providing Protestant Christians in the GDR with materials that helped orient them to respond to this new situation in a way that united reliable information with their faith perspective.

What was presented in summary fashion in the "Message to the Churches" was extensively developed in three sections in the "Orientation Helps." Section II, the heart of this document, provided a comprehensive response to the planned introduction of military instruction, and at the same time defined the position and task of the churches' responsibility for peace in this situation. The following particular positions were defined in the churches' response:

—opposition to "security thinking marked by anxiety and a sense of threat," because it leads to actions which heighten similar anxiety on the other side and lead to counter-threats;
—opposition to "the danger that obligatory military instruction of young people tends to accustom them to the use of military means for resolving conflicts, which in the long run could prove a hindrance for their genuine readiness to support disarmament";
—opposition to the serious endangering of youth's capacity for peace, because the intended military instruction "presupposes the possibility of a military conflict between East and West," and the induction into "military modes of thought" decisively reduces "the possibilities of peaceful overcoming of conflict"; and
—opposition to the contradiction between an external policy of peace and *détente* and an internal educational policy based on military security, which could cast a shadow over the believability of the peace policy of the GDR.

The protest of the Protestant churches did not stop the introduction of military instruction. Nevertheless, it has not

remained without effect; joined with the "Education for Peace" study and action program provided by the Protestant Federation, it has:
1. offered a genuine restraint against discrimination of children who refuse to take part in the military instruction; and
2. helped the great majority who do participate to do so critically, seeking to bring elements of peace education into the discussion, such as the role of the UN and the significance of the Helsinki Final Act.

Peace Decades

Peace decades (period of ten days) have proven to be special crystallization points in the peace activities of the churches in the GDR since 1980. Developing out of a youth initiative, which was held for the first time in 1980 under the theme "Make peace without weapons" (*Frieden schaffen ohne Waffen*), they have become activities of the entire congregation. Coming at the end of the church year in November—traditionally a time of repentance and reflection in our churches—they lead the community of Jesus Christ to place its Lord's peace mission in a special way at the center of its work, its celebration and its influence on society.

One theme unites these activities each year. The way has been clearly marked since the beginning of the 1980s:

"Make peace without weapons" was the motto of the first "peace decade" in 1980.

"Justice-Disarmament-Peace", were three catchwords whose inevitable interrelationship united the thought, activity and prayer of evangelical congregations in 1981.

"Anxiety-Trust-Peace", were again three catchwords in dialectical relation that motivated the congregations in the autumn of the following year.

"Make peace from the strength of the weak": This 1983 slogan related to experiences of powerlessness and vulnerability and used the biblical "Servant of the Lord" songs in Isaiah 42–53 and the New Testament theme of "My strength is powerful in the weak" to attack despair and hopelessness.

"Life against Death" in 1984. Biblical references used were the Noah story (Genesis 6–9) and the promise of Jesus, "I live, and you shall also live."

From the very beginning of the first peace decade, a part of that program was directed toward answering the question, "How do I become a Christian conscious of my political responsibility?" The "peace days" are to help answer this question through information, guidance for action and the experience of worship.

The drive toward concrete actions, especially among our youth, is a special challenge to the peace work of the churches in our country. The churches have found in it a great treasure of good will, of creative unrest and of driving imagination that opposes apathy—"There's nothing anyone can do"—and flippancy—"It won't be so bad." But it also has aroused the suspicions of the government that it may be an attempt in the church (perhaps under the class enemy's influence) to split the unified peace movement of the GDR. At the same time, the church has had energetically to compete against the influence of some Western press coverage and commentary that tends to exploit everything that arises in the area of the church's autonomous peace witness as an "independent peace movement" and as political opposition against "the system." A certain kind of blind activism also has had to be discouraged.

To clarify all of this both in our church and in our society was a central concern of the peace decade in 1983. The Synod of the Federation of Churches responded in this way:

> The desire for peace elicits creativity. Many persons attempt, with spontaneous actions, unusual ideas and various sign-events, to clarify and carry out the total about-face which is necessasry today.

Examples of this creativity include new forms of prayer for peace (fasting and times of silence), peace workshops, peace celebrations and peace games, peace letters between citizens of different nations and actions directed toward equitable sharing.

Critical inquiry remains necessary as to whether or not the

paths trod and the means applied really lead us further on the way to peace. Unusual ideas and spontaneous actions can be important triggers for thought, can represent learning stages on the way to peace and may persuasively make clear a willingness for peace. They run the danger, however, of being misunderstood and misused. For this reason, the effect and consequences of such plans must be carefully considered. The synod underscored the statement of the Conference of Evangelical Church Leaders that it is important to be alert for signs and evidence of changes of consciousness, to seize them and build upon them.

An example of imaginative and spontaneous action which led to misunderstandings and also to misuse but also finally to learnings, is the badge "swords into plowshares."

The badge itself was part of the materials prepared by the Federation of Protestant Churches for the *Friedensdekade* (Ten Days for Peace) held November 3–13, 1981 with the theme "Justice-Disarmament-Peace." The badge carried the picture of the well-known sculpture that the Soviet Union had given the UN, which stands in its park beside the East River—a man beating a sword into a plow (reflecting the prophetic promise of Isaiah and Micah). That this sign, which in no sense was intended as a badge, received so enthusiastic and widespread a reception is in part to be understood by the fact that it becomes ever more difficult in the GDR as elsewhere dialectically to unite increased arms programs and militaristic tendencies with the perspective of a world without weapons, which is also a socialist motif.

On the other hand, it cannot be denied that this sign of a genuine concern for peace and commitment to disarmament was misread as a badge of opposition and of a so-called independent peace movement in the GDR, a development in which Western mass media played a primary role in the style of the cold war. The churches in the GDR, therefore, had to both distance themselves from this misinterpretation and misuse, while at the same time deciding to defend the wearers of the badge against the rigorous measures the state took against them. At the beginning of the next *Friedensdekade* in 1982 under the theme of "Anxiety-Trust-Peace," the Synod of the Federation, in the fall of 1982, responding to the campaign against the use of this badge, declared:

> The *Friedensdekade* 1982 will take place under the theme "Anxiety-Trust-Peace." The conference has approved this theme and authorized the use of the symbol "Swords into Plowshares" for the church's programs again during this *Friedensdekade* and for the printed materials prepared for them. . . . The conference thanks all of the young people who have worn this symbol as a sign of peace, and who have not allowed themselves to become embittered by the measures taken against them but have given an account of the hope that is in us.

The symbol "Swords into Plowshares" has continued, despite all the difficulties encountered, to be the sign of the "Ten Days for Peace" of the Protestant churches.

Continuing Peace Activities of the Evangelical Churches in the GDR

"Peace decade" cannot mean only thinking, learning, working and praying for ten days out of the year, but also being strengthened, gaining insights, building communications and practicing cooperation, which are to be lived and to become effective 365 days a year. In many member churches of the Federation of Protestant Churches in the GDR, there are so-called peace workshops. Here, as during the "peace decades," communal living is practiced (along with fasting and prayer). There are also information booths, materials are exchanged, authors read and speeches given which lead from demonstration toward argumentation.

A particular mission of the church in socialism is to find—under the actual circumstances in a socialist society—specific forms of cooperation with other social forces which respect our autonomy, do not seek to co-opt us and allow our peace witness uninhibited opportunity. To be named here in particular are the Peace Council of the GDR, the Committee for

European Security and Cooperation, the Association for the United Nations and the Solidarity Committee of the GDR. True possibilities for participation must be developed here, especially for activities which the churches in the GDR want to put into operation for development in the Third World and in the area of ecology. We see the support of economic justice and peace with creation as basic peace activities.

The Protestant church in the GDR was given a great opportunity for exercising social influence in the public sphere during the Luther year of 1983. The *Kirchentag* movement in the GDR proved itself once again as a resource for peace work. Even the theme of the seven regional *Kirchentage* in the Luther year was a peace theme: "Risk Trust". Central to the questions voiced were those concerning disarmament—"Your enemy needs peace"; and peace with creation was put into words—"Our grandchildren want to live too." And the fact that peace is not possible without justice became the declaration of the entire Christian community as they gathered by the thousands in public streets and market places to say: "I'm fed up that others go hungry!".

The central concern and activity in which churches and Christians are irreplaceable remains prayer for peace. At the center of every "peace decade" there is a prayer service for peace in the world. The liturgy is prepared cooperatively with the Protestant church in the Federal Republic of Germany, and all of the churches in the ecumenical community with which we have bilateral peace dialogues are invited to contribute elements appropriate to the situation in which they perform their respective peace service. A part of the intercessory prayer of 1980 was:

> We thank You that You have brought hostile nations closer to each other and have led them toward cooperative work; we acknowledge to You our indifference, and the fact that we have not clearly overcome old prejudices. Lord, help us to be good neighbors to all nations, that we may not see in others the enemy, and that we may resist demonizing on both sides.

We thank You for the years in which weapons have been silent in Europe; we acknowledge the lack of gratitude shown in our holding on to our divisions and intensifying our differences.

Lord, show the nations ways to security without mutual threat, so that the military competition may come to a stop and disarmament become possible.

We thank You for the efforts of many politicians toward *détente* and for their desire to limit armaments; we acknowledge our lack of imagination and love to solve conflicts without hostility and violence. Lord, bless with success those who seek dialogue. We ask You for the success of the conference in Madrid: that the politicians may listen to each other, meet with each other in openness, and contribute to the growth of trust between the nations.

The Federation of Protestant Churches in the GDR formulated their own intercessory prayer for the Second UN Special Assembly on Disarmament in 1982 and gave it to the congregations. In several congregations a prayer chain was established, i.e., members prayed around the clock for the duration of the assembly. In one town a remarkable incident took place: In the high chancel of the cathedral a group was gathered in prayer at midnight. A policeman, who found the light through the church windows at this unusual hour suspicious, found his way into God's house. The following exchange took place:

> Question: "What are you doing here?"
> Answer: "We're praying."
> Question: "Are you authorized?"

We are authorized! We have a mission. Prayer is the most noble peace service of Christians everywhere in the world. In each of our worship celebrations it has its definite, established place. Here belongs also the prayer for those who suffer for the sake of their peace witness and for those who are serving prison sentences because they have refused military duty for reasons of conscience. They are prayed for by name in our churches, based on an intercessory list. The question of military service for Christians with its related issue of conscientious objection, now for the first time under the conditions of modern armies with nuclear weapons, has been a continuing issue for the Protestant churches in the GDR. Thus the Synod of the Federation of Protestant Churches declared in 1984:

> We cannot simply accept the stationing of new missiles in Western Europe and the corresponding measures taken within the states in the Warsaw Treaty. Military means, including service in the army, is seen less and less by many of us as a sensible way to secure peace. We request our government insistently to validate alternative concepts of security on the basis of common security. We request the Conference of Church Leaders to urge all of our ecumenical partners that they also use their influence against the policy of deterrence in their countries and support a return to detente. The Synod emphasizes that in the situation of increased tension the dialogue between churches that bridges the East-West blocs has special importance.

The so-called construction units were established by the National Defense Ministry in 1964 as a result of the churches' efforts. They make possible service without weapons, although within the national army. The core of present negotiations by the churches lies in this issue of providing an alternative civilian service (in agricultural or forestry service, health care or other social service).

The Conference of Church Leaders emphasized in their report to the synod of the Federation in September 1984 that in the previous twenty years,

> . . . thousands of Christian young men had provided a sign of their love for peace through their service in the military "construction units." They have given witness in their lives to Jesus' command to be peacemakers. The soldiers with the spade on their shoulder-strap have stimulated many to consider their responsibility for peace. The church has to thank these men that they have given "hands and feet" to the witness for peace.

Dialogues with the Government

"Exercising influence over governments" is a standing challenge raised in all ecumenical assemblies that deal with the vital question of peace. The churches are called upon to seek dialogue with their governments and to remain in contact with them concerning current questions of securing peace. The Protestant Church in the GDR sees this as a call to influence the government of its own country. It sees little sense in "speaking out the window" or pointing fingers at the other side.

Taking a position on the vital questions of the nation is an accepted right of the church. The political mandate to which the church subjects itself is free of clerical claims. The Federation of Protestant Churches, as a community of witness and service, thinks of this as part of its service.

At the same time, this fits the sense of the Preamble of the World Council of Churches, which states that it belongs to the constitutional functions and goals of the World Council "to give expression to the common task of the churches to serve human beings in need, to pull down the barriers that divide human beings, and to call the human family to live together in justice and peace."

International documents such as the Helsinki Final Act also point the church explicitly toward this task when it expressly states in Principle IX "that governments, institutions, organizations and persons are accorded a relevant and positive role in contributing their cooperation for the achievement of these goals."

In the GDR this takes place not only in occasional negotiations with the government over particular questions, but also in a continuing process of so-called *Sachgespräche* (dialogues on issues), which have progressed ever more strongly from pure information to an actual process of dialogue. They have reached a partnership-like exchange of ideas, in statements and replies and in mutual explanation of current different positions. They know no taboos!

The basis of these discussions has often been ecumenical

documents on which we ourselves as member churches have worked and which contain concrete questions, suggestions and demands. The peace work of our own churches in the GDR, contacts with other churches and church associations, and participation in relevant study processes—for example, the World Council of Churches' "Program for Disarmament and Against Militarism and the Arms Race"—have brought about an increased consciousness of the problems and an expertise that enables the church to articulate its own position vis-à-vis that of the government. In such conversations it is a matter of making ethical convictions politically viable. The church's fundamental support of *détente* and disarmament is linked with concrete suggestions to those in positions of political responsibility; the innovative impulse of church peace initiatives is translated into the impulses of political action.

Thus the Protestant church in the GDR, in dialogue with the government—i.e., with experts of the foreign ministry, including disarmament experts—has presented for discussion its rejection of the spirit, logic and practice of deterrence. In these discussions the Church has, for example, interpreted its understanding of the political concept of "common security" as an alternative security concept in accord with the Gospel understood as "intelligent love of the enemy." The church also relates its perspective to certain aspects of the foreign policy of the Warsaw Treaty nations: their cooperative political declarations, the reply of the GDR government to the Swedish proposal for creating a nuclear-free zone in middle Europe, the trust-building measures in accordance with the Helsinki Final Act, etc. Questions growing out of these issues are thoroughly discussed. Some examples are:

1. Where does the dilemma arise between announced political intentions ("limitation of destruction," the "Coalition of Reason") and the continuance of armament automatism (stationing of medium-range missiles in the GDR and Czechoslovakia)?
2. How can this dilemma be resolved?

3. How can the conviction that the testing, production, stationing and deployment of nuclear weapons is a crime against humanity be translated into an international and national ban of these weapons?
4. Where are we in the mutual recognition of the capacity of both great world systems for peace as a prerequisite for redirecting military-oriented production into civilian-oriented production?
5. How compatible are the building of trust and the extensive practice of secrecy?
6. What is now the major emphasis in the realization of trust-building measures discussed in Stockholm?
7. What is the relationship of the concept of common security to the concept of peaceful coexistence?
8. What is the government doing in the area of the United Nations' Disarmament Campaign; what possibilities are there for the churches to contribute to this campaign?

In the background of such dialogues, church leaders take opportunities publicly to address the government concerning its responsibility for peace, as, for example, the address of Bishop Horst Gienke of Greifswald to Swedish Prime Minister President Olof Palme and GDR State Council Chairman Erich Honecker during Palme's GDR visit in the Marienkirche at Stralsund; or Bishop Dr. Rathke's address to FRG Chancellor Helmut Schmidt and Erich Honecker in the Güstrow Cathedral. Such speeches address the responsibility of governments to fulfill their mandate for the well-being of humanity.

At the beginning of the Conference on Trust-Building Measures, Security and Disarmament in Stockholm, within the Helsinki process, the Federation of Evangelical Churches and the *Arbeitsgemeinschaft* (working committee) of Christian Churches in the GDR turned to the participating nations with the urgent request to come to agreement through negotiation. Here, the church acted only with the authority of a supplicant, devoid of all the worldly power that in the traditional German alliance of throne and altar was certainly at one time its to command.

Based on the fundamental conviction that peace is indivisible, that domestic peace and foreign peace belong together, the questions of inner peace, which are relevant to foreign policy, also belong in the peace dialogue between church and state.

Seeking to exercise direct influence upon government through dialogue is a central component of the Federation of Protestant Churches' perception of its peace mission. This dialogue, of course, doesn't receive any spectacular press coverage, not because it is secret diplomacy, but because it seeks to build trust. Its efficacy is thrown into question when the contents, duration, and results of such dialogues are run through the mills of the cold war.

The congregations are instructed thoroughly; but this is not a one-way street "from above to below." It is much more a matter of developing from the congregation's questions, experiences and perceptions the conception for particular dialogues, the themes to be discussed, the questions which must be asked and the impetus which must be given.

At the same time it can occur, as in the suspenseful days of fall 1983, that a congregation addresses itself directly to the chairman of the state council:

> . . . Like many citizens of our nation, we feel particularly threatened by the escalation of atomic armaments in Europe. We are greatly concerned that, in the need for ever-greater deterrence and defense, it could come to the no-longer calculable risk of an atomic war. We are filled with horror that after the stationing of new American atomic missiles in Western Europe—an act condemned by all of us—corresponding counter-measures are being introduced in our territory as well, and we and our children must live directly with atomic missiles. . . .
>
> We want to support you, and at the same time urgently request you to do all in your power to bring the negotiations in Geneva to a successful conclusion, and to continue and expand the dialogue between the two German states, so that trust can grow as a basis for a security partnership—according to your words—a "coalition of reason."

For us as Christians, the key to overcoming tensions lies in trust-building between states. It appears to us that the willingness to make unilateral concessions based on trust, that is, not demanding exact reciprocation, might be the only possibility for peace and security today. This conviction arises for us out of the New Testament, in particular out of the Gospel of Jesus.

We know that the teachings of Jesus, above all those concerning the love of neighbor and of enemy, have been considered politically impractical, indeed, as irrational. Nevertheless, in view of a deadly armament-spiral, a liberating impulse could be discovered in them: to create trust through measures which amount to a unilateral concession, in order that this deadly automatism might be destroyed. Even when we know that you are politically and ideologically led by different fundamental ideas, we see it as our inner duty to bring these ideas out of the Christian tradition as a contribution to the great peace discussion in our land. . . .

This letter from the Dresden-Loschwitz congregation was printed verbatim in the leading newspaper, *Neues Deutschland*, which is the organ of the Communist Party. As far as we can see, it was not printed out of propagandistic motives or as an obligatory act of *Vater Staat* ("Father State") for the Christian population. Rather, we observe a genuine expectation toward the church on the part of the government. Results of such exchanges find their way onto the agenda of international conferences.

Beyond the Borders

The churches in the ecumenical community form a transnational reality that enables them to be effective as real peace factors beyond the borders of nations and systems. The churches can benefit from a wide network of national and international connections to inform themselves and thereby obtain a reasonably accurate image of reality without propagandistic distortions. Precisely in crises, when diplomatic channels fail, the churches can (while remaining loyal to their own states) keep communication going and, if necessary, offer their good services for unofficial contacts. Given their image of the human being based on the Gospel, the churches are better able than other organizations to offset clichés, to question enemy images and to reveal the reality behind ideological concepts. As churches, they need never fear "losing face." They are in a position to discern in all their depth the other side's feelings of being threatened, and to make these feelings clear to their own people. Thus the ecumenical movement may be designated a peace movement par excellence.

The Federation of Protestant Churches in the GDR is part of this worldwide peace movement. It makes use of the possibilities provided by the multilateral networks associated with it in ecumenical councils, in various ecumenical gatherings, and above all, continuously in its bilateral ecumenical network of communication:

Dialogue with the British Council of Churches

The trigger instance was the Falkland War, during which the churches in both countries attempted, together and in their own national contexts, to exercise influence in the direction of peace.

Further possibilities for the churches to influence peace based on this "model" should be investigated.

Dialogue with the Protestant Church in the Federal Republic of Germany

Consultations have taken place since the united statement on the occasion of the 40th anniversary of the outbreak of the Second World War.

Point of emphasis: analysis of the particular situation of the relationship between the churches in both German states and the consequences thereof for their peace mission.

Dialogue with the Netherlands Church Council

Point of emphasis: The question of nuclear disarmament in Europe and the strife over the stationing of Euro-strategic missiles in Western Europe and tactical missiles in the GDR.

Dialogue with the Polish Ecumenical Council

Particular motivation: Reconciliation with the Polish neighbors.
Point of emphasis: Education toward peace.
Special peace project: Participation in the building of the Children's Health Center in Warsaw, which was established as a memorial for the children killed in World War II in Europe (including two million Polish children).

Dialogue with the Russian Orthodox Church

The foundation is theological discussions (the Zagorsk dialogues) with their special exchange of ideas in the socio-ethical area, including church and society.
The round table discussions initiated by the Russian Orthodox Church since 1983 have been particularly fruitful for the fulfillment of the peace mission of the church. Special subjects considered have been the economic and moral implications of nuclear armament and the military armament of outer space.

Dialogue with the National Council of Churches of Christ in the USA

This dialogue was triggered by the threatened introduction of neutron weapons in 1978. Rather than taking part in a propagandistic protest, the Federation of Evangelical Churches in the GDR invited its genuine church partner to discuss this threat because it considered the influence of the NCCC-USA on government and public opinion in the USA to be effective.

Since that time, three further dialogues have taken place. A particular point of emphasis in the third dialogue was the freezing of nuclear weapons ("freeze") with its military and economic implications. Written exchanges also have had a particular place in this dialogue process: the National Council of Churches was exhaustively informed of the anxiety of people in the GDR over the installation of Euro-strategic missiles.

The border-crossing ecumenical peace activities of the GDR Federation build upon the peace work of the congregations and their results end up back in them. Their findings are also conveyed, however, directly to the government of the GDR as "instruments" of peace-making.

In Conclusion

Work for peace is and will be done by the Protestant churches in the GDR—and that means in a socialist society—independently and responsibly, motivated by the Gospel in a way that not only finds the Gospel an impulse but also a constant guiding principle (plumb line) for practical action. Hope is a crucial contribution that churches and Christians may make to the earthly political business of achieving, securing and maintaining peace. The Christ who is our peace is at the same time the hope of the world.

Protestant churches and Christians in the GDR see their task as letting Christianity's great visions of hope enlighten the possibility of a world without weapons—so that it might also influence those who sit in seats of worldly power:

—The lamb shall lie down with the lion: trust;
—Swords shall be beaten into plowshares: disarmament for the sake of righteousness;
—"God shall wipe away all tears from their eyes" (Rev. 7:17): security.

These are admittedly eschatological visions. But what should stop us from transforming their motive power into real utopias and bringing it into the earthly business of peacemaking? The concept of "common security," for example, is such a real utopia that has already come a long way from the standpoint of its political possibility. The Protestant churches in the GDR recognize this as their responsibility.

The United Nations has decided that 1986 will be an International Year of Peace. The Federation of Protestant Churches in the GDR will continue its ongoing peace program by developing its own programs for that year within the World Disarmament Campaign of the United Nations.

The Political Efficacy of the Church's Responsibility for Peace in the German Democratic Republic

by Günter Krusche

I. THE CHURCH IN THE GDR FACES THE PEACE QUESTION

The church's testimony for peace in the German Democratic Republic became concrete for the first time after World War II in its response to the "Battle Commission" of the central committee of the Free German Youth, which had called for volunteer military service in the newly established national defense army. In a statement issued in Berlin-Brandenburg in 1961, church leaders called upon pastors to make "the inner predicament of youth" their own.[1] This predicament was intensified by the introduction of universal military service on September 20, 1961.

The church's efforts at that time concentrated exclusively on pastoral care. The church insisted that members of the army should have freedom of religion and of conscience, and should be free to take part in worship services. The church

---

Dr. Günter Krusche is General Superintendent of the Church of Berlin-Brandenburg, German Democratic Republic.

addressed the interpretation of the oath of allegiance and the problem of conscientious objection and requested occasional exemption from military service for young men in theological training.[2]

The establishment of "construction brigades" in the army by an order of September 7, 1964 served to expand the church discussion. On the one hand, a certain relaxation of tension occurred, due to the possibility of alternative service for conscientious objectors; on the other hand, the controversy concerning a truly civilian alternative service was fueled anew by the military character of the construction units. Much time was to pass until a true alternative was worked out.[3]

In the long run, the church could not evade theological reflection on the peace theme because alternative service for "construction soldiers" touched only one aspect of the church's responsibility for peace—and that unsatisfactorily—the defense of conscience. Since only a few youth took advantage of this solution, the question of a "service of peace" had to be considered in a larger context. "The Church and all its members are charged to serve the world in the direction of peace—also in the area of political and social responsibility," stated a church memorandum of 1965.[4] The individual ethical limit of the question was consciously transcended. Under the threat of nuclear destruction, conscientious objection was recognized as the "clearer sign"[5] of Christian responsibility for peace. Yet the fundamental right of the state to maintain an army in order to secure peace was not challenged—indeed, the state's desire for peace was not questioned at all. Yet "criticism of the state" was not ruled out as a task of the church. The church promised its support for "all efforts toward disarmament and the protection of peace," yet wanted its support of the "conscience oppressed by military service" to be understood also as a "testimony to peace."[6]

The founding of the Federation of Evangelical Churches in the GDR brought a new quality to the discussions concerning the church's responsibility for peace. The church had to deal more comprehensively with the subject of peace, not only because of the expansion of military training (which was required in the ninth and tenth grades of polytechnical high schools after September 1, 1978), but also due to the growing interest in peace among those unaffiliated with the church. The church's concern now clearly reached beyond individual ethics into the area of social responsibility because the federation understood itself emphatically as "a community of testimony and service" in socialist society.[7] This self-understanding required consideration of peace questions on a total social scale.

The federation's Committee on Church and Society applied itself precisely to this challenge.[8] Working together with the section on peace questions of the federation's Committee on Theological Studies, the committee addressed the subject of peace in all its breadth in a number of pamphlets and resource materials.[9] The synod and the Conference of Church Leaders have also increasingly affirmed the church's responsibility for peace—often under the pressure of actual challenges.[10] The church found support both in ecumenical peace efforts of the World Council of Churches, the Lutheran World Federation and the Conference of European Churches and also through participation in the 1973 and 1982 World Conferences of the Forces for Peace, both held in Moscow.

The signing of the Helsinki Final Act opened up a new, broad area of responsibility for peace. Soon after its signing on August 1, 1975, the first "Post-Helsinki Conference" of the Conference of European Churches took place in Bukow. The GDR churches became increasingly engaged in these Post-Helsinki Conferences, as well as in "The Churches' Human Rights Program for the Realization of the Helsinki Final Act." A working paper of the federation, delivered in March, 1981 at a consultation on human rights of the advisory group of the Commission of the Churches on International Affairs (CCIA) of the World Council of Churches, also directed attention to the inseparable connection between peace *détente* and the realization of human rights.

In summary, one may say that the peace discussion in the churches of the federation has concerned itself increasingly with the political implications of the peace question. The

"Statement on the Current World Political Situation," developed by the churches of the federation for the January 28–31, 1980 conference in Budapest of the World Council of Churches, with member churches from the socialist countries of Europe, is particularly telling in this respect. Here we find this important statement: "The churches' task in respect to peace is derived fundamentally and directly from the proclamation of the Gospel. Today, however, it arises also from the fact that the churches' members are a world-wide ecumenical community."[12] This observation makes it clear that responsibility for peace is a central question for GDR churches, which is determined for them by their attitude toward the Gospel. This statement, however, does not come simply out of the socio-ethical tradition of the Evangelical churches in German-speaking areas, and cannot be explained without reference to their participation in the ecumenical movements' testimony for peace.

II. THE PEACE QUESTION IN THE ECUMENICAL CONTEXT

Awareness of the theological significance of a heightened commitment to peace has grown in the World Council of Churches as well. Putting life on earth in total jeopardy through the deployment of nuclear weapons has been compared to racism. It was denounced as "a crass negation of the Christian faith"[13] by the Fourth WCC Assembly at Uppsala, and was defined as an "ethical heresy"[14] by its general secretary, Dr. Visser 't Hooft.

My own testimony in the WCC International Hearings on Nuclear Disarmament in 1981 in Amsterdam made this point: "In this context the ecumenical movement would have to ask itself whether it should not sharpen the consciences of the member churches of the World Council of Churches by declaring the deployment of nuclear weapons as *status confessionis,* as did the Lutheran World Federation in its full assembly in Dar es Salaam in 1977 in denouncing apartheid.

The identity of the church is truly at stake when it is faced with the question whether the life of many innocent human beings and even the future of our earth may be determined according to political objectives."[15]

An important step in the direction of an unambiguous stance on the peace question was taken by the Christian world conference "Life and Peace," which took place by invitation of Swedish Archbishop Olof Sundby April 20–24, 1983 in Uppsala.[16] The message issued by the conference, passed only after intense debate by the full assembly, based Christian concern for peace upon the Gospel of Jesus Christ, itself a "message of peace." Christianity gains its identity and unity by representing the cause of peace.

> We, who come from various different churches, see a great sign of hope in the efforts toward the unity of Christendom. Precisely at this point in history, where divisions threaten the mere survival of humanity, the Holy Spirit moves his people to discover and publicly acknowledge this unity.[17]

The connection between "peace and justice" also was stressed at Uppsala, an emphasis entirely in keeping with the "comprehensive" understanding of peace which has developed recently in the ecumenical community.

> The struggle for peace holds little sense for the victim of injustice, as long as that struggle is not bound to the struggle for justice. . . . The peoples of the Third World warn us that the struggle for peace encompasses more than overcoming the dangers of violent conflict.[18]

The doctrine of the "just war" was interpreted at Uppsala: It has "always proceeded from a moral anti-war standpoint."[19] In other words, it never justified war; rather, it supported its limitation. The only possible conclusion was drawn: "We are therefore fully in agreement that a nuclear war, which, like every war, would escalate quickly, can never be justified."[20]

Particularly intense debate took place at Uppsala on the "doctrine of nuclear deterrence." It was agreed that this doctrine, undefined as it is, can no longer contribute to maintaining peace. It is becoming "in every respect ever more questionable and dangerous." The formulation however, still betrays something of the heated debate:

> *Most of us* believe that, viewed from a Christian standpoint, a dependence upon the threat of and possible use of atomic weapons as a means of avoiding a war is unacceptable. *Some of us* are ready to tolerate nuclear deterrence *only as a last resort*, as long as no alternatives are found. *For most of us*, however, the possession of nuclear weapons *is irreconcilable with our belief in God*, our *understanding of creation* and our *membership in the universal body of Christ*. Nuclear deterrence is by nature dehumanizing; it escalates fear and hate and strengthens the confrontation between 'the enemy and us.' The majority of us believe, therefore, that the mere existence of these weapons contradicts the will of God. Obedience to this will of God demands that all of us undertake decisive efforts toward their elimination within a definite period of time.[21] (emphases added)

For a considerable majority at the conference, therefore, not only the threat of the use of atomic weapons was unacceptable, but even "the possession of nuclear weapons" was considered irreconcilable with the trinitarian faith. At this point the conference came close to proclaiming the *status confessionis;* yet here again, it became clear that insistence upon particular formulations does not encourage consensus. The disagreement was reduced finally to a "matter of opinion" as to whether the "threat" of use may still be termed a sensible political tool or not. In any case, even advocates of a policy of deterrence by nuclear weapons think this valid only "within a limited period of time." This means that nuclear weapons are fundamentally irreconcilable with the will of God, and are ultimately to be rejected.

In an analysis of the discussion on peace among churches in the Federal Republic of Germany,[22] the role of the churches is seen above all as a "forum for the discussion of the politics of peace and security. . . . This function is irreplaceable at the moment in the Federal Republic."[23] "Fundamental criticism" as well as room for "the representatives of uncomfortable positions and critical minorities" must have a "legitimate place" in the churches. "Initially, utopian-sounding alternative security concepts can also be discussed among churches, particularly since there is no direct pressure for action in this case."[24] But then the critical observation is made that "the consensus concerning the fundamental goals of peace politics established in the Church's stance remains without consequence so long as those principles are not mediated, on the one hand, on the level of situational analysis, and on the other hand, on the level of strategies for action."[25]

This critique describes the dilemma of the ecumenical peace discussion as well. The WCC public hearing in Amsterdam in 1981 was undoubtedly a forum for opinions, but what operational criteria emerged from it? Olof Palme, Swedish prime minister and chairman of the so-called Palme Commission, pointed out that "the decisions concerning these questions cannot be based on strategic or military considerations . . . Fundamental political and moral values come into play."[26]

III. THE CHURCHES IN THE GDR AND THE *STATUS CONFESSIONIS*

The significance of these questions for the churches and Christians in the GDR emerges in the first place out of their general dismay over the dangers of nuclear war on the "seam" between socialism and capitalism, the "antagonistic social orders" established in the two Germanies. It arises also out of the ecumenical engagement of the Evangelical churches in the GDR. For this reason, the Federation Synod in Halle passed a resolution based on a report of the Conference of Church Leaders on September 28, 1982. Entirely in keeping with the course of the ecumenical discussion, the synod formulated three questions which "cannot remain unanswered in the long run:"

> a) "Are Christians permitted to take part in preparations for defense with atomic weapons when it is certain that such defense irretrievably destroys what is to be defended?"

b) "Are Christians permitted to participate in threats with weapons which themselves make the catastrophe probable that Christians are supposed to prevent?"

c) "Can Christians and churches still justify the use of weapons as a means of securing peace and the defense of one's neighbors in the face of the unimaginable horror of a possible war?"[27]

In this context, the synod expressed the desire that an investigation be commissioned "for the clarification of the concept *status confessionis* in connection with the question of peace. This investigation is to take place in an ecumenical context."[28]

The Reformed General Convention in the GDR expressed agreement with the church leaders' project of clarification only a month later, on November 9, 1982. It emphasized particularly:

a) the observation that the "peace question" is not a passing theme for the Church, but rather, "proceeds much more from the center of the Gospel" (see Thesis I);

b) the connection between military armaments and the economic oppression of, above all, the hungry and poverty-stricken of the world; and

c) the increasing obligation for peace discussion created by the declaration of the *status confessionis,* which is seen as an "invitation to faith and a call to the binding decision of the profession of that faith." This understanding of the *status confessionis* is expressly confirmed. The "common understanding of the Gospel" declared by the *Leuenberger Konkordie* ('38) is not to be called into question by the current argument, but rather realized through it.[29]

The proclamation of the *status confessionis* however, does not relieve one of the obligation to:

—identify the *situation* which calls for the witness to faith,
—clarify the *position* in which it is imperative to witness,
—describe the concrete *goal* of that testimony,
—disclose the *particular strategy* (goal and partial goals), and
—seek *dialogue* within the particular associations, congregations or churches.

Because, however, the concept of *status confessionis* or *casus confessionis*, owing to its various usage in the history of Protestantism (it has not existed in the Catholic Church to date) and its numerous meanings, leads more often to conflict concerning its applicability than to actual profession of faith, its further use probably should be avoided. For it is not a matter of merely articulating the *status confessionis*, but rather of effecting it as an act of specific testimony that may indeed be covered by the authority of the church.

The major objections in the current dispute concerning the *status confessionis* are not directed toward the specific professions of faith of individual Christians and their identification with politically concrete demands and actions. They are rather directed against the church's "public and unambiguous" (Dar es Salaam) call to political commitment. This was exactly the EKD objection against the Program to Combat Racism of the World Council of Churches in 1970.[30]

That the church is called to a specific testimony in the question of peace cannot be doubted. No one has in earnest contradicted the statement of the Reformed church leadership that "the peace question is a faith question"[31] when the statement is predicated on the belief that "Jesus Christ is our peace."

The conflict begins when the question becomes the concrete form of obedience—a matter no longer of preaching, but of doing—such as political decisions concerning the production and use of nuclear weapons. A recent case is NATO's resolution to deploy new medium-range nuclear missiles in Europe. Clarification of the technical questions demands only informed dialogue—dialogue open to arguments from everyone, since both Christians and non-Christians are affected and challenged by the arms race. However, resolution of political conflicts concerning peace requires information so that individual Christians will not be left to their own resources. "The call for peace based on the Gospel demands from the churches and from each individual Christian a serious testing of everything which in the current world situation reduces tensions, promotes trust and serves peace."[32]

The decision for or against a concrete political witness must withstand a serious testing as to whether, in the given situation and at the present time, such an act of "public and unambiguous" testimony does indeed promote peace. For profession cannot simply replace reflection.

Thus we stand before the task of creating a church peace strategy.

IV. THE NECESSITY OF A PEACE STRATEGY FOR THE CHURCH IN THE GDR

Realization of the responsibility for peace gives those who act responsibly a specific direction. For peace does not exist; peace should exist! The service of peace requires commitment to politics and political reasoning. It is necessary to realize the essential difference between *shalom* as an eschatological promise and peace on earth, but this may not be understood in a way that relegates *shalom* only to the next world. Peace on earth is subject to "eschatological limitation." It can be surpassed, it is always threatened, and it is an ongoing task, but it is not insignificant, nor merely a matter of personal discretion. Obedience and discipleship are demonstrated in the taking of responsibility for peace, as in all historical responsibility.

"Christ is our peace" (Eph. 2:14) is the testimony of the congregation, which then must draw conclusions from it for peace on earth. Dispensing with a politically viable strategy for action signifies only the irrelevance of Christian faith for the political sphere, which is then left to the "autonomy" of the so-called dictation of circumstances. "The relevance of faith to the world requires sober insight into the power of laws in history in order for the freedom of faith to establish itself. The kind of sobriety needed is as remote from any kind of legal fatalism as it is from any flippant suspension of actual powerful, inevitable consequences. The way of Christian freedom goes through history, not through secret ways around it."[33]

Three fundamental goals were established for the WCC hearing in Amsterdam in November 1981 to contribute to a peace strategy:
1. to evaluate the problems which arise from the escalation of the arms race, as well as from the concept of deterrence and limited atomic war, and to investigate the effects of the suspension of efforts toward atomic disarmament;
2. to further develop Christian reflection on several of the most important problems in this area; and
3. to search for ways in which churches, Christian groups and others can work toward a more positive approach to atomic disarmament, and how they themselves can best obtain practical successes.[34]

Information, reflection and directions for action are necessarily and inextricably bound together. "What can the Church do for peace?"[35] is therefore a necessary question; its answer requires the creation of a church peace strategy. Awareness of the danger to peace in the face of the atomic arms race should not obscure the political task that the steps toward peace constitute. In the words of Wolfgang Huber, "The insight is spreading, that it is time for a new politics of peace."[36] Even the declaration of *status confessionis* becomes politically relevant only when that particular witness to faith is part of a reasonable peace strategy; in other words, when a statement follows the "No without any yes"[37] pointing out how we should then proceed.

By definition, a strategy for action consists of quantifiable, concrete and debatable steps.[38] The setting of goals, strategy planning, the organization of activities and the attendant analysis of the process ("feedback")[39] are the basic elements of a theory of action. A peace strategy must therefore disclose its desired goals, describe concrete measures toward peace and name conditions under which peace is politically conceivable. Only then will church contributions to peace become worthy of public debate: positions would be clarified by thinking through and playing out the political possibilities; the comparable could be compared. It may prove to be the case that a worldwide consensus in matters of peace is far from consensus, but an intensive, patient dialogue of the antagonists is itself a step toward peace. It could, states an EKD memorandum, "strengthen the sense of proximate solutions."[40]

Albrecht Schönherr recently (1982) demonstrated in his contribution to the *Festschrift* for Bishop Kurt Scharf of Berlin[41] that the priority peace concern of the Evangelical Churches in the GDR from the beginning was not the individual ethical question "whether a Christian may take up arms or not", but based on the Berlin-Weissensee peace Synod of 1950, was oriented to the more comprehensive question: "What can the church do for peace?".[42] The 1982 Halle Synod of the Federation of Evangelical Churches in the GDR dealt explicitly with questions of the individual Christian in the congregations[43] and pleaded for individual freedom of faith and conscience, particularly for young people.[44] Nevertheless, the synod declared the church itself responsible when it comes to threats to peace:

> New weapon systems are said to make an atomic first-strike possible; new strategies seek to insure its success. This threat to all life through excessive armament poses a challenge to our faith. If we accept it without response, we enter into contradiction with God the creator, for His commission obliges us to preserve creation and forbids the right to destroy it. For this reason it is a matter here of *obedience or disobedience to God*.[45]

(emphasis added)

The division of theological studies of the federation created a tool for the churches in its "Report on Peace Questions," to help make responsible persons competent on all levels of peace questions. In this report, the head of this division, Joachim Garstecki, worked through the most important results of peace research to make them accessible to the churches.[46] He, too, sees the church's responsibility for peace as extending to the concretely political:

The tension between eschatalogical promise and political reality, between the peace of God and the world's peace, requires churches and Christians to seek direction for their own action on the field of ethical judgements, which cannot be gained through a fixation on political action. Christian peace ethics is the attempt to find answers—through productive mediation between theological knowledge and secular reason, between utopia and force of circumstances, between "Gospel" and "law"—to the question "What should I do?" Only as a consequence of this mediation do hope and responsibility for the future, openness and readiness, willingness to take risks and planning, become categories of a reflective "Christian world responsibility" conscious of its possibilities and limitations.[47]

The concept of "common security," which the churches of the federation support, is the result of such a "productive mediation between theological knowledge and secular reason" (Garstecki), and as such a contribution to the peace politics debate. It is, states Hans Ruh, "a strategic concept which does not maximize one's own power, but rather optimizes common security in its own self-conception."[48] Its consequence is a process of "step-by-step" disarmament. The suggestions of the churches in the GDR follow along these lines. In the conference report of the Halle Synod, church leaders were not content wih the "rejection of the spirit of the system of deterrence"[49]; but risked suggesting several "political measures" which effectively amount to partisanship in support of previously suggested measures in the disarmament debate. One could conclude that the churches in the GDR have lost their anxiety about touching the political sphere.

The rejection of the spirit of the system of deterrence should become effective not only in verbal explanations and exemplary action, but also in political plans through concretely discriminating judgments. Such judgments must submit themselves to political argumentation.[50]

A formal suggestion in the report of the federation's section on Theological Studies, "Security, Partnership and Freedom in Europe: the Task of the German States, the Responsibility of the German Churches" (published March, 1983),[51] seeks to be politically effective in the sense of the above-cited criteria. This suggestion replaces the principle of mutual deterrence with the principle of "common security" from the report of the Palme Commission.[52] It builds upon the synod's "rejection of the spirit and logic of deterrence" in Halle in 1982.[53]

Two fundamental requirements for the possibility of peace and security in Europe are named, in agreement with the Palme Report:

- a) military détente on the basis of the progressive reduction and disengagement of both military blocs in Europe, and
- b) political and economic stability in both parts of Europe. This places a special task on both German states[54], because massive armed forces confront each other on their territories.

The churches' responsibility for peace must presuppose that in the foreseeable future, no political alternatives to the contemporary political and military constellation are thinkable. Therefore the study calls for affirmation of one's own social order and of peaceful coexistence. The advantage of this proposal lies in its political concreteness and appropriateness to the given social situation, something which no peace strategy may overlook. Yet the concept is ruled by a vision, for "it is necessary to establish the vision of a peaceful European society—Europe as a life community composed of its various peoples, cultures, social and political systems and associations—over and against the apocalyptic vision of a European nuclear catastrophe," according to the report.[55] The churches in both German states have a "particular responsibility for this discussion"[56]:

> The churches in both German states can make the European dialogue possible; they stand at a point in the history of Europe which can be occupied by no other church. They stand at the point where the guilt for Auschwitz and the possibility of nuclear catastrophe intersect.[57]

The basic ideas of this study were collected in a document made public, with the signatures of church men and women of both German states,[58] at the peace forum of the *Kirchentag* in Hannover.[59] It ends with the appeal: "We ask all Christians who acknowledge their responsibility for peace in the church and in society, to contribute to it according to their means, in order that the concept of common security may be translated into practical peace politics. Time is pressing."[60]

Characteristic of this initiative is the desire for concrete political measures which

—are active in contemporary circumstances;
—lie within the realm of the politically feasible and politically wise;
—already now demonstrate peace and trust-building; and
—place common security (security partnership) over mutual deterrence.

V. RESPONSIBILITY FOR PEACE AND THE STRUCTURE OF THE CHURCH

The realization that the church witnesses for its Lord not only through its preaching, but also in its witness in life and practice is nothing new in the ecumenical community. The conviction that structures, too, "preach" was introduced in the World Council of Churches' study "Mission as a Principle of Structure,"[61] with its critical edge directed against "morphological fundamentalism."[62]

The church in the GDR, like all churches, exists as an empirical church under complex circumstances,[63] and in a variety of forms.[64] Just as the socialist society in the GDR, although based upon the principle of democratic centralism, is far from monolithic, so the life of the church also takes different forms in relation to society. Indisputably, the church is moving in the direction of "diaspora,"[65] and therefore in the direction of smaller congregations;[66] but the process of "de-churchification" has progressed variously. The *Volkskirche* (national church) still exists in structure and, residually, in people's consciousness: regional churches and parish districts still reflect the territorial system of sovereign church rule; official clerical acts still have great significance for participation in the life of the church, even if the majority of funerals demonstrate the end of popular church-oriented religiosity.[67] This process, which Marxist sociology of religion continues to interpret as evidence of the "dying out of religion,"[68] rather has been from the standpoint of the church, an extensive learning process[69] which has led to a new definition of its relationship to the state and society.[70]

Just as the church found its way only with difficulty into the new situation of the post-Constantinian era[71] and worked its way through its non-reflective anti-communism by a theological re-evaluation of its own past,[72] so the church saw itself after the founding of the federation as facing the task of "finding its place"[73] in relation to socialist society: "Not beside, and not against socialism," but rather, "in socialism."[74] A position paper of the Committee on Church and Society, "The Witness and Service of the Evangelical Churches and Christians in the Socialist Society of the GDR,"[75] which remained controversial and was circulated only as a "paper for discussion," bore witness to the struggle over "the acceptance of the given situation."[76] The results of this struggle set the tone for committee member Heino Falcke's report before the 1972 synod in Dresden, "Christ liberates—and so a Church for Others,"[77] which brought into play for the first time the phrase "concretely discriminating cooperation": "Thus we are freed from the fixation on a self-perception of socialism which permits only a flat yes or equally flat no."[78] A mode of "critical participation" was thus opened for the church.[79] "The church in socialism would be the church which helps the Christian citizen and individual congregation to find a way of freedom and faith's commitment, and thus make an effort to seek the best for the whole," Evangelical Church leaders observed. (Schwerin, 1973).[80]

In the March 6, 1978 dialogue with the executive board of the Conference of Evangelical Church Leaders, the chairman of the state council of the GDR recognized completely the autonomy of Christian responsibility for the world. Both dialogue partners also agreed, however, that much remained to be done. "The relationship between church and state is as good as the individual Christian citizen experiences it 'in the street,' in his own social situation."[81]

The peace question, because of its highly political character, necessarily became the touchstone and stress test of this new relationship between church and state. This was true from the point of view of the socialist state because the rejection of the "spirit and logic of deterrence"[82] appears directed against an essential element of its defense strategy and may be suspected of intending to weaken defense preparedness. It was true from the standpoint of the church, because the church interprets its peace witness in the service of society as "not directed against socialism," but rather as "seeking the best for the whole."[83] For peace is indivisible.

Some lack of clarity in the church's peace witness was also created by the sheer extent of peace activities on all levels of church life. These activities grow out of deep concern and dismay and out of the consequent desire for responsible activity for peace, but they are often—to the point of indistinguishability—carried out by persons, primarily youth, for whom such activities are simultaneously an expression of dissatisfaction with the government, of political opposition or of inner emigration (often as an initial step to actual emigration). In the actual carrying out of the peace effort in congregations, it is hardly possible "to separate the wheat from the chaff," nor does this appear to be required. As a recognized free area in society, the church has the responsibility to be "the voice of the voiceless." As the "church for others," the church in the GDR has constantly resisted the demand to be solely a "means of transmission" of state demands, "and thus become itself an organ of the state."[84]

VI. THE CHURCH'S OPPORTUNITIES IN THE GIVEN POLITICAL SITUATION

With the process of secularization the church as an institution is receding socially into the background, while church groups determine the life of the churches more powerfully than ever before.[85] In place of the closed church institution there is increasingly open activity. Under such circumstances, the individual Christian gains a new and great significance. As a "lay person,"[86] he or she is the witness "in the world," who must necessarily step out of the institutional structure; he or she is an authentic witness to the faith insofar as he or she must bear alone the risk of his or her action. The Synod of Saxony had to tell its youth, "we are no longer in the position of being able to protect you from the consequences which the wearing of the 'Swords into Plowshares' patch can bring these days."[87] The institutional church can assist insofar as it can inform, train, and give pastoral support to individuals and groups.

The general concept of the program "Education toward Peace" (1978)[88] was thus intended to initiate a learning process, provide expert information, supply politically engaged persons with arguments and strengthen the willingness to take risks. Congregations have partially rearranged their work programs to concentrate on this peace effort. Though it is not to be expected that the organized church in the GDR would adopt a role like the historic "peace church,"[89] it has proven again and again that without the assistance of the institutionalized church, particularly on the highest level, the individual Christian's responsibility for peace at the local lay level is not sustainable. The bishops can say what others are forbidden to say. This discrepancy between the "upper level" and the "base" is in various ways burdensome to the peace effort in the GDR churches.

Some peace groups in the GDR approximate what Wolfgang Huber has called "initiative groups,"[90] and some recognize in them the modern equivalent of the "radical, charismatic wandering preachers"[91] from the time of the New Testament. But it is questionable whether the peace groups which are so mixed in membership may so easily be identified with a circle of dedicated disciples who lived in the spirit of the Sermon on the Mount (Matthew 5:1–12), and who obeyed the call uncompromisingly to imitate Jesus (Matt. 10:5–15, 16–33; 16:24–28). In spite of this, such peace groups perform the task of questioning the church's existence as church and the earnestness of the church's own imitation of Christ. Local congregations are often overtaxed in attempting to create the social space such groups need. Regional cooperation is needed to keep them critically participant within the larger community of the church. The organized church should in no case seek to rid itself of this critical minority. Their questions are directed toward church and state. By making room for these questions, peace is served in an important way through communication, even in the concrete sense of social reconciliation. For these are the questions of the younger generation concerning the lifestyle and moral principles of the older generation. The silence of governmental authorities regarding these activities indicates that the other side, too, recognizes at least the "safety-valve" function of such meetings.

The universal dimension of the *ecclesia* also becomes decisively important in fulfilling the church's responsibility for peace. The peace effort of GDR churches is often indebted to the ecumenical community for impetus for its own activity. Our churches take part in the ecumenical movement and in this way communicate their experiences to the worldwide community of churches.[92] The decisive aspect of the ecumenical community is, of course, its universality, its transnational character. Following Ephesians 2, where Christ is affirmed to have "broken down the enmity which stood like a dividing wall," reconciliation in a divided world must be recognized as one dimension of peace. Seen historically, the ecumenical movement is a peace movement. In the tension between the universality of the church and the particularity of the churches, the church as the body of Christ is in solidarity with fallen humanity. Trusting in the unity given in Christ, the church can name the tensions and contradictions that endanger peace; and, unencumbered by political power and free of direct pressure to act, may suggest alternative solutions, as well as ask for understanding of "the other side."

Within the framework of ecumenical encounters it is possible to interpret and clarify the policies of one's own land, and yet to accept critical objections and inquiries. This results most authentically from an attitude of "critical participation" (Falcke), in contrast to either uncritical repetition of official government statements or an indiscriminate opposition that only confirms already-existing prejudices. The churches' dependency on the social system in which they participate is always painfully apparent as well. This experience aids in better understanding politicians with responsibility, keeps one from making impossible demands on them, and thereby protects one against an attitude of resignation.

The church, which relies on Christ as the basis of peace, understands itself on all levels and in all dimensions of its responsibility for peace as a confessing congregation. It stands or falls according to its witness for Him. He called it to be a community of "peacemakers" (Matt. 5:9). He established it as a sign of hope, the "city on the hill" (Matt. 5:14). Its action has exemplary character.[93] The church's responsibility for peace, too, lies under the "eschatalogical reservation": It has not yet arrived at its goal; it has no established solution to offer. It knows that it may not overestimate its own potential. "In certainty of the peace which God himself has promised and which comes to us with His rule in our lives, we are warned against delusion and false optimism in our actions."[94]

The most fundamental basis for the church's responsibility for peace, as for its entire world responsibility, is its witness to Jesus Christ. The church's responsibility for peace then cannot be discharged through the occasional declaration of the status confessionis; it requires a permanent process of witnessing.

VII. SUMMARY

The church in the GDR as an institution has no direct influence on the political processes in this socialist society. The principle of separation of church and state in the socialist interpretation precludes any direct political influence by the church. Yet the church influences society indirectly in a variety of ways.

The church is a factor in creating public opinion. The church's positions receive great attention in society, in both governmental and social organizations. Positive statements concerning political events and processes are particularly welcomed by representatives of the state. However, critical positions are also taken very seriously, even if this is not always admitted openly. In any case, in confidential conversations between representatives of the church and the government, problem situations can be openly expressed and often clarified.

On the other hand, the church is increasingly receiving the attention of critical groups, as we noted above, and is employed as a free social space in society. Such groups as "Women for Peace," "Homosexuals for Peace," ecological groups and even "punks" are concerned with peace problems, and ask for sanctuary and support. Conscientious objectors, members of the political opposition and dissidents ask for legal aid and support as well—even when they do not belong to the church. This circumstance often leads to an identity crisis on the part of congregations and peace groups, and questions concerning the specific character of Christian peace service become more insistent.

A further factor affecting the social efficacy of the church is the presence of the laity in society. Many Christians work in responsible capacities in society: in the universities and colleges, as Christian teachers or even as officials of the Christian Democratic Union (CDU), a party which attempts, in close cooperation with the ruling United Socialist Party of Germany (SED), to advocate Christian concerns in society, although without changing the fundamental principles of that society.

When Christians stand up for peace either as individuals or as a group without representing the viewpoint of the ruling party (the SED), they are considered enemies, or at least misled, and are treated accordingly. The results of church peace events (such as the "Peace Workshop"[95]) also come easily under the suspicion of being counter-revolutionary, subversive activities. Church leadership is repeatedly warned against supporting "enemies of the state." The independent peace witness of the church is tolerated only as long as it doesn't interfere with official peace politics. However, the contradiction between a Christian service of peace based on the Sermon on the Mount and Marxist ideas of class conflict that require a clear image of the enemy necessarily leads to tensions.

The role of the Western mass media must also be seen in this context. In vast areas of the GDR, and above all in the capital, Berlin, the influence of Western media is immense. In their coverage of church peace activities, they naturally emphasize those aspects critical of state policies, thus making their influence ambivalent: on one hand, many activities are made known to a larger public, but on the other hand, church activities are given an accent which the church does not intend. The church in the GDR does not want to be portrayed as a political opposition movement because it does not understand itself in this way. It intercedes for persecuted and disadvantaged human beings and their rights on the basis of its faith, not out of political motives. For this reason, the church has often recently been critical of Western press coverage.

The peace work of the churches is aimed chiefly at peace witness in society and education toward peace within its congregations. Knowing that inner and outer peace are two sides of the same reality, the church works at "consciousness-raising" and increasing the capacity for peace among its members; they are to be empowered to contribute to society constructively and critically out of their concern for peace.

The church in the GDR is aware of its limited means for bringing about political peace and the limited power of its members. But it trusts in the "power that is strong in weakness" (2 Cor. 12:9). This motto of the "Peace Decade 1983," (a period of ten days) which was celebrated in all congregations of the Evangelical Church in the GDR from November 6–16, 1983, should not be understood simply as a formula of religious impotence; rather, it represents a sound political judgment and understanding of reality:

"Make peace out of the power of the weak"
(*Frieden schaffen aus der Kraft der Schwachen*).

NOTES

1. Letter of the Evangelical Church leadership of Berlin-Brandenburg, October 9, 1961.
2. The dialogue between representatives of the GDR government and the Evangelical churches of the GDR took place March 12, 1962. It came about by request of church representatives. A report is found in the 73. *Rundbrief von Landesbischof Mitzenheim an die Pfarrer der Evangelisch-Lutherischen Landeskirche in Thüringen*.
3. "Instructions of the National Defense Council of the GDR concerning the Establishment of Regulations in the Area of the Ministry for National Defense" (September 7, 1964), *Gesetzblatt der DDR*, 1, No. 11 (September 16, 1964).
4. "For the Churches' Service of Peace—Advice for Pastoral Care of Servicemen" November, 1965 (for private circulation within the churches only), mimeograph. Reprinted in: *Kirchliches Jahrbuch* 93/1966 (Gütersloh, 1968), pp. 249ff. Quotation from p. 250.
5. *Ibid.*, p. 256.
6. *Ibid.*, p. 260f.
7. Order of the Federation of Evangelical Churches in the GDR, June 10, 1969, Article 1(2). Reprinted in: *epd-dokumentation*, 1 (Witten/Frankfurt/Berlin, 1970) p. 34.
8. An expert study group (*Facharbeitskreis*) on peace questions was integrated into the Committee on Church and Society; together with the Committee on Peace Questions of the Section on Theological Studies (ThStA), it attends to contemporary problems.
9. The most important publications are listed here. They are all available only in mimeograph form and as aids for use within the church:

    Arbeitsmappe; Erziehung zum Frieden: Stimuli and suggestions for parish activities on the theme of education toward peace. Compiled by the Section on Peace Questions and *Facharbeitskreis* of the Federation of Evangelical Churches in the GDR, (1976).

    Handreichung: Gemeindetag Frieden: "Was macht uns sicher?" (July, 1979).

    Rahmenkonzept: Erziehung zum Frieden: Contains "Points of Emphasis in Educating toward Peace" and three additional enclosures; conceived in line with a resolution of the Conference of Church Leaders, July 1978.

    Grundfragen eines politischen Wirksamwerdens von Christlichem Friedensdienst. Revised edition of a presentation at the September, 1981 conference, together with *Ausarbeitung: 'Pazifismus' in der aktuellen Friedensdiskussion*, passed in the closed session of the Conference of Church Leaders on March 14, 1982, and placed at the disposal of member churches.

In addition, mention should be made of the contributions (e.g., *Gesellschaftliche Diakonie*) of the Section on Theological Studies (ThStA), for example, "For Discussion Concerning the So-called 'Euro-strategic Weapons,' a Sketch of the Problem" (October, 1981).

Since February–March 1981, the following texts have been published by the ThStA's Section on Peace Question's *Information und Texte:*

Nos. 1/2: Declaration of the Synod of the Netherlands Reformed Church concerning nuclear weapons, etc.

Nos. 3/4: Report concerning the WCC Public Hearing in Amsterdam, November, 1981.

No. 8: Declaration of the leadership of the Reformed Federation in the Federal Republic of Germany, June 1982.

10. The introduction of the subject "Socialist Military Education" into the ninth and tenth grades of general schools beginning September 1, 1978 was such a challenge. "The practice of military safeguarding of peace as it is followed in the GDR (defense assignments, security interests, alliance duties) and the tendencies toward alternative methods of securing peace recognizable in church statements and initiatives [Advice of the conference concerning military education (1978), the "peace decade" (1980/81), and the campaign "Social Service of Peace" (1980/81)], allow a church-state conflict to come to the fore: a conflict to which the state responds by limiting church powers and with the expectation of a clearer support of socialist peace politics," *Grundfragen*, etc. 3(2.2).

11. The humanitarian questions of the Helsinki Act, including the question of religious freedom, were the direct cause behind the resolution of the Fifth Assembly of the World Council of Churches in Nairobi concerning "Disarmament—The Helsinki Agreement—Religious Freedom" (Nairobi Report, 181ff.). Inquiries of Western assembly participants brought about an unsatisfactory debate over the question of religious freedom in the Soviet Union. Consideration of the problems which resulted from this debate produced the report "The Churches' Human Rights Program for the Implementation of the Helsinki Final Act." This program is not the product of the World Council of Churches, but rather of the Conference of European Churches and the National Councils of Churches in the USA and Canada. It is not identical with the activities of the advisory group for human rights of the CCIA, which is responsible for global problems in the area of human rights.

12. "Statement Concerning the Contemporary World Political Situation," in *Kirche als Lerngemeinschaft*, 262ff.

13. *Uppsala Report*, 68.

14. *Ibid.*, 337.

15. Günter Krusche, "Trust instead of deterrence," testimony as a "witness" before the open hearing in Amsterdam (Free University: November 23, 1981), printed in *Information und Texte*, No. 4.

16. Some 150 church leaders and Christian experts from 62 countries took part in the conference, which took place at the University at Uppsala. Participants and other church leaders were called upon to deliver their "message" to their gov-

ernments. This occurred in the GDR on August 11, 1983 at the Bureau of Church Affairs.
17. "Life and Peace—Christian World Conference: The Message," adopted by the conference on April 23, 1983, Uppsala: April 20–24, 1983. (Notes 18–21, which follow, are based on the German text)
18. *Ibid.*, p. 3.
19. *Ibid.*, p. 4.
20. *Ibid.*
21. *Ibid.*, p. 4f.
22. "Christen zur Friedensdiskussion. Analyse des Diskussionsstands der innerkirchlichen Friedensdebatte" (shortened version of an article by Theodor Risse-Kappen: "Christen zur Friedensdiskussion—Kontroversen in den Kirchen der Bundesrepublik," originally published as "Friedensforschung aktuell" (No. 2, Spring 1982, Hessische Stiftung Friedens-und Konflikt forschung (HSFK), ed.) in *epd-dokumentation*, No. 31a/82 (September 7, 1982).
23. *Ibid.*, p. 6.
24. *Ibid.*, p. 7.
25. *Ibid.*
26. Quoted from a tape of the speech.
27. Resolution of the Synod of the Federation of Evangelical Churches in the GDR in response to the September 28, 1982 oral report of the Conference of Evangelical Church Leaders (mimeograph) p. 1.
28. *Ibid.*
29. Position of the Reformed General Convention in the GDR to the declaration of the Reformed Federation, "Das Bekenntnis zu Jesus Christus und die Friedensverantwortung der Kirche" (typescript) p. 1f.
30. Letter of the council chairman of the EKD, Bishop D. Hermann Dietzfelbinger, dated December 15, 1970, to Dr. E. C. Blake, general secretary of the World Council of Churches. Reprinted in *epd-dokumentation*, No. 40/70, p. 18.
31. *Ibid.*, p. 1.
32. 1978 pamphlet of the Federation of Evangelical Churches in the GDR: H. Falcke, "Friedenszeugnis in kritischer Partizipation." "The Evangelical Churches in the GDR and Peace Problems": Lecture held April 24, 1982 in DüsseldorfKaiserwerth in the context of the International Bonhoeffer Committee. Printed in: Hans Pfeifer, ed., *Frieden—das unumgängliche Wagnis. Die Gegenwartsbedeutung der Friedensethik Dietrich Bonhoeffers* (Munich, 1982), p. 78. Also quoted: A. Schönherr, "Was kann die Kirche für den Frieden tun? Friedensbemühungen der Evangelischen Kirchen in der DDR," in: V. Deile, ed.: *Zumutungen des Friedens. Kurt Scharf zum 80. Geburtstag* (Reinbek: 1982), p. 163ff.
33. W. Dantine, "Der Welt-Bezug des Glaubens," in W. Dantine and K. Lüthi, eds., *Theologie zwischen gestern und morgen. Interpretationen und Anfragen zum Werk Karl Barths*, eds. W. Dantine and K. Lüthe (Munich, 1968), p. 295.
34. *Before It's Too Late* (Geneva) p. 36.
35. A. Schönherr, "Was kann die Kirche für Frieden tun?" op. cit., p. 156ff.

36. W. Huber, "Wann ist es Zeit für ein Nein ohne jedes Ja?" *Zumutungen des Friedens*, p. 100.
37. Pastoral letter of the General Synod concerning the question of nuclear armament, dated November 1980, printed in *Wort an die Gemeinden zur Kernbewaffnung: Brief, Erläuterung und Bericht. Neue Materialien der Nederlandse Hervormde Kerk* (Neukirchen-Vluyn, 1982), p. 3, etc.
38. *Operationforschung. Technik, Praxis, Philosophie* (Berlin: Wissenschaftliche Schriften der Humboldt-Universität zu Berlin, 1968), Vitalij Stoljarow, *Zur Technik und Methologie soziologischer Forschung* (Berlin, 1966), p. 8ff.
39. Günter Krusche, *Neue Erkenntnisse über gesellschaftliche Leitungstätigkeit und ihre Bedeutung für die Kirche*, Official publication of the Evangelical-Lutheran Church in Saxony (1968), p. 34ff.
40. *EKD Memorandum*, p. 67.
41. *Zumutungen des Friedens*, p. 155ff.
42. *Ibid.*, p. 156.
43. "—Are Christians permitted to take part in preparations for defense with atomic weapons when it is certain that such defense irretrievably destroys what is to be defended?

—Are Christians permitted to participate in threats with weapons which themselves make the catastrophe probable that Christians are supposed to prevent?

—Can Christians and churches still justify the use of weapons as a means of securing peace and the defense of one's neighbors in the face of the unimaginable horror of a possible war?"
(Resolution of the Synod of the Federation of Evangelical Churches in the GDR responding to the oral report of the Conference of Church Leaders, Sept. 29, 1982, p. 1.)
44. *Ibid.*, p. 3.
45. *Ibid.*, p. 1.
46. *Information und Texte* since February/March 1981 (see footnote 27). The Section on Peace Questions works in conjunction with the *Facharbeitskreis* on peace questions of the Committee on Church and Society, and with the ad-hoc committee on disarmament; other appointments come about as needed.
47. J. Garstecki, "Zwischen Wirklichkeit und Möglichkeit: Auf der Suche nach Frieden", Supplement 1 to March 5, 1981 letter of the *Arbeitskreis Halle* (Cath.) p. 5.
48. Statement by Hans Ruh at the fourth Post-Helsinki Consultation of the Conference of European Churches (Madrid, 1980), quoted in Garstecki, op. cit., p. 3.
49. Conference report, *Mitteilungsblatt des Bundes 1982*, No. 5/6 (September 16, 1982), p. 35.
50. *Ibid.*, p. 36.
51. Section on Theological Studies of the Federation of Evangelical Churches in the GDR, Essays *B-9* (March, 1983).
52. Independent Commission on Disarmament and Security, Olof Palme (Swedish prime minister), chairman.

The Church's Responsibility for Peace in the GDR 175

53. See footnote 1, among others.
54. B-9, p. 10ff.
55. Ibid., p. 18.
56. Ibid.
57. Ibid., p. 19.
58. Those who signed from the GDR were: Elisabeth Adler, Heino Falcke, Günter Jacob, Günter Krusche, Walter Romberg, Albrecht Schönherr, and Christof Ziemer; Signers from the FRG were Günter Brakelmann, Volkmar Deile, Erhard Eppler, Brigitte Gollwitzer, Helmut Gollwitzer, Wolfgang Huber, Kurt Scharf, and Helmut Simon.
59. Saturday, June 11, 1983.
60. Document titled, "For a new security policy in Europe," (typescript), p. 2.
61. H. J. Margull, ed., *Mission als Strukturprinzip* (Geneva, 1965), 127ff: "Not only biblical testimony, but also the structure of the congregation are *expressions* of the working of the Holy Spirit. Neither in the letter of Scripture nor in the church's structure does the Holy Spirit find a timeless manifestation of itself." (Hans Schmidt), p. 128.
62. Ibid., p. 129.
63. Günter Krusche, "Die institutionelle Wirklichkeit der Kirche in der DDR," In *Barmen III*, v. I, pp. 37–46. Originally published in *LM* 1976 (15), pp. 39–43.
64. Günter Krusche, "Einheit und Pluralität der Kirche" *ThV XI* (Berlin, 1979), p. 129–137, revised version of a lecture held before the Synod of the Evangelical-Lutheran Church of Saxony on March 20, 1976 (Official Publication of the Evangelical-Lutheran Church in Saxony, 1976/B), pp. 33–38.
65. W. Krusche, "Die Gemeinde Jesu Christi auf dem Weg in die Diaspora," speech delivered at the third session of the seventh Synod of the Evangelical Churches in the district of Saxony (Fall, 1973); " 'Diaspora': Zum gegenwärtigen Gebrauch des Begriffes, Studie der ThStA beim Bund der Evangelischen Kirchen in der DDR, 1975," in *Kirche als Lerngemeinschaft*, pp. 186–205.
66. "Wir werden kleiner," in " 'Diaspora'," 186; W. Büscher, "Unterwegs zur Minderheit: Eine Auswertung konfessionsstatistischer Daten," in: *Die evangelischen Kirchen in der DDR: Beiträge zu einer Bestandsaufnahme*, ed. R. Henkys, (Munich, 1982), p. 422ff.
67. R. Henkys, "Volkskirche im Übergang," in *Die evangelischen Kirchen in der DDR*, ed. R. Henkys, (footnote 285), p. 437ff.
68. This is supported by W. Timofejew, *Kommunismus und Religion: Über die sozialen Prinzipien* (Berlin, 1975): "To the extent to which relations in practical, everyday life are built in human society, relations which, as Marx predicted, 'represent clear, rational relations between human beings and nature,' the conditions for the existence of religion disappear. Karl Marx stressed that 'religion, itself empty, exists not by means of heaven, but by means of earth, and it falls apart when the perverse reality, whose theoretical basis it is, disintegrates.'

The atheistic propaganda which the communists carry on is supposed to help believers arrive more quickly at the scientifically-based Marxist worldview." (p. 216)

69. A. Schönherr, "Die Kirche als Lerngemeinschaft," Address to the Synod of the Federation of Evangelical Churches in the GDR (Hermannswerder, 1974).
70. Günter Krusche, "Neubestimmung des Verhältnisses zu Staat und Gesellschaft in den sozialistischen Ländern Osteuropas," in *Die Evangelisch-Lutherische Kirche*, ed. V. Vajta, Die Kirchen der Welt, v. 15 (Stuttgart, 1977).
71. G. Jacob, "Der Raum für das Evangelium in Ost und West," in *Kirchliches Jahrbuch* 1956 (Gütersloh, 1957), 10ff.
72. J. Hamel, *Christ in der DDR*, Buchreihe 'unterwegs' 2/1957; J. Hamel, *Christenheit unter marxistischer Herrschaft*, Buchreihe 'unterwegs' 7/1959.
73. "Finding its Place," *Kirche als Lerngemeinschaft*, pp. 161–221.
74. Report of the Conference of Evangelical Church Leaders to the synod of the federation in Eisenach (July, 1971), printed in extracts in *Kirche als Lerngemeinschaft*, p. 172.
75. The paper was put before the Conference of Evangelical Church Leaders in its session of January 12–13, 1973. It was decided "to release the paper as stimulus for discussion to committees of the federation and to other groups working on the questions." The tensions which developed in connection with the position paper and in preparation for the federation synod in Dresden (1972) led to the removal of representatives of the "extreme positions."
76. This formulation from the first draft of the paper of committee chairman Günter Krusche was not kept.
77. H. Falcke, "Christus befreit—darum Kirche für andere," *Zum politischen Auftrag der Christlichen Gemeinde (Barmen II)*, p. 213ff.
78. *Ibid.*, p. 226.
79. Thus it is formulated in H. Falcke, "Friedenszeugnis in kritischer Partizipation: Die evangelischen Kirchen in der DDR und die Friedensproblematik," in: *Frieden—das unumgängliche Wagnis. Die Gegenwartsbedeutung der Friedensethik Bonhoeffers*, ed. Hans Pheifer, p. 59ff.
80. Report of the Conference of Evangelical Church Leaders delivered to the federation synod in Schwerin (May, 1973), *Kirche als Lerngemeinschaft*, p. 185.
81. *Kirche als Lerngemeinschaft*, p. 217.
82. Report of the Halle conference, *Mitteilungsblatt*, p. 35.
83. Reference is to the formulations of Eisenach (1971) and Schwerin (1973).
84. Fifth Barmen thesis, *Barmen II*, p. 15.
85. Christa Drummer, "Gruppenbeziehungen in der Gemeinde. Erkenntnisse der Gruppensoziologie und Folgerungen für die Gemeindearbeit," *ZdZ*, No. 6 (1970), 206–213 (bibliography).
86. Concerning the importance of the laity for the missionary congregation, cf. Hans-Ruedi Weber, "Mündige Gemeinde," *ÖR*, No. 9 (1960), pp. 3–20; also Hans-Ruedi Weber, "Kirche in Todesgefahr. Einige Lehren aus der nordafrikanischen Kirchengeschichte," *Aufruf und Aufbruch* (Berlin, 1965), pp. 89–98.
87. Letter of the Synod of the Evangelical-Lutheran Church in Saxony to youth (March 24, 1982).
88. See footnote 9.

89. J. Hempel, "Further Contemplation of Christian Responsibility for Peace" (activity report, Part III), presented to the 1982 fall synod of the Evangelical-Lutheran Church of Saxony, p.8: "Although in our time pacifist initiatives belong to a living Christian church, the church may not raise pacifism to the principle of its teaching. In the past year in Buckow, the Conference of Church Leaders termed Christians' service in the armed units of the *Volksarmee* (people's army) as a still-possible courageous act."
90. Huber, op. cit., p. 47f.
91. Gerd Theissen, *Soziologie der Jesusbewegung*, ThExh 194 (Munich, 1978).
92. "Weltverantwortung im ökumenischen Kontext," *Kirche als Lerngemeinschaft*, op. cit., p. 223ff.
93. Günter Krusche, "Weltfriede und Friede Christi," address to the General Convention of the Berlin district, May 26, 1982 (Manuscript), p. 9f.
94. *Kirche als Lerngemeinschaft*, p. 262.
95. "Peace workshop," "peace seminar," "peace station": these and similar designations have become common in reference to these sorts of public gatherings.

What the Church in Poland Did for Peace, 1980 to 1983

by Joachim Kondziela

I. THE CHARACTER OF THE ROMAN CATHOLIC CHURCH IN POLAND

The National Character of the Church

The Catholic church in Poland is historically linked with the Polish nation. It grew together with it. The church is an integral component of Polish national culture. It has been from the beginning, and is today, the primary factor uniting Polish society. The church has played this role especially during those periods when the Polish state did not exist: the partitions during the eighteenth and nineteenth centuries and the Nazi occupation of 1941–45. In those times, the church was the only representative of the Polish nation as a whole. The church today maintains this historic role of representing the nation.

Professor Joachim Kondziela is Dean of the Division of Catholic Social Sciences, University of Lublin, Poland.

The Dialogue-Oriented Character of the Church

The function of uniting and representing the nation required the Catholic church in Poland to be an open church. The extremely mild course of the Reformation in Poland—"a state without stakes"—testifies to that. The development of the Age of Enlightenment in Poland also indicates this feature of the church; Catholic clergy were outstanding representatives of the Enlightenment in Poland. A deeply humanist culture undergirds the tendency in Poland to find unifying solutions to social and political conflicts. Extremist Jacobinism never took root in Polish political life, essentially because of the activity of the church.[1] This dialogue-oriented character of the Polish church became clearly apparent in the post-World War II period, in which the church coexisted with a state espousing a Marxist-Leninist system.

The Mass Character of the Polish Church

The relatively uniform religious character of the Polish state with its new boundaries in this postwar period increased the strength of Catholicism in Poland and contributed to its increasingly "national" character. The saying, "a Pole is a Catholic and a Catholic is a Pole" becomes understandable in these circumstances. In a Marxist-Leninist state that deprived the church of sufficient access to mass media for a long period of time, the church found a solution in intensive activities of a pastoral nature: mass pilgrimages and huge services worshipping the Virgin Mary. Hundreds of thousands of the general populace gather in Czestochowa while hundreds of thousands of working men go to Piekary in the Silesian industrial region. The church in Poland in this way acquired great proficiency in addressing and influencing the masses, speaking both to the entire Polish society and in defense of the interests of the entire society.

The High Social Status of the Church

Political developments in Poland between August 1980 and December 1981 were essentially characterized by a national protest against an arbitrary and arrogant mode of exercising authority. Therefore this evolving protest movement could appeal to long-established national traditions and symbols and seek support in a church that embodied those values. The Solidarity movement sought legitimation from the Catholic church in Poland as the continuingly credible social force it is.

The church had to play both the role of mediator between the state authorities and Solidarity and that of an agent calming the radically anarchist takeover tendencies of extremists. Particularly important were the numerous speeches of the late Cardinal Stefan Wyszyński, then primate of Poland. Especially decisive was the primate's speech on August 26, 1980 in Czestochowa to hundreds of thousands of pilgrims, which really addressed the Polish nation as a whole when he said: "If this assistance [of the Virgin Mary] was ever necessary, then it is even more so today, when the nation comes closer to an awareness of its responsibility, i.e., to learning its duties and rights in its homeland. All this requires good judgment, caution and the spirit of peace and work; without the latter there is no appropriate solution to the situation."[2] One should stress here the personal commitment of the then terminally-ill primate in averting a national strike in March 1981, during the period when military exercises of the Warsaw Treaty forces were taking place in Poland and social tempers were running high. A strike at that time could have led to the outbreak of civil war and consequently to the disruption of the balance in Europe.

Following the institution of martial law in Poland on December 13, 1981 the church maintained its social position as a mediator between the authorities and the society and as the representative of the nation. The great social authority of the church is not questioned by anyone, either inside or outside of Poland.

II. THE INTERRELATIONSHIP OF DOMESTIC AND INTERNATIONAL PEACE

An Apparent Lack of Commitment to World Peace

The Roman Catholic church in Poland has not committed itself to any very public actions for international peace. There is no church-based peace movement in Poland; nor have there been any substantial declarations from either the church hierarchy or lay organizations cooperating with the Polish bishops. The only exception was the Warsaw Christian Forum for Peace in Europe, which convened in Warsaw September 1–2, 1979 with the circumspect blessing of Primate Wyszyński. This forum was an initiative of the three Catholic lay organizations represented in the Polish parliament, (Sejm): The Pax Movement, the Christian-Social Association and the Polish Catholic Social Union. There were only two follow-up sessions of this forum in 1980 and 1981, both dedicated to the problems of education for peace. It has not met since, although its secretariat still exists.

Another rare example, confirming the scarcity of such initiatives, was the well-known speech by Cardinal Wyszyński in the cathedral of Cologne during his visit to the Federal Republic of Germany in 1978. It was a speech of almost prophetic character and remains relevant. An important passage from that speech is worth quoting here to illustrate the wisdom with which the leader of the Polish Catholic church, although he seldom spoke on the subject, perceived the danger of putting peace in jeopardy:

> Europe must again recognize that it is a new Bethlehem for the peoples and nations of the world, from which the King and

Prince of Peace, the sole savior of the human family, will come amidst contemporary wars and rumors of wars. Europe, which received a peace through the Universal Church the world is not able to give, cannot continue to be a munitions factory, an international arms market and supplier; it must not continue to be a firing-range for war experiments that inflict self-torment on peoples and nations.[3]

The implications of that speech become clearer when one considers that at that time, discussion concerning the deployment in Europe of the new U.S. Pershing ballistic missile and the ground-launched cruise missile had begun in the German Federal Republic.

The discretion with which the Polish church has addressed the issues of international peace has been dictated by its concern to maintain the credibility of the church on this issue. In the period after 1945, official propaganda in Poland led to the cheapening of the word "peace." The fact that the USSR came up with numerous peace initiatives while remaining a symbol of atheism and source of resentment for many Poles, made peace initiatives by the Catholic church very problematic. Poland's political situation took a different turn after World War II than many Poles under the influence of the Polish government in exile in London and the Polish "underground" had expected, making it difficult for the Catholic church to join national initiatives for international peace. The Catholic church in Poland, however, followed an indirect, extremely consistent, road on this issue.

Identification with the Apostolic See's Peace Teachings

The Catholic church in Poland safeguarded its identity and integrity by following in a particularly attentive way the voice of Rome on issues of international peace. Whatever the Vatican said on this issue met with very strong response in Poland. This was the case with the John XXIII encyclical,

Pacem in terris, the constitution of Vatican Council II, *Gaudium et spes*, and with the teachings of Paul VI on peace, especially the encyclical *Populorum progressio* and his famous messages for the World Day of Peace he established for the Roman Catholic Church.[4] As far as it was possible, the documents were published, but the press runs were too small to talk about a broad promulgation of the church's social thought on peace. The messages of Paul VI published by the Apostolic See on the World Days of Peace found response in Poland, though this response was largely confined to the press, rather than finding resonance in the society at large. The dissemination of the international ethic and teachings of the church on peace have begun to gain momentum, however, in recent years. The fact that a Pole is the pope has undoubtedly contributed to that. John Paul II's speeches, including those on the subject of international peace, are listened to with great attention and meet with acceptance by the Polish populace.

It is important to note the particular function of papal teachings on peace in the Polish situation. They make it possible for the Polish church to take a stance on the issue of world community so strongly stressed by the social teachings of the Church, beginning with the teachings of John XXIII, as well as on global problems related to peace. The social teachings of the church make it possible to overcome the peculiarly self-centered behavior manifested especially in recent years, when domestic problems have absorbed most of the attention of Poles and decreased their sensitivity to world problems.

Papal teachings on peace, because of their authority and credibility, have great potential for stirring Polish awareness of international problems and developing pro-peace attitudes. The social teachings of the Apostolic See also create credibility for initiatives launched by Catholic groups in Poland. Lay Catholics organized in the Polish Catholic Social Union, the Christian Social Association, the Pax Association and other smaller groups like that connected with the *Tygodnik Powszechny* weekly in Cracow, have been devoting a great deal of attention in recent years to the popularization of the social teachings of the church, including those concerning international peace.

These three associations of lay Catholics acted together for the first time when they organized the Warsaw Christian Forum for Peace in Europe, mentioned earlier. The Pax association collected and edited the papal messages for the World Day of Peace. Periodicals published by lay Catholics (one daily and some weeklies and monthlies) print documents including teachings of the church for peace, as far as limited space and resources allow. The Center for Documentation and Social Studies (the intellectual arm of the Polish Catholic Social Union) runs a Peace Research Center, which in addition to its research conducts attitude-forming activity to popularize problems of peace. These include materials prepared by the Peace Research Center to meet the needs of the clergy in pastoral care.[5] The center has close cooperative ties with the chair for Catholic Social Doctrine in the Catholic University in Lublin.[6] Courses and seminars have been offered in this university for the last ten years on peace problems, within the framework of the regular course on "International Relations and Catholic Social Doctrines and Social Ethics."

Elements of church teachings on peace are also part of the instruction in the church's catechism classes. It must be added that the teaching program on peace of these classes is still much too general and theoretical. Nevertheless, the possibility of propagating a deepened concept of peace and promoting peaceful attitudes through that channel is still very great. Such a program should refer to the great Polish tradition of tolerance and to the Polish initiative for a nuclear-free zone in Europe. There is also an urgent need for the church to use its moral authority to revise the still current stereotypes of Germans, Russians, Ukranians, Czechs and Jews. Such an effort, if undertaken by the church, would make a great contribution to preparing Polish society for peace by creating a better understanding of people in East and Central Europe. A beginning in this direction was made by John Paul II in his speeches during his first and second visit to Poland, e.g. the speeches in Gniezno and Auschwitz in 1979, and in Wroclaw and the Mount of St. Ann in 1983. More teaching on peace in seminaries is very important. Everybody in Poland knows that without a peace-oriented clergy, especially younger clergy, there would be no effective education for peace in this country. Recent declarations of the Polish episcopate give grounds to hope that the expansion of the peace content in seminary teaching will become more and more noticeable.

The Church's Primary Focus on Domestic Peace

The Catholic church in Poland has continued in the last three years, as it has for centuries, to be an enormous social force enjoying the firm support of the entire society. The masses listen to its voice. The church sustains this high credibility both because of the content of its teaching and its proven attitude toward Polish society. The church has never betrayed the Polish people nor abused the confidence the society has given it in the past. It did not collaborate with the enemy during the Nazi occupation, unlike, for instance, the church in Slovakia, or, to some degree, in France. The church in Poland continues to be trusted by Polish society as a channel for socially important information, including that related to world peace.

It is important to realize in this regard the scope of the "apparatus" of church influence. Religious instruction is offered to young people from 6 to 18 years of age. Attendance is good in general. It has increased considerably over the past three years, especially among secondary school pupils. Centers of pastoral care in academic communities work well. The Sunday mass with the Sunday sermon is an important channel for communication and educational influence. Since the mid-1970s, and especially since August 1980, when Solidarity came into existence, and then following the December 1981 imposition of martial law, communiqués from the conferences of the episcopate and pastoral letters from local bishops have been read to churchgoers.

The Church as a Moderating Force

The church conducts a continuous dialogue with the masses. In spite of the complexity of the domestic situation in Poland in the years 1980–1983, the church successfully counseled the masses to adopt peaceful attitudes. In this period, the Catholic church in Poland did not exploit its authority or social position. The church was not and is not eager to "Khomeini-ize" Polish society, though recent times offered such opportunities more than once. The church acted to moderate the course of the post-August 1980 revolutionary developments, and did the same after martial law was instituted in December 1981. On the one hand, it stressed the common good of the society which must not be exposed to danger; while on the other hand, it emphasized the inviolability of human rights and the need to restore them by the quickest possible lifting of martial law. At the same time, throughout the three-year period, the church appealed to the public not to resort to violence as a means of working out confrontations. Emphasizing nonviolent conduct and stigmatizing violations of human rights, the church appealed for national agreement and reconciliation of the entire nation.[7] Playing the role of a mediator and the representative of the nation, the church made a valuable contribution toward defusing tensions and conflicts.

The church's contribution to social peace in Poland thereby earned it approval from society, from state authorities and from foreign countries. Never in the entire postwar period did the church enjoy such extensive recognition by the state authorities as it did under martial law. The church not only mediated internal conflicts, but to some extent mediated between the Polish government and Western countries. Thanks to this role, the economic sanctions imposed by Western countries after December 13, 1981 were not so painful, for the church was the addressee of foreign aid, which it distributed often with the help of the state. It is noteworthy that the church also gained the approval of the Apostolic See for this role. The elevation of Archbishop Jozef Glemp, the primate of Poland, to cardinal in the period of martial law, was an act of approval for his policy of internal peace and reconciliation.[8]

Throughout these recent difficult years the church in Poland continually emphasized the need to keep peace, and to a large extent, the church really contributed to saving the peace. By consistently following this line, it also acted for international peace.[9] Undoubtedly, destabilization of the political situation in Poland would have entailed destabilization in Europe and the world. Because of Poland's strategic position in the heart of the Warsaw Treaty nations, unrest in Poland might easily evolve into a conflict between NATO and the Warsaw Pact. Under the wise guidance of Primate Glemp, the church in Poland was aware that peace in Europe as well as world peace depends to a great extent on peace in Poland.

A Model for Supra-Systemic Peace Dialogue

As a laboratory experiment of dialogue between Catholics and Communists, or to put it more exactly, between the Catholic church and the Marxist-Leninist state, Poland is working out a model of coexistence between two different ideologies of world scope. This is extremely important if one considers that NATO and the Warsaw Pact polarize the world not only militarily, but also perhaps primarily in ideological terms. For the first time in history the world is divided along ideological lines. Acting as a moderator, the Catholic church in Poland is working out nonviolent ways of resolving these most difficult ideological conflicts, which also carry political implications. The Catholic church in Poland and the Marxist-Leninist state are looking for ways of institutionalizing the resolution of such conflicts.

An example of such an institution is the so-called Joint Commission, a venue for regular meetings of representatives of the church and the state since 1980. The commission not only did not suspend its activity in the period of martial law, but even stepped up its work.[10] An important role was played also by the meetings between Primate Wyszyński and Prime Minister Wojciech Jaruzelski on March 26, 1981 and between Primate Glemp and Prime Minister Jaruzelski on July 11, 1981, April 25, 1982, June 6, 1983, and January 5, 1984. The memorable Glemp-Jaruzelski-Wałesa meeting of November 4, 1981 was also an important event.

The dialogue between the church and the Marxist state in Poland is effective. The Polish example may suggest that permanent supra-ideological dialogue is possible when its object is vital humanist values. And peace is certainly one such value.

III. MAINTAINING THE STATUS QUO IN EUROPE

The peace activity of the church in Poland is also implicit in its invariably firm stance on the Polish western territories, those former German eastern territories that were returned to Poland after World War II following centuries of German occupation. Since 1972 the Apostolic See has had the same clear stance regarding Poland's western borders along the Odra and Nysa Luzycka rivers. Throughout the almost forty-year history of the Polish People's Republic, notwithstanding the different viewpoints of the church and state on many other issues, there has always been complete agreement on the western territories.

The Polish Catholic church formulated the problem of the western territories in terms of an existential value when the problem arose in polemics with West German Catholics, and for some time during the pontificate of Pius XII even in defiance of the Vatican. Were the territorial status-quo in Europe to be questioned, as has been done by West German federal minister of the interior Zimmermann and minister Hans Mayer of Bavaria, the church in Poland would not change its stance on this issue. Because the Polish western territories are not only an essential matter for the Polish nation, but at the same time are a stabilizing factor of European order, as confirmed in the Final Act of the Helsinki Conference on Security and Cooperation in Europe, the Polish church's continual defense of them is an important guarantor of peace in Europe. The Catholic church in Poland has full approval of the Polish society on this issue and would be able to rally the whole Polish society for the defense of this cause.

The issue of Polish western territories is a typical example of how one can legitimize peace as an existential value. The invariability of the stance of the church on this issue and its vital interest in the *ex definitione* peace problem was demonstrated during the last visit of Pope John Paul II in Poland.[11] The pope paid visits to Wroclaw and the Mount of St. Ann, both places that fell to Poland after World War II and are a symbol of the post-Yalta and Potsdam order in Europe.[12]

IV. THE GRAND DISCOURSE FOR PEACE—POPE JOHN PAUL II'S PILGRAMAGE TO POLAND, JUNE 16–22, 1983

The entire pilgrimage visit of Pope John Paul II was conceived both by the pope himself and the leadership of the Polish Catholic church, especially by Cardinal Glemp, as a mass catechization of peace. Rallying the masses around the papal visit, the church was able to mobilize them to a large extent in support of both external and internal peace.

Mass Character of the Papal Discourse for Peace

Millions of people were waiting for the Pope along his pilgrimage route. This was true in Warsaw; in Niepokałanow, where the newly created Saint Maximilian Kolbe lived and worked; in Czestochowa, where more than two million people attended the celebration of the six-hundredth anniversary of the presence of the revered image of the Mother of God, "Matka Boska" of Jasna Gora, a national sanctuary for Poles; in Poznan, in the Katowice region where over one million mostly blue-collar miners and steel workers listened attentively to the pope's words; in Wroclaw; on the Mount of St. Ann near Opole; and in Cracow. Not less than one million people attended the celebrations in each of these places. In addition, millions more "participated" in the papal discussions for peace, thanks to television coverage of many of the events. Polish streets were generally empty during the television broadcasts because most of the people were watching. All of the papal homilies were also broadcast complete and live by Polish radio.

Many daily papers and weeklies also carried full texts or excerpts of the papal speeches. The circulation amounted to millions of copies. The Catholic weeklies, *Gość Niedzielny* (circulation 200,000), *Niedziela, Tygodnik Powszechny, Lad, Kierunki, Za i Przeciw* and the Polish edition of *Osservatore Romano* printed full texts of the papal speeches. Several publishing houses are working on book editions of them. Though the press runs will be rather limited (not to exceed 50,000 copies in each case), they will have the advantage of being of more lasting character, and thus may be reread many times. This material will help to continue the Christian discourse of peace established by the pope.

Peace as the Central Theme of the Papal Pilgrimage

The very fact that the papal visit came about as the result of the joint efforts of the Polish Catholic hierarchy and the Polish government endowed the visit with a peace character. The aim of the papal visit was national reconciliation. This was obvious almost from the first moment of the visit. The Pope expressed it very clearly in his speech at the Okecie airport in Warsaw. Referring to the kiss he had bestowed on Polish soil after stepping down from the plane, he said: "I compare kissing my native soil with a kiss placed on a mother's hand. May this be also a kiss of peace for all those who, in whatever way, will be a part of this great community on pilgrimage with the Polish pope. *Pax vobis!* Peace to you, Poland! My homeland!" This became the motto for the entire papal pilgrimage. It was planned in advance by the pope and the Polish Catholic hierarchy, as was evident in the millions of pictures of the pope with the inscription, "Peace to you, Poland! My homeland!" that were distributed. Considering the Apostolic See's commitment to the cause of world peace, one could not have expected the pope in Poland to act otherwise than in favor of internal peace in Poland.[13]

The Content of the Peace Discourses of John Paul II

The papal teachings were meant, as has been already stated, primarily to *educate people for internal peace*. This thought appeared in nearly all of the more than a dozen papal addresses. The pope pointed first of all to the dignity of all persons and their rights, which are matched by respective duties, as the groundwork for social peace. He stressed the need to set up active participation in social and political life, for participation protects the society against frustration and social unrest. In Wroclaw the pope pointed to the need for mutual trust between the authorities, whose function is that of servant to the society and the nation. The pope spoke of trade unions and workers' self-management as among the associations that should be established and guaranteed. Thus the papal discourses affirmed social justice broadly conceived as prerequisite to internal social peace. Crowds cheered when the pope voiced these principles. Characteristically, however, the same crowds of the faithful dissolved and went home in peace and order. There were no major demonstrations, nor did the social unrest hoped for by extremist groups of both the "left" and the "right" materialize. Society was freed by the papal visit from the accumulated psychic tensions, which had a social effect in Poland. The people could identify themselves in public with a certain set of fundamental humanistic values during demonstrations which followed a peaceful course.

The Method of Securing Internal Peace

According to the teachings of John Paul II, "dialogue on a national plane" is the sole effective method for maintaining internal as well as international peace. The pope emphasized this method in his address to state authorities in the Belvedere, the official residence of the Polish State Council, which was broadcast live nationwide, when he said:

> A dialogue for peace must be established . . . in order to resolve social conflicts. In order to seek the common good. While bearing in mind the interests of different groups, it is possible to lead to *peaceful agreement* through dialogue, through the democratic observance of freedom and fulfillment of duties by all, thanks to the structures of participation and many means of reconciliation . . . (e.g., in disputes between employers and workers, in the manner of respecting and integrating the cultural, ethnic and religious groups which make up the nation). When, unfortunately, dialogue between the government and its people is absent, social peace is threatened or even absent; it is like a "state of war." But history and present day observations show that many countries have succeeded or are succeeding in establishing a durable agreement in resolving the conflicts which arise within them, or even in preventing them, by acquiring means of dialogue which are truly effective.[14]

Dialogue, preached the pope, is the only possible, right and efficient means for dealing with the tense situation in Poland. By the same token, John Paul II rejected any solution based on violence, no matter which side might resort to it. The firm "no" addressed to violence was underlined by the pope again in Niepokalanow, a locality connected with the life and work of St. Maximilian Kolbe, who gave his life for a fellow inmate in Oswiecim (Auschwitz) by being starved to death in a bunker. Referring to the sacrifice of Saint Maximilian, the pope appealed to his listeners in the words of

Saint Paul: "Do not be overcome by evil, but overcome evil with good" (Rom. 12:21). This is the only way, he said, one can overcome "that civilization of death which, especially at certain moments of the present day, shows its menacing face." The example of Maximilian Kolbe proved that "love is stronger than death."

During the beatification of Brother Albert Chmielowski and Father Rafal Kalinowski toward the end of the pilgrimage to Poland, John Paul II said:

> Father Rafal and Brother Albert, during their lives, reached those heights of holiness that the church today confirms, by way of love. There is no other road that leads to those heights. Today Christ says to them: "You are my friends. I have called you friends, for all that I have heard from my Father I have made known to you" (John 15: 14–15). This all is summed up in the commandment of love.

These words define the pope unequivocally in favor of nonviolent methods in resolving conflicts, methods he wanted to teach his compatriots.

The Necessity of Dialogue for Ensuring World Peace

During his discourse for peace in Poland the pope did not lose sight of world peace. He recalled the threat involved in the arms race. He referred to the candid report on the inestimable destruction of a nuclear war prepared by the Papal Academy of Sciences and directed to the governments of the Soviet Union, the United States of America, Great Britain and France, and to the secretary general of the United Nations. The pope affirmed dialogue for peace as necessary for our times. Referring to his message for the World Day of Peace on January 1, 1983: "The Dialogue for Peace—a Challenge for Our Times," he said:

> This message refers to experiences of the past to show that dialogue for peace, especially in our time is necessary. It is also possible: "People are finally capable," the message reads, "of

overcoming divisions, conflicts of interests, even if the oppositions seem to be radical . . . if they believe in the virtue of dialogue, if they agree to meet face-to-face to seek a peaceful and reasonable solution for conflicts.

The pope viewed the Polish issue in the context of international dialogue. To stress this fact, he quoted the words of Paul VI, the pope to whom Poland owes the normalization of the church administration of the western territories: "A prosperous and peaceful Poland is in the interest of tranquility and sound cooperation among the peoples of Europe . . ." The pope later made clear that the term "sound cooperation" refers to relations with countries in both the East and West. It was as if the pope wished to stress the point of the special significance of Poland's geopolitical and cultural position in a dialogue between the West and East, which by virtue of such a position must be carried out in peace and "sound cooperation." A passage referring to the Polish Catholic hierarchy is significant in this regard: "I also know that the Polish episcopate constantly makes tireless efforts to ensure that the principle of dialogue proclaimed by the church may become a fruitful basis both for internal peace and for good cooperation between Poland and the other nations of Europe and the world." Undoubtedly, this was an expression of the pope's appreciation of the Polish Catholic hierarchy's stance, despite the criticism of extremists at home and abroad, and quite frequently, by foreign mass media.

This dialogue, as the pope stressed in Wroclaw, may lay the groundwork for agreement between yesterday's enemies if it follows the principles of "reciprocal understanding and reconciliation." He cited the case of Poland and Germany expressed in the many contacts between representatives of churches in two nations that had been at odds for centuries. This "sound cooperation" must be based on mutual trust and truth.

All the dimensions of social life, such as the political and the economic, and naturally the cultural dimension and every other, are based definitively on the fundamental ethical dimensions of truth, trust and community. Thus it is in the family. Thus it is also, on another scale, in the nation and the State. Thus it is, in the final analysis, in the whole human family.

One can stress at this point that both Poland's distant past and recent past connected with World War II give the church in Poland a mission of reconciliation among nations. This mission, confirmed by the Polish pope, should consist in service for rebuilding confidence among nations. It is a mission of educating societies in the spirit of peace.

There are no differences between the church and the state on this issue. It was the initiative of the government of the Polish People's Republic in the thirty-third session of the United Nation's General Assembly that led to the adoption of the "Declaration on Preparation of Societies for Life in Peace" on December 15, 1978. It is not simply a coincidence that the papal message for the twelfth World Day of Peace, January 1, 1979, issued by the Polish Pope John Paul II, dealt with the same theme: "We Shall Achieve Peace by Preparing for Peace."[15]

How the Papal Pilgrimage Contributed to Peace

1. The Catholic church in Poland and the Apostolic See demonstrated their service and commitment for peace in Poland, in Europe and in the world by this papal pilgrimage, as also by the previous one of 1979. This was realized by the state authorities and the neighboring states.
2. The church managed, to a large extent, to increase peaceful attitudes and dampen negative emotions in the society. By pointing out the need for reconciliation, agreement and solidarity among people, it thwarted attempts by extremist groups.
3. The entire Polish society carried out the commandment of nonviolence in an exemplary way. The church apparently persuaded the populace that there is no alternative to dialogue, on a national and an international scale, at the present time. The peaceful course of the pope's pilgrimage also influenced the decision to lift martial law on July 22, 1983.
4. The church showed that it is a responsible guarantor not only of internal peace but also European peace, in view of Poland's

geopolitical position between the world's two mightiest and antagonistic military blocs. The church's role as a guarantor of peace in Europe was duly noticed and appreciated by the USSR, as was expressed by Soviet officials during the ensuing visit of General Jaruzelski to Moscow.

5. The ability of the church to rally masses of people, and especially young people, to attitudes fundamental for humanity—truth, justice, human rights, democracy, peaceful dialogue, nonviolence, solidarity among people and nations—was demonstrated in a convincing way.

Hence we arrive at a more far-reaching conclusion: it is possible to rally broad masses of people for the cause of world peace with the assistance of the church, provided that the church is able to present itself as a credible social force, an autonomous force speaking on behalf of society, i.e., on behalf of the existential values of the society.

It seems possible, for example, to rally mass support for European nuclear-free zones in Poland, which is traditionally interested in building bridges between Eastern and Western Europe. In this concept, the value of peace appears as an autonomous one fairly independent of the great powers, while including directly the interests of certain nations. Mobilizing churches for such a concept seems reasonable and would prove to be of immense ecumenical importance because it would involve the Orthodox, Roman Catholic and Protestant churches.

A visit by the Polish primate to the USSR would provide a good opportunity to discuss the pease issue in a broader context. During his visit to Hungary in autumn 1983, the primate was asked by journalists whether he would visit the Soviet Union. Cardinal Glemp was not surprised by such a question and answered that before going to Moscow, he would like to visit the Roman Catholic church of Lithuania. In the meantime, Patriarch Pimen of the Russian Orthodox Church visited Warsaw in May 1984, on invitation of the Polish Orthodox church.

The Polish primate could use the occasion of a visit to the USSR historically at first, to assure the Soviets that the Polish Catholic church is firmly interested in supporting internal peace in Poland, thus preventing destabilization on the western flank of the USSR. He might also make it clear to Soviet officials that the Polish church, like the universal church, is not devoted to anti-communism and anti-Sovietism; that it should be regarded as a reliable partner in preserving peace, both internal and external. The Polish church's activities in organizing financial support for Polish agriculture, with the help of churches from Western Europe and the USA, aimed at improving the economic and by that means the political situation in Poland, could be another argument to convince the Soviet leadership of the Polish church's realistic stance and peaceful orientation.

Finally, the problem of how to get the churches involved in the process of building nuclear-free zones in Europe should be discussed in Moscow by the Polish hierarchy. Such a proposal would be, on the one hand, an implementation of the late Cardinal Wyszyński's testament regarding peace in Europe, given in his sermon in the cathedral of Cologne; and on the other hand it would be, because of the well-known "Rapacki Plan" for a nuclear-free zone in central Europe, a very Polish approach for securing international peace. "Baptized" by the Polish Church, it would be given the credentials of the high moral authority which the Polish church authentically exercises, especially when seen as the church of today's pope.

At this point, one may only speculate whether such possibilities will become reality. What must be said, however, is that nobody for whom the survival of humanity is the highest value should miss such historic opportunities. There may be only a little time left. . .

NOTES

1. Neal Asherson, *The Polish August: The Self-Limiting Revolution*, London: Penguin, 1981. Especially the postscriptum, p. 278 ff.
2. Stefan Kardynal Wyszynski, *Kosciol w Sluzbie Marodu* (Church in the Service of the Nation), Rome, 1981, pp. 12–13.
3. *Chrześcijanin w świecie* (The Christian in the World), No. 75, 1978, pp. 84–85.

What the Church in Poland Did for Peace, 1980–1983   199

4. The pastoral letter of the Polish Catholic episcopate for the 16th World Day of Peace, December 2, 1982, is an example.
5. The materials include a part devoted to pastoral care: instructions for parish work for peace, the holy mass for peace, concepts of lessons on peace issues for religious instructions, homilies and sermons and prayers; and an auxiliary part: message for the World Day of Peace, a discussion of the message, other documents concerning the teachings of the church on peace problems, articles devoted to non-violence, disarmament, etc. The materials are prefaced by Bishop W. Miziołek, chairman of the episcopate's Commission for Pastoral Care.
6. For the time being, the director of both is Joachim Kondziela.
7. Communiqué from the 183rd Plenary Conference of the Episcopate of Poland of February 26, 1982 (two months after martial law had been instituted). The Primatial Social Council, appointed by the primate at the beginning of 1982, also helped in working out a social agreement. Composed of lay Catholics, it prepared guidelines for a social agreement. See also the letter from the primate to the Polish bishops on April 8, 1982 and the Guidelines of the Primatial Social Council on Social Agreement of April 5, 1982 (mimeographed text).
8. John Paul II in his speech "To the Episcopate of Poland," delivered during his pilgrimage on June 19, 1983: "I address here Cardinal Józef Glemp primarily, the archbishop of Gniezno and Warsaw, the successor to the primatial see. We all realize that together with the grand dignity, a heavy burden was laid on your shoulders, dear Primate; all of us can feel this burden in a way, especially in the face of the developments in the homeland. In this situation, the collegial unity of the conference of the episcopate, which offers support to every bishop, does so especially to the Primate, and assumes particular importance."
9. Communiqués from the meeting of the main council of the episcopate of Poland on August 27, 1980, August 13, 1981 and December 15, 1981, as well as communiqués from the meetings of the Plenary Conference of the Episcopate of Poland.
10. The joint commission was established in 1980 and has met about 25 times to date. The first meeting of the commission under martial law was held on January 18, 1982; the dialogue between the church and the state continued in spite of the discrepancies and differences.
11. "A prosperous and peaceful Poland is . . . in the interest of tranquility and good cooperation among people of Europe. I take the liberty of beginning my speech with the same words that I used in this same Belvedere Palace in June 1979, during my previous visit to my homeland. I repeat these words because they were said by a great friend of Poland, Pope Paul VI, to whom the Church in our country owes the important work of normalization in the northern and western territories. I repeat them also because these words reflect, so to speak, the constant quintessence of what the Apostolic See thinks of Poland." Pope John Paul II's speech addressed to the state authorities on June 17, 1983.
12. A passage from a speech delivered on the Mount of St. Ann on June 21, 1983 by Pope John Paul II: "And so today the path of my pilgrimage takes us through Wrocław, where we have venerated Saint Hedswig, daughter of the German

nation and at the same time the great mother of the Polish Piasts at the end of the 12th and the beginning of the 13th century. And from Wroclaw, we reach the land of Opole to pause in the land of the Piast whose name is linked to the foundation of Jasna Gora and the gift of the Image of Jasna Gora in the years 1384–92, Ladislaus II, Prince of Opole. . . ." (The Piasts were the first dynasty of Polish monarchs who ruled Poland until 1370.)

13. In this context one can also interpret the reiterated appeals by the pope and the church for lifting martial law, against violence, and for restoration of basic civil rights and freedoms. It is also worthwhile to consider the impact of developments in Poland on the Madrid Conference.

14. Much of what the pope said on this occasion referred to his message for the World Day of Peace of January 1, 1983, "The Dialogue for Peace—A Challenge for Our Times." He stressed that he had taken the liberty to send this message also to the Polish state authorities.

15. The topic for this message had been chosen during the last months of the pontificate of Paul VI, and published in the weekly *Osservatore Romano* on August 28, 1978.

Structural and Functional Possibilities for the Churches to Influence Disarmament Issues in Poland

by Janusz Symonides

I. CHURCH-STATE RELATIONS IN POLAND

The Constitution of the Polish People's Republic of July 22, 1952 defined the legal status of the churches and other religious bodies through such principles as freedom of conscience and religion, freedom to exercise religious functions by all the churches and religious associations, and the separation of church and state. All churches have rights in the territory of Poland.

There are thirty-seven churches and religious communities in Poland. The Polish Ecumenical Council associates eight Orthodox, Protestant and Old Catholic churches. The largest of these is the Polish Autocephalous Orthodox Church with 320 clergy, 233 parishes and about 480 thousand believers. The Lutheran Church of the Augsburg Confession has 92 clergy and nearly 72,000 believers. The Evangelical-Reformed

---

Professor Janusz Symonides is Director of the Polish Institute of International Affairs and Professor of International Law, Warsaw University.

Church has four clergy and about 4,500 believers. The Polish Catholic Church has 116 clergy and about 33,000 believers. The Old Catholic Church of the Mariavites has twenty-nine clergy and about 25,000 believers. There is also the Polish Christian Baptist Church with sixty clergy and about 6,000 believers and the United Evangelical Free Church with 256 clergy and about 10,000 believers.

Outside the Polish Ecumenical Council, the Seventh-Day Adventist Church has sixty-four clergy and about 7,000 believers. There are also non-Christian religious bodies: the Moslem Religious Union with about 2,000 believers, the Religious Union of the Jewish Faith with about 2,000 believers, and two Buddhist Unions. The non-Roman Catholic churches in Poland in total comprise only about 660,000 believers in 1,381 congregations.

The important position of the Roman Catholic church in Poland is determined not only by the number of its believers—the vast majority of Poles are Catholics[1]—but also by its over one thousand-year-long history that has influenced the destiny of the nation and contributed so much to Polish national culture. Its continuing widespread impact on the thinking and attitudes of the society at large makes the Roman Catholic church in Poland a significant social force.[2]

Relations between the minority churches and the state authorities have long been good[3] as a result of the minority churches endorsing the Polish *raison d'état* as well as promoting pro-state attitudes among their believers and clergy. Relations between the Roman Catholic church and the state, on the other hand, have gone through various stages and the normalization process has not been free from obstacles.

The party and the government both have sought normal relations and accord with the Roman Catholic church, which implies a recognition of the church as an enduring element of the Polish reality. The state has no intention of destroying the church while expecting the church likewise not to undertake actions against the socialist system and the state. Thus the normalization of mutual relations hinges on the church and state agreeing on the fundamental interests of the nation, the state and world peace.

During the turbulence of the eighties, this stance has been repeatedly confirmed. The resolution adopted at the Ninth Extraordinary Congress of the Polish United Workers' Party (PUWP-Communist) in July 1981 states: "The Congress voices its respect and appreciation of the patriotic attitude of the Catholic church and other religious communities, characterized by a high sense of responsibility for Poland, and declares itself in favour of further constructive development of dialogue and cooperation between the state and the church for the sake of our socialist homeland's welfare."[4]

The policy and practice of dialogue and accord were not broken even by the introduction of martial law. In his first speech after martial law was declared, General Wojciech Jaruzelski stated that the idea of national accord was being fully supported, diverse world outlooks would be respected and the patriotic attitude of the church was appreciated. During a meeting between General Jaruzelski and Primate Józef Glemp on January 9, 1982 both expressed intentions of normalizing life in the country;[5] and the communiqué from the session of the Joint Commission of the Representatives of the Government and the Episcopate on January 18, 1982 stressed the importance of cooperation between the state and the church for accelerating the emergence from martial law.[6] The church hierarchy took this position despite their negative attitude to the very fact of the government having introduced martial law.

During the seventh plenum of the PUWP Central Committee, the first to be held during martial law, General Jaruzelski discussed state-church relations and said:

> It is no secret that differences of opinion existed and still exist. The supreme interest of the nation and the state includes a continuous, patient overcoming of divergences and the widening of the field of mutual accord. . . . The differences in world views crucial for the inner, personal sphere of man's emotional experience cannot be an obstacle to seeking a common denominator for social and state matters, and continuation of a profitable dialogue.[7]

Primate Glemp also pointed to the need of solving all the difficult problems of the country by way of dialogue; and the significance of dialogue was underlined in the communiqué following the session of the Joint Commission of the Representatives of the Government and the Episcopate of August 8, 1982: "The present situation in the country which still faces difficult problems was discussed. It was agreed that their solution could only take place in conditions of peace and by way of dialogue."[8]

The relations between the church and the state have also comprised a large and fruitful sphere of cooperation. The state recognized long ago the need to cooperate with the church in strengthening the family, counteracting negative moral phenomena, promoting understanding of the supreme value of the common good and consolidating the society for the security and welfare of Poland.[9] Professor Adam Lopatka, head of the Office for Religious Denominations, said: "It is possible and desirable that the cooperation between the state and the other churches and religious communities proceeds on the level of concern for the independence of Poland, the integrity of its territory and its security, and on the level of the struggle for peace and halting the arms race. . ."[10]

II. INSTITUTIONAL POSSIBILITIES FOR CHURCH-STATE DIALOGUE ON PEACE AND DISARMAMENT

There can be no doubt that international issues occupy much space in the relations between the Holy See and Poland. Although Poland does not maintain diplomatic relations with the Vatican, groups for permanent working contacts have existed since 1974. They are led by Minister Plenipotentiary Jerzy Kuberski, representing the Polish government, and Archbishop Luigi Poggi, representing the Holy See. Their direct contacts with foreign affairs departments create possibilities for taking up not only Polish-Vatican problems but also broader international issues. In the preparations for the 1983 visit of Pope John Paul II, for example,

Archbishop Poggi visited Poland in March 1983 and was received by the Polish minister for Foreign Affairs, Stefan Olszowski. The communiqué following the meeting indicated that among the aspects of international policy discussed were threats to peace, security and cooperation in Europe created by the arms race. Archbishop Poggi gave the foreign minister the pope's message for the sixteenth World Peace Day titled, "The Dialogue for Peace, A Challenge for Our Times."

The next level of contacts are those between the secretary of the Council for Public Affairs of the church and the Polish minister for foreign affairs. These contacts, too, create favorable grounds for discussion of broader issues. For example, during discussions in Poland between Archbishop A. Silvestrini and Foreign Minister S. Olszowski, May–June 1983, the belief was expressed that Pope John Paul II's visit would prove beneficial for the cause of international peace and accord. The dangers threatening peace in Europe and the world at large were pointed out, and the need to increase efforts for dialogue and international cooperation was stressed.

A special occasion for taking up the issues of peace was created by John Paul II's last visit in June 1983. This visit of the pope from Poland to his homeland was the subject of numerous articles and analyses which, however, didn't always note the peace aspect of the visit.

The Polish government's invitation to the pope, issued by the president of the Council of State, Henryk Jabloński, stated that the Polish nation, mindful of its historical experiences and aware of the threats to humanity, expected the papal visit to be propitious for efforts to maintain peace, halt the arms race and forestall nuclear catastrophe. This theme was reiterated by President Jabloński in his welcoming address.

John Paul II devoted much attention to the issues of peace in his speech of June 17 during a meeting with the state authorities in the Belvedere Palace. The Pope reviewed efforts of the Holy See for peace; pointed out the twentieth anniversary of Pope John XXIII's encyclical *Pacem in terris*; and emphasized the conclusions of the Pontifical Academy of Sciences on the terrible consequences of the use of nuclear weapons. He also spoke of the church's celebrating each New Year's Day as a World Day of Peace and recalled that year's message, "The Dialogue for Peace, A Challenge for Our Times," which his representative had already given the foreign minister. The pope also expressed his desire that Poland might always take her proper place among the nations of Europe, between East and West, and that conditions of good cooperation with all the Western nations be reestablished. He expressed his conviction that such conditions could be reestablished.

Questions of world peace were one of the topics on the agenda of the two direct talks between Pope John Paul II and the premier, General Jaruzelski. The government press spokesman said that the talks centered around a shared concern about the fate of the country, world peace and international cooperation.[11] President of the Council of State Jabloński mentioned with gratitude in his farewell speech to Pope John Paul II the pope's repetition on Polish soil of an appeal for peace and the confirmation of the Polish attitude toward the western and northern territories.

Similar possibilities can be discerned in the recent dialogues between state authorities and the hierarchy. The first meeting between General Jaruzelski and Cardinal Glemp took place on July 11, 1981, just four days after Bishop Glemp's appointment as primate of Poland. On August 13 of the same year the primate met with the first secretary of the PUWP Central Committee, Stanislaw Kania, and on November 4 a meeting was held between General Jaruzelski, Primate Glemp and the chairman of Solidarity, Lech Wałesa. The first meeting after the introduction of martial law between General Jaruzelski and Primate Glemp was held on January 8, 1982 followed by meetings on April 25, 1982, November 8, 1982 and May 9, 1983. For obvious reasons, these meetings were devoted to important internal problems, including national accord and dialogue with the society, as well as preparations for the visit to Poland of Pope John Paul II. It may be assumed that these meetings of the premier and the primate paved the way for future discussions of efforts to halt the arms race.

Another sphere for dialogue and cooperation between the Polish hierarchy and the Polish government is the Joint Commission of the Representatives of the Government and the Episcopate, reactivated in August 1980. It has adopted a long-range program of work and established working groups with specialists from both sides. At present there are six working groups, including a group for publications and journals, a group for education, and a group for combating alcoholism. The activity of the commission and its groups, in the opinion of the government, consolidates the atmosphere of mutual matter-of-fact dialogue and helps in settling current problems. The commission has twice expressed an opinion on international issues, condemning the economic sanctions by Western states against Poland.[12] Perhaps a working group on peace and disarmament could be established within this joint commission.

Other religious communities also maintain contacts with the government. Premier Jaruzelski met on December 10, 1981 with the board of the Polish Ecumenical Council, and on September 15, 1982 with its presidium. In February 1982, the premier also received a delegation of the World Council of Churches.

The Roman Catholic church and the other religious communities may influence the official state stance in matters of disarmament not only in this direct way, through what may be called institutional dialogue, but also indirectly by helping shape believers' attitudes and engagement in matters of peace. The elements of general education for disarmament include daily pastoral activity, religious education, religious seminars and the curriculum of theological schools, as well as the use of church publications.

A broader impact on the society has also been enhanced by giving the Roman Catholic church access to Polish radio since September 1980 to broadcast the Sunday mass. Since January 1982, on every first and third Sunday and on the most important church holidays, Polish radio also broadcasts worship services of the churches in the Polish Ecumenical Council. This means that each of the churches has opportunity to broadcast four services a year.[13]

The shaping of peaceful attitudes toward the most crucial problems of the contemporary world may be done through religious education. The Roman Catholic church includes this aspect in its religious teaching program, especially in secondary schools.[14] In the cycle "The Christian in the Contemporary World," these issues are discussed in detail. For example, the source material for catechetical instruction developed by Father W. Koska[15] in part six devoted to "The Church and World Problems," discusses such issues as the church and technological progress, peace and war and the presence of the church in the world. The teacher's book for catechism in the Catholic faith, under the heading of "The Christian in the Contemporary World," examines in detail subjects like these: are all people brothers? what consolidates brotherhood among people? thou shalt not kill; the world for all; peace to all the people; in the service of peace.

Lectures on the problems of peace are included within Catholic social science in diocesan and monastic seminaries for the priesthood and are also included in the curricula of the higher theological schools. There are four such institutions in Poland: the Catholic University of Lublin, the Academy of Catholic Theology, the Pontifical Academy of Theology and the Christian Academy of Theology, this last serving the churches of the Polish Ecumenical Council.

Research on peace issues is prominent in the Catholic University of Lublin's Department of Social Sciences, notably in the framework of international political relations and Catholic social science and a special section devoted to international ethics. Among the university's researchers, Professor Joachim Kondziela, Ph.D. has contributed especially to the presentation of the church's stance on peace.

Among the publications of the Academy of Catholic Theology, the book by Father S. Olejnik, *The Morality of Social Life*,[16] provides an interesting discussion on international community, the phenomenon of war and the arms race and a condemnation of total war.

Possibilities for education for peace through the religious press are provided through the 124 religious journals published in Poland. Some 103 are Roman Catholic and the rest belong to the other religious communities. Journals connected with the episcopate do not include a daily newspaper (the daily *Slowo Powszechne* with a circulation of 100,000 is published by the Pax association) but do include a number of weeklies, with the largest, *Gość Niedzielny*, boasting a circulation of 200,000; two fortnightlies: *Posłaniec Warmiński* and *Lad Bozy;* ten monthlies including *Więź, Apostolstwo chroym, Rycerz Niepokalanej,* and *Przeglad Powszechny;* bi-monthlies, quarterlies and annuals. Twenty-six Catholic journals with a joint circulation of 25,000 are published by Catholic dioceses, and serve as a link between the ecclesiastical authorities and the clergy.

Religious journals offer a broad presentation of the churches' standpoints on peace and disarmament, including messages, homilies and the pope's speeches. They also present the stance of the Apostolic See and the World Council of Churches on the most important contemporary problems, including nuclear weapons.

Another important mode of disseminating Pope John Paul II's philosophy of peace are Polish publications, which are partly biographical, but in large part are devoted to documentation of his trip. Many of these publications are brought out by state publishing houses. The State Scientific Publishers recently published a collective work: *The Philosophy and Social Thought of John Paul II.* There can be no doubt that the feelings cherished by Poles for their pope greatly facilitates their reception of his views on peace.

Ecumenical developments in Poland have enhanced the possibilities of the churches' influence on matters of disarmament. Progress in relations between the Roman Catholic Church and the Ecumenical Council may be seen in mutual visits paid by the council and the primate, in regular meetings of the Joint Commission of the Polish Ecumenical Council and the Polish Episcopate, as well as ecumenical services joined by the primate in 1982 and 1983. A symbolic expression of these relations is the plan to erect in Majdanek—at the initiative of its Catholic bishop, Msgr. Pylak—a world temple of peace for various religions and for nonbelievers. This temple is intended to be an ecumenical place in the service of reconciliation, peace, brotherhood, and prayer for a world free from wars and hatred. It is supposed to serve three kinds of unity: unity between Christians, unity between various religions and the unity of humanity.

The Roman Catholic Church and the other churches and religious communities maintain lively contacts with churches abroad. These contacts broaden the possibilities of the churches' approach to problems of peace. The sermons of the late Primate Cardinal Stefan Wyszyński during his visit in 1978 to the Federal Republic of Germany with a delegation of the Polish episcopate were important in this regard, as are the ongoing discussions of the Polish Ecumenical Council and the Council of the Evangelical Church in the Federal Republic of Germany.

III. THE ROLE OF LAY CATHOLIC AND CHRISTIAN ASSOCIATIONS

In People's Poland, despite sporadic discussions, there are no Christian or Catholic parties or trade unions. An important component of the present political system, however, is its coalition nature. Given the leading role of the PUWP, participation in the exercise of authority is granted to the United Peasant Party and the Democratic Party, as well as groups of lay Catholics who actively accept the socialist state: the Polish Catholic Social Union, the Pax Association and the Christian Social Association.

The common trait of these Catholic social groups is their endorsement of the social changes in Poland, although their motives for doing so differ. Some accept socialism as the height of social development, while others accept it on grounds of political realism. A basic interest of these groups is to create optimum conditions for the church to proclaim its evangelical message and to promote Christian ethics in a socialist society. These groups belong among those forces in Catholicism which are concerned that the church adapt to the contemporary world in accordance with the teachings of the Second Vatican Council. They seek to intellectualize Catholicism, to strengthen the place of the Catholic intelligentsia and to stimulate its social work. They endeavor to promote ideological pluralism in the socialist state and to secure complete political rights for people who consistently stand by their Christian world outlook.

These Catholic social associations constitute a kind of intermediary between the church on the one hand and the state on the other, while their relations to the Catholic hierarchy differ. In the case of the Polish Catholic Social Union, Cardinal Glemp said on the occasion of a reception for its chairman, Janusz Zablocki, that the church deals with social lay Catholics "acting in liaison with the Church."[17] Pax is founded on Polish patriotism, a Catholic worldview and a struggle for a progressive, pluralistic socialism.[18] The Christian Social Association stresses its independence from the episcopate and its ecumenical formula as a movement not only of Catholics but all Christians.[19]

These associations of lay Christians and Catholics are represented in the Sejm (Polish parliament). At present, Pax has six representatives, while the PCSU and the CSA each have four. Pax deputy A. Klafkowski and Christian Social Association deputy K. Morawski are also members of the Council of State. The chairman of the Pax Association, Z. Komender, is a deputy premier. The deputies representing the associations are also members of the Sejm commissions, and especially important from the point of view of peace, they participate in the work of the Foreign Affairs Commission.

The Polish associations of lay Catholics and Christians also publish journals and newspapers in their own publishing houses. The Pax Association publishes the daily *Slow Pow-*

szechne and three weeklies, *Kierunki, Katolik,* and *Zorza,* as well as a monthly, *Zeszyty Naukowe.* The Christian Social Association publishes three weeklies: *Za i Przeciw, Hejnal Mariacki* and *Tygodnik Polski.* The Polish Catholic Social Union sponsors a weekly, *Lad,* and a monthly, *Chrześcijanin w Świecie.*

Much of the activity of these lay Catholic associations involves issues of peace and international security, especially in Europe. The Polish Catholic Social Union established a Center for Peace Research which cooperates with the Polish episcopate. The center, headed by Professor J. Kondziela, conducts studies on international peace with special attention to the social teachings of the church. The Center also gives high priority to issues of education for peace, international ethics and disarmament. Seventeen seminars organized to date have taken up problems like Polish-German relations and the international activity of the Apostolic See.[20] In 1978 the Center played host to a Polish-German symposium on "Education for Peace" and in 1980 to a Polish-American seminar on "Human Rights and Peace." It also organized a seminar with the Club of Catholic Intelligentsia in Lublin to mark the twentieth anniversary of Pope John XXIII's encyclical *Pacem in terris.*

The associations of lay Christians and Catholics also express their attitude toward mounting threats to peace. An example is the declaration "For a Safe Europe—Against New Armaments", adopted by the main board of the Christian Social Association on December 8, 1979, which appealed to Christian organizations in Western Europe to oppose the deployment of new nuclear missiles and to support all means serving the cause of a durable *détente,* disarmament, constructive cooperation and contribution to a broader and better mutual understanding.[21]

The PCSU, CSA and Pax jointly sponsored the Warsaw Christian Forum for Peace in Europe in September 1979 with participants from all of Europe and the USA on the subject "Christians and the Responsibility for Peace." The forum also organized, in May 1980, an international symposium in Warsaw on "Methods of Education for Peace."

The PCSU participates in the congresses of the international peace organization Pax Romana, in conferences of the European pontifical organization *Iustitia et Pax*, (Justice and Peace) and in the work of the Committee for Continuation of European Meetings of Dialogue and Cooperation.

The CSA participated in the World Conference of Religious Workers for Saving the Sacred Gift of Life from Nuclear Catastrophe, held in Moscow in May 1982. A symposium organized by the CSA was held on September 9–10, 1983, with Christian participants from both East and West, on "The Responsibility of European Christians for Peace and Security on Our Continent."

All three associations participate in the work of the Polish Peace Committee, whose representatives are members of the World Peace Council. Representatives of the PCSU, Pax and CSA participated in the World Peace Assembly in Prague in June 1983.

In summary, the role played by the lay Christian and Catholic associations in influencing the state's disarmament policy consists in creating possibilities for indirect representation of the churches' and the hierarchy's stance in the Sejm and its Commission for Foreign Affairs, the council of state and the government. The associations' research work, meetings and scientific conferences are also significant for developing a better understanding of the churches' stance on disarmament, and they elaborate ideas and material to be eventually used by the churches. The fact that the associations have their own press which takes up issues of war and peace and presents the social teachings of the church widens the possibilities for educating the society for peace. It should be added that the international activity of the associations indirectly enlarges contacts, exchange of opinions and dialogue on problems of disarmament between the churches in Poland and abroad.

IV. NEW POSSIBILITIES IN THE "PATRIOTIC MOVEMENT FOR NATIONAL REBIRTH" (PRON)

Ways for the churches to influence state decisions on disarmament should not overlook a new and important institution in the political system of Poland, the Patriotic Movement for National Rebirth (*Patriotyczny Ruch Odrodzenia Narodowego*—PRON).

PRON emerged in response to the need for accord and national rebirth and aims at seeking solutions for socialist renewal. The history of the movement is not long. In mid-1982, the Polish United Workers' Party, the United Peasant Party and the Democratic Party, together with the three Christian and Catholic associations issued a Declaration on the Patriotic Movement for National Rebirth. The expressed intent of the movement is to lead the country out of crisis and consolidate the socialist ideals of social justice, people's rule, and the rule of law and human dignity. Participation in this movement is open to all who acknowledge that there is no other way for Poland than socialist development and no other reliable guarantee of Poland's independence than its alliance with the Soviet Union and its participation in the community of socialist states.

The declaration clearly affirmed the place and role of Catholics and Christians in the movement:

> There can be no divisions into party members and non-party members, believers and nonbelievers in the work for Poland. All citizens have equal rights and duties. We pronounce ourselves in favor of the possibility for an unfettered promotion and taking up of key positions by non-party members who abide by the Constitution of Poland.

The signatories also stated that the Patriotic Movement for National Rebirth

> will offer room for Catholic and Christian activists as well as activists of different faiths. Polish society is aware of the Church's

authority. Therefore the cause of national rebirth should and can be increasingly served by a constructive dialogue between the State authorities and the Episcopate of the Roman Catholic Church and other churches and religious groups.

An Initiating Commission to establish the movement was set up on September 15, 1982, chaired by non-party Catholic writer Jan Dobraczyński. Among its accomplishments are the appeal submitted to the Sejm to lift martial law, release the interned and take up work on an amnesty. Toward the end of 1982 the Provisional National Council of PRON consisting of 327 persons was established. It included a number of Catholic and Christian activists, and Jan Dobraczyński was elected its chairman.

The Polish Autocephalous Orthodox Church, the Lutheran Church of the Augsburg Confession and the Old Catholic Church have representatives in the council. Clergy of the Roman Catholic church do not participate in the council; Cardinal Józef Glemp stated on December 24, 1982:

> We (Poles) must recover from the crisis ourselves. But in unity. Unity can be achieved only in the course of a dialogue and the dialogue may only be in truth. Let the civic committees for salvation emerge. Priests will not join the committees, because their task is to pave the way to national unity according to the truth of the Gospel. Organization of unity according to civil truth should be entrusted to lay Catholics.

The Provisional National Council adopted guidelines for action: to build agreement among Poles over the basic national and state issues; to act in favor of internal peace; to restore to Poland her due place in the world; and to consolidate and expand the movement.

PRON received its final shape in its first congress held in Warsaw May 7–9, 1983. The congress adopted a program stating directions, methods of activity and statutory principles. The delegates also adopted an appeal to the nation, "A Peace Appeal." Numerous themes from the congress' proceedings relate to the place of the movement in the political system of Poland, the role of Catholics and other Christians in the movement and questions of peace and disarmament. It was repeatedly stressed during the discussions that PRON is to be a durable element of the socialist political system, a voice for public opinion, an organizer of consultations and an initiator of political actions which will meet the needs and expectations of the society and the government.[22] It was noted that for the first time in the history of the Polish People's Republic, a political event of such importance as the PRON congress was attended with equally decisive voice by PUWP members, members of other political parties, members of Catholic and Christian associations and non-party members. In one of the speeches, PRON was seen as a substantial step toward the practical implementation of a "historic compromise," an agreement between Marxists and Catholics, as well as a broadly conceived social accord and cooperation of all Poles of good will.[23]

General Jaruzelski said during his speech at the congress:

> We are not treating cooperation with the church as a temporary and tactical necessity. We want it to be useful for the state and the nation. . . . Broad masses of lay Catholics have actively participated in building People's Poland since its very beginning. Such foundations provide the possibility not only of simple coexistence but constructive cooperation in specific fields.

Do the decisions and resolutions of the first congress of PRON create institutional possibilities for the churches' influencing the policy and official stance of the state on internal and external issues? This question may be answered affirmatively both with regard to the adopted program assumptions and the composition of the movement itself.

The resolution on the directions and methods of action of PRON states clearly that the movement's objectives include the expansion of the society's influence on the activities of the organs of the authority by: 1) participation in the election of representative organs and influencing the deputies and councillors; 2) participation in the law-making process; 3) power to examine and consult the organs of administration; and 4) the expansion of the social basis of management and exercising authority.[24] The movement is to see to it that the masses of non-party citizens have full opportunity to take part in the public life of the country.

With regard to issues of Poland in the international arena, the movement shall inspire and support the activities of state authorities and social organizations to deepen a general knowledge about the world, the scope and mechanisms of threats to peace and international security as well as disarmament negotiations and initiatives. PRON pronounced itself against spreading hostility and national, racial, ethical or religious prejudices, and as in favor of cooperation with progressive movements in all the world which share common goals.[25] The Peace Appeal adopted during the congress took note of the role of the churches in the struggle for peace and opposition to the arms race, and recognized that resistance to militarism and the arms race is expressed not only by politicians and governments in many countries, but also by protests of whole nations, peace organizations, and churches. Special attention was given to the messages of Pope John Paul II in this regard.

The National Council of PRON elected at its first congress is 400 strong and includes 120 representatives of the Polish United Workers' Party, 49 members of the United Peasant Party and 36 members of the Democratic Party. Besides the participation of the Orthodox, Lutheran and Old Catholic churches mentioned earlier, the Christian and Catholic associations also have representatives: Pax, 30; the Christian Social Association, 20 and the Polish Catholic Social Union, 12. Its vice-chairmen include Z. Pilecki of the CSA, W. Lewandowski of Pax, A. Elbanowski of the PCSU and J. Ozdowski, a lay professor at the Catholic Academy of Theology who is also deputy speaker of the Sejm. The congress elected the Catholic Jan Dobraczyński as chairman. The composition of the authorities of the Patriotic Movement for National Rebirth thus justifies a thesis about the possibility of the influence of the churches and lay Catholics and Christians in PRON.

To implement the program of action of PRON, the National Council on June 10, 1983 set up a number of commissions including a 60-person Commission for Peace, International Security and Foreign Cooperation. The commission started work on drafting a program of action to implement the resolutions of the congress, which provide for supporting all actions of Poland aimed at disarmament and halting the arms race, *rapprochement* between nations and their better understanding, and serving the cause of peace. Also envisaged are inspiration and backing of state activity in this field. The commission includes representatives of the Lutheran Church of the Augsburg Confession, the Old Catholic Church and the Polish Autocephalous Orthodox Church. The Christian and Catholic associations are also widely represented in the commission.

V. CONCLUSIONS: THE CHURCHES' NEW POSSIBILITIES

The preceding discussion demonstrates that the churches in Poland enjoy not only an opportunity to present their stance on armaments, but also the possibility of starting dialogue and cooperation over this matter with the state. This cooperation in the cause of peace may already be seen in the conspicuous convergence of the Polish declaration on the "Preparation of Societies for Life in Peace" submitted in December 1978 by the Polish government to the UN General Assembly and the subject of the twelfth World Day of Peace, "We Shall Preach Peace through Education for Peace," endorsed by Pope Paul VI in August 1978. The Polish government initiative made use of Pope John Paul II's message on this matter and received the support of the permanent observer of the Vatican to the UN. During the debate over the draft of the declaration on the preparation of societies for life in peace, the Vatican's observer stressed that the Apostolic See is particularly interested in the education of societies in the spirit of peace.

While the churches' stance on peace and disarmament has long been dominated by declarative appeals for peace and condemnation of war, violence and the arms race, more recently the churches have been taking more concrete positions against nuclear armaments. The Church of England recently received wide attention in the Polish mass media during the 1982 debate of its working group report on "The Church and the Bomb." The report recommended unilateral nuclear disarmament of the United Kingdom. Though the church rejected this radical unilateral action it called upon its government and disarmament negotiators to make efforts for genuine disarmament and appealed to the NATO states to adopt a "no first use" policy for nuclear weapons.

The initiative on the question of nuclear disarmament taken up by the U.S. Roman Catholic hierarchy has also become widely known in Poland. Its pastoral letter calls for freezing of nuclear arms production and seeking more effective means of nuclear disarmament. This question was the subject of a discussion in the Vatican January 18–19, 1983, attended by representatives of many national episcopates. The Canadian Council of the Churches, which includes the Roman Catholic Church, the Episcopal Church, the Presbyterian Church and the Lutheran Church, also sent a pastoral letter to all Christians in Canada, rejecting the policy of nuclear armaments and the thesis that nuclear war is inevitable.

One could ask why there is as yet no pastoral letter of the Polish episcopate, nor a joint stand of all Polish churches on the question of nuclear armaments. There are at least two reasons: first, it probably follows from the churches' quite justifiable and great preoccupation with domestic peace within Poland; second, it appears related to the fact that huge peace movements compel the churches in other countries to take up these crucial issues, and there is as yet no such broad and spontaneous movement in Poland.

NOTES

1. Official sources do not give the number of Catholics in Poland, but according to church records, about 86 percent of the Poles belong to the Roman Catholic Church. (cf. a survey by the Profs. J. Kondziela and W. Piwowarski.)
2. In their analyses of the sources of the Roman Catholic Church's power in Poland, authors point especially to the wise policy conducted by the Primate S. Wyszyński over a thirty-year period after World War II. cf. J.E. Will: "Church's Enormous Power Gives Poland Hope," *Chicago Sun-Times*, January 9, 1982; J. Szczepański: Wizyta (The Visit), *Polityka* July 23, 1983.
3. W. Myslka, M.T. Staszowski, eds: *The Policy for Denominations: Background, Conditions, Implementation*, Warsaw 1975, p. 441ff.
4. The Ninth Extraordinary Congress of the Polish United Workers' Party. July 14–20, 1981 *Documents and Materials*, Warsaw 1981, p. 255.
5. *Trybuna Ludu*, January 11, 1982.
6. *Rzeczpospolita*, January 19, 1982.
7. *Trybuna Ludu*, February 25, 1982.
8. *Slowo Powszechne*, September 8, 1982.
9. The Resolution of the PUWP Eighth Congress, February 11–15, 1980. *Basic Documents and Materials*, Warsaw, 1980, pp. 200–201.
10. A. Lopatka, op.cit., p. 23. Among the other fields of cooperation, he also enumerated the dissemination and consolidation of moral attitudes; actions toward improvement of the nations' hygiene and health; consideration for order and esthetic values; combatting alcoholism, drug taking and hooliganism; actions aimed at consolidating the family, strengthening respect for good work, care for the old people and others in need of care.
11. *Rzeczpospolita*, July 23, 1983.
12. *Rzeczpospolita*, July 16, 1983.
13. As stated in the 1980–83 report by the chairman of the Polish Ecumenical Council, Prof. Witold Benedyktowicz. The survey of the Polish radio reports there are about four million listeners to these broadcasts.
14. *The General Program of Catechization on Secondary School Level* (grades 1–4), 1971, pp. 32–34. It is worth noting that the program of teaching religion in secondary schools is attended by about 30 percent of the students.
15. Rev. W. Koska: *Chrześcijanin w świecie wspólczesnym* (The Christian in the Contemporary World), Poznań: St. Wojciech Bookstore, 1982, p. 133ff.
16. Rev. Stanislaw Olejnik: *Moralonsé zycia spolecznego* (The Morality of Social Life), Warsaw: Academy of Catholic Theology, 1970, p. 260ff.
17. *Lad*, July 10, 1983.
18. Z. Komender, "Fundamentalne zasady naszego ruchu. Kultura, Oxwiata, Nauka" (Fundamental Principles of our Movement. Culture, Education, Science) in: *Zeszyty Naukowe PAX*, no. 2, 1983, p. 8.
19. *Za i Przeciw*, No. 29, 1957.
20. The center also conducts research activity and the following monographs are being elaborated under its auspices: H. Wuttke, PhD., *Chrześcijanie niemieccy a*

Churches and Disarmament Issues in Poland 221

pojednanie z Polska (German Christians and Reconciliation with Poland); A. Mura, PhD., *Polska-RFN. Zbilzenie a podrecznik szkolny* (Poland—the FRG: *Rapprochement and the School Textbook*); Associate Professor R. Buchala, PhD., *Stolica Apostolska a pokój* (The Holy See and Peace); Father F. Mazurek: *Prawa czlowieka a pokój* (Human Rights and Peace); Associate Professor S. Kurowski, PhD., *Gospodarezo-spoleczne i moralne uwarunkowania pokoju światowego* (Socio-economic and Moral Determinants of World Peace); O.H. Rawalski: *Moralonśé apokój* (Morality and Peace).
21. Christian Social Association: *Information Bulletin*, no. 11/12, November–December 1979, p. 44.
22. Program report delivered by Jan Kostrzewski at the First Congress of the PRON, *Materials and Documents*, Warsaw 1983, p. 13.
23. Cf. pronouncements by Marian Krzeminski, *Lad*, Warsaw, May 29, 1983.
24. Directions and Methods of the PRON activity. The First Congress of the Patriotic Movement for National Rebirth. *Materials and Documents*, Warsaw, 1983, pp. 40–41.
25. *Ibid.*, p. 44.

Insights for the Churches

by James E. Will

The dominant purpose of this study has been to assess and enhance the efficacy of the ecumenical peace witness and action of the churches. The editor, of course, can begin this process only as a U.S. churchperson, and given U.S. pluralism, can only suggest some learnings that many others will have to augment. It is hoped that many in European and Canadian churches will also be able to learn much that is helpful from this study, and that it will contribute to an increasing process of responsible ecumenical interaction in peace witness and action.

Philip Everts points at the conclusion of his paper to one of the most exciting aspects of the "new peace movement": its transnational and truly non-aligned character. He also suggests that the churches are "eminently qualified to be transnational actors because they transcend the state system." One may or may not agree that nation-states as such are an obstacle to world peace, as Dr. Everts suggests. In the long run, world peace may well require a new international political order with transfer of some sovereignty to a world government; but in the shorter run we must witness and work for peace within a world politics of balancing power between states and the blocs they have created.

The reality that churches transcend the state system while living within sovereign nation-states requires congruent growth in the churches' capacities to act more effectively *both* in their national contexts *and* in the "transnational, truly non-aligned" peace witness of the ecumenical church. What wisdom may be distilled for U.S. churches as we address the possibilities and difficulties of this double challenge?

The Necessity of an Ecumenical National Peace Strategy

The most substantive peace issue facing contemporary European and North American churches is their relation to the growing moral doubt undermining the policy of nuclear deterrence in all of our societies. This study makes it clear that the churches in these four European societies have been creating the theological basis and legitimating the political analysis for such moral doubt. It is not necessary to repeat here what has been plain to read in the preceding essays.[1] Much the same process of thought also has been going on in many U.S. churches. The tacit political consensus of the last twenty years supporting the theory that possession of nuclear weapons is necessary to prevent their use by the other side is crumbling under the weight of the moral implications of the massive terror it depends upon.

What is not yet as clear in our churches as among those of our European colleagues is the necessity, therefore, of supporting a political alternative for this failed policy. As Everts and Hogebrink put it, "the 'no' to nuclear deterrence will have to be translated gradually into a 'yes' to certain alternatives." (Everts and Hogebrink, p. 80) A large part of Günter Krusche's paper summarizes the ongoing reflections of the churches in the German Democratic Republic that have convinced them of their need for a "peace strategy." (Krusche, p. 158f.) The churches have increasingly accepted the chal-

Insights for the Churches 225

lenge to enter the peace politics debate with their own "productive mediation between theological knowledge and secular reason." (Krusche, p. 161) They have thus decided to support the strategic concept of "common security" as advanced in the report of the non-aligned Palme Commission. Dr. Krusche concludes that the churches in the GDR "have lost their anxiety about touching the political sphere." (Krusche, p. 161) Professor Huber, on the other hand, reviews the failure of the churches in the FRG to reach consensus on five points of political controversy, a situation more similar to that of our churches in the United States. (Huber pp. 108–111)

The Dutch Interchurch Peace Council (IKV) began to address its political alternative to nuclear deterrence as early as 1977, stimulated by the U.S. Professor Osgood's ideas about gradual and reciprocal initiatives in disarmament. (Everts and Hogebrink, p. 33) After careful analysis of the possibilities congruent with the size, character and power of the Netherlands, the IKV proposed a peace strategy of unilateral denuclearization for their state that advocated removing all nuclear weapons from the Dutch armed forces and Dutch territory. This strategy was thought to be sufficiently unambiguous and large enough to have significant international impact, while small enough in purely military terms not to destabilize the military balance. At the same time, it was thought to be the maximum for which majority domestic support could be generated. (Everts and Hogebrink, p. 34)

Public opinion polls in the Netherlands have shown that a majority of the Dutch population support the unilateral removal of all nuclear weapons from the Netherlands and that as many as two-thirds oppose the deployment of the new NATO cruise missiles. (Everts and Hogebrink, pp. 55, 56) Yet the elections of 1981 and 1982 showed that security policy issues were less determinative of Dutch voting behavior than domestic economic issues. Thus there has been as yet no decisive breakthrough at the political level for support of the Dutch churches' peace strategy. (Everts and Hogebrink, pp. 45–59)

Some of the public opinion data in the Netherlands support a point central to the emerging peace strategy of the churches in the German Democratic Republic. Christa Lewek writes that the GDR churches do not intend to "change the power structures and balance of power in Europe," but rather to "make the prevailing ones capable of peace." (Lewek, p. 125; cf. Krusche, p. 162) The same Dutch polls that show a majority supporting unilateral denuclearization of the Netherlands also show strong support for membership in NATO and the need to maintain military equilibrium between East and West. (Everts and Hogebrink, p. 55) Thus a church peace strategy in any of our societies, if it is to gain sufficient domestic support, must neither aim, nor be interpretable as aiming, at destabilization of existing balances of power between East and West.[2] It is a moot question, but I think that it may never be appropriate for the church as such to function in *realpolitik* in so direct a way. The moral dimensions of the church's peace strategy are fatally obscured when churches allow themselves to be drawn so completely into power politics.

This means, somewhat paradoxically, however, that the churches must be concerned for power factors as they formulate their peace strategies. If one does not aim to destabilize power balances, then the peace strategy must be congruent with the power position of the state in which the church exists. What is appropriate as a peace strategy in the Netherlands, then, would likely not be appropriate for the churches in the USA or the USSR. Unilateral denuclearization of a superpower is obviously destabilizing. Neither, of course, does this mean that the churches in a superpower may simply support the status quo of its security policy.

The major churches in the USA are ever more forcefully articulating a *peace witness* that is morally undermining the state's strategy of nuclear deterrence; but they have not yet begun to articulate an alternative *peace strategy*. Given our social and denominational pluralism, this may prove to be ecumenically impossible; in any case, it will be much more difficult than in the smaller, more homogenous societies of the Netherlands and the German Democratic Republic. But it must be attempted if we are to hope that our peace witness will become politically effective. Issues such as first strike, first use and bilateral freeze are already on this strategy agenda in the USA. Equitable arms reduction proposals in the context of negotiations, confidence-building measures in the context of the Helsinki process and cultural measures for overcoming "enemy images" appear to be other elements necessary for such a strategy. All or most of these, and perhaps others, await to be shaped into a coherent peace strategy for which the churches can seek ecumenically to rally political support. The ecumenical structures of the National Council of Churches will be crucial in this enterprise, but the churches themselves will have to take full responsibility for any strategy articulated in this "communion of communions."

The Educative Value of Ecumenically-Sponsored National Peace Weeks

At the center of the reports on peace witness and action from the Netherlands and the GDR are descriptions of their *Friedensdekaden*, or peace weeks, which are akin to the even longer-established *Kirchentag* (and *Katholikentag*) in the Federal Republic of Germany, but more sharply focused only on issues of peace. The Dutch Interchurch Peace Council was formed in 1966 by the nine major churches in the Netherlands to promote peace work in the congregations and to speak and act on behalf of the churches in matters of peace, justice and human rights. Their major activity from the beginning was promotion of annual peace weeks, in which local churches in all cities, towns and villages participated. (Everts and Hogebrink, p. 32) The Federation of Evangelical Churches in the GDR, responding to an initiative of their youth, have sponsored such peace weeks in November every year since 1980. (Lewek, p. 133f.) This peace week model also began to take root in the Federal Republic of Germany at the same time, being held in 120 places in 1980 and growing to 4000 in 1981. (Huber, p. 99) This extensive educational effort at the national level provided the consciousness-raising and conscientization necessary to the subsequent peace strategies of these churches.

The ecumenical churches in the USA have already learned from these initiatives of their European colleagues. Through the leadership of the National Council of Churches in the USA, the first "National Week for Pursuing Peace with Justice" was organized in May 1983. Ten member churches and eleven national ecumenical organizations cooperated in its organization. Its success led to seven additional national religious bodies joining in the second national week in May 1984, in which at least 20,000 local congregations in every state participated. The National Conference of Catholic Bishops, the Union of American Hebrew Congregations, Church Women United and the Executive Committee of the Leadership Conference of Women Religious were among the 28 churches and national groups which joined in the organization of this week.[3]

It is evident that a powerful instrument is being forged in these national peace weeks for an ecumenical witness for peace with justice across religious, theological and confessional lines. Thus the Interunit Committee for International Affairs of the NCCC-USA reaffirmed its commitment to this program in September 1984; but its still-precarious position may be seen in that the interunit committee had to overturn a subcommittee recommendation that the National Council of Churches give up its coordinating functions because it could not afford the budget required to fulfill them. It remains to be seen whether the churches in the USA will recognize the value of this week for their national peace witness and provide the necessary resources for its continuing ecumenical coordination. The degree to which we learn from the experience of our European colleagues may play a significant role in this decision.

The fact that 28 groups are already involved in the planning and coordination of such a week in the USA indicates the pluralism of our peace witness and related peace movements. We probably never will be able to achieve the theological coherence that has informed the themes of the peace weeks in the GDR formulated within its Federation of Evangelical Churches (cf. Lewek, pp. 133–134); nor should we seek it in so pluralistic a society. It is at this very point that we may be encouraged by the analysis of Professor Symonides as to why there has not yet been a large national effort of all Polish churches against nuclear armaments. There are, of course, a number of important reasons, as his and Professor Kondziela's essays reveal. Symonides suggests, however, that huge peace movements in a way compel the churches in other countries to take up these crucial issues, and there is as yet no such broad and spontaneous movement in Poland. (Symonides, p. 219; cf. Kondziela, p. 182f) The peace movement in the USA is increasingly broad and certainly spontaneous. Thus the churches have a momentous opportunity for national peace education in the USA if they are wise enough to help provide the correlation and coherence needed. Without the cumulative educative affect of such national efforts, as we may learn from our European colleagues, there may be little hope for the churches' peace witness to mature into a politically effective peace strategy at the national level in the USA.

The Relation of the Churches' Peace Witness to the Political Center

The political center in all five of the quite various societies under our consideration has supported an East-West security policy of peace/deterrence through nuclear strength for the last two or more decades. That "center," of course, is constituted quite differently by the "democratic centralism" of the communist parties in Poland and the GDR than it is by the electoral politics of the three Western democracies. Nevertheless, they have adopted almost mirror-image security policies that have locked them into the nuclear arms race. As defined by Robert McNamara while U.S. secretary of defense during the Kennedy administration, this policy saw security as lying in "mutual assured destruction," that is, "the certainty of suicide to the aggressor—not merely to his military forces, but to his society as a whole."[4]

National security was thus based on the morally appalling

threat to destroy an entire society; but the mere threat was not enough, for its credibility requires the government's "unwavering will," as McNamara put it, "to *use* its nuclear weapons if necessary." After the ratification of the partial test ban treaty in 1963, public nuclear concern in the political center almost disappeared for twenty years; so George Kennan could write when he accepted the Einstein Peace Prize in 1981:

> We have gone on piling weapon upon weapon, missile upon missile, new levels of destructiveness upon old ones. We have done this helplessly, almost involuntarily, like the victims of some sort of hypnotism, like men in a dream, like lemmings headed for the sea.

Kennan's powerful metaphors might be translated to say that for two decades the political center of U.S. (and European) societies remained unconcerned, if not unthinking, about the morally and socially destructive implications of a policy of "peace through growing nuclear strength." During this period the mainline churches were almost equally quiescent on the nuclear issues, concentrating their peace concerns for a time on opposition to the Vietnam war.

It is almost surprising, therefore, that the peace strategies of all the European churches studied seek coalition with at least some elements of the political center. Given the democratic centralism of communist-led states, it may be less surprising that this is the preferred, perhaps only feasible method there. What may be surprising to U.S. citizens, however, is the array of institutional possibilities for the churches to influence the communist-led political center through what might be called "elite networks" in Poland (Symonides, pp. 204–207), and the continuous process of church-state dialogues in the GDR. Professor Kondziela even thinks that the "suprasystemic peace dialogue" now being institutionalized in Poland may prove an internationally important model for world peace (Kondziela, pp. 188, 189), and envisions the possibility of the Polish church rallying mass support for a nuclear free zone in Europe in a way that might also relate to the policy-making center of the Polish government and the Warsaw Pact centered in the USSR. (Kondziela, pp. 197, 198) It is also obvious that the array of important subjects discussed with the foreign ministry by the churches in the German Democratic Republic go to the heart of nuclear weapons policies, including a nuclear free zone for Central Europe. (Lewek, p. 141)

Churches in the U.S. find closer analogies, however, with the experience of the churches in the Netherlands and the Federal Republic of Germany. Hogebrink and Everts noted that if popular protest is to have political impact it needs to build a coalition with the center in Dutch politics (Everts and Hogebrink, pp. 42, 43); and they carefully analyzed this process. Factors that appear especially significant are the decline of the "confessional" vote in the political center, the emergence of "critical" groups (*actiegroepen*) representing specific interests and the consequent growing inability of the traditional political parties to translate diverse demands into coherent political programs. This has provided the political configuration within which the peace movement and the churches have come to play a more influential role in the debates over international security policies and nuclear weapons. (Everts and Hogebrink, pp. 27, 28)

The church-related peace movement, to be effective in the political center, must understand itself as a "coalition type" organization seeking maximum possible support, rather than a "prophetic minority" only witnessing to an alternative lifestyle. The Dutch IKV has thus undertaken a "long march through the institutions": women's organizations, the Central Federation of Trade Unions, the soldiers' trade union, local city and village councils and professional groups—especially physicians. Many groups not heretofore politically concerned or active have become committed to de-escalation of the arms race. (Everts and Hogebrink, pp. 44, 45) To the degree that the problem of nuclear weapons has become a major issue in Dutch election campaigns, it has been due to strong pressures from below engendered by this coalition rather than directly due to the efforts of the political parties themselves. Leaders of the major parties are often strongly tied to positions developed in bloc politics—NATO for the

Netherlands—and are unable to resolve the internal divisions in their parties over these issues.

Some of this analysis appears to have direct analogies in the U.S. political process. Given our broad two-party system, lack of political coherence in the platforms and programs of our parties is endemic—although this is more clearly the case for the Democratic Party, which has become increasingly comprised of a coalition of various interest groups. The Republican Party remains at this point more consistently representative of the established economic groups grounded in the U.S.'s traditional capitalistic ideology. Thus the Democratic Party appears currently to be the the political arena most available to be influenced by a broadly-based peace coalition. This was borne out by the endorsement by the "Freeze Voters" (a spin-off committee from the National Freeze Campaign), e.g., of the candidacies of Walter Mondale for president and Paul Simon for senator in Illinois. These actions were not so much old-style partisan politics as they were the consequence of astute analysis by a peace coalition as to where they might have the most effective impact on the U.S. political process, successfully in one case and unsuccessfully in the other.

U.S. churches, however, face great difficulty in exercising any direct influence, even as part of a peace coalition, in the electoral process. Externally, the constitutional and traditional separation of church and state makes the endorsing of particular candidates virtually impossible; and internally, the lack of any "national church" tradition has led to a very strong opposite tradition of leaving direct political decisions entirely to the consciences of individual members. If the NCCC-USA were to become as politically active as the Dutch IKV, the polarization described by Everts and Hogebrink in Dutch churches and society would be mild as compared to the furor that would emerge in U.S. churches. In my opinion, the dissolution of the NCCC-USA and schism in some of the major churches would be a probable result.

Thus if the peace witness of U.S. churches is to be effective in the U.S. political center, it will have to relate pastoral care to political responsibility with great sensitivity. Prophetic interpretation of the moral dimensions of political decisions concerning nuclear arms will have to be linked at every point to the most open group processes, articulated in a comprehensive peace education that reaches from the personal/interpersonal to the social/political and rooted in the churches' experience of and commitment to reconciliation.

The Need for Comprehensive Peace Education Grounded in Reconciliation

Although it may not yet be widely recognized in our churches, politically efficacious peace witness by the churches in the U.S. is as precarious here as it is anywhere in Western or Eastern Europe. To be sure, constitutional guarantees and institutional pluralism protect its possibility. But the individualism celebrated in our pluralism and the national ideology expressed in our civil religion endanger its actualization. For the church to foster political power in support of nuclear disarmament is to court social and economic endangering of its total program of evangelism and pastoral care. Every responsible leader in mainline churches knows and fears this danger.

U.S. churches may have to become as self-conscious about our social location of being "a church in capitalism" as the churches in the GDR have become about being "a church in socialism." (Lewek, pp. 121, 122) This should mean for us, as it does for them, that we do not want to be a church above capitalism, against capitalism, or for capitalism—nor by any means a capitalist church. We may very well make our own the position articulated by the GDR Federation of Evangelical Churches:

> The Church must therefore always make clear that its position is not above the divisions in the world, but rather in the midst of its conflicts, among the human beings to whom it is sent. In these conflicts the church is neither judge nor supporter of any one side. It is given the task of reconciliation. (Lewek, p. 122)

Adequate theological understanding of the task of reconciliation, of course, does not allow that kind of adaptation or outright co-option that compromises our understanding of the Gospel's implications on any crucial issue. So it shall mean for us, as it does for our German colleagues, "critical cooperation" with leaders of our society's political center. And the peace questions shall be for us, as for them, "the touchstone and stress test of this relationship." (Krusche, p. 165)

If a growing proportion of U.S. church members are not only to support but to participate in this kind of critical cooperation in our socio-political location, they will have to be prepared by as comprehensive a mode of peace education as has been devised by our GDR colleagues. The sixteen points in which Christa Lewek summarizes their curriculum reaches from the personal to the political. (Lewek, pp. 129, 130) And prayers for peace will have to become as regular and natural a part of our communal liturgical life as it is becoming in theirs. In this regard, I doubt if there was any mainline congregation anywhere in the U.S. that had a prayer chain around the clock during the whole of the UN Special Assembly on Disarmament in 1982, as the East German churches had. (Lewek, p. 138) My experience was that most of our congregations did not even know that there was an assembly until they read in their newspapers that our president had used it as a forum again to denounce the Soviet Union.

U.S. churches may perhaps find more direct learnings from the more similar society of their colleagues in the Netherlands. Everts and Hogebrink reported a recent opinion survey of supporters of the Christian Democratic Party, their political center there. No less than 69 percent said that their party's position on nuclear arms was "not so clear" to them, indicating how ambivalent and ambiguous the political center has become on nuclear issues. And 58 percent agreed that it is a good thing that the churches speak out on the issues of the cruise missiles. In a poll conducted by Daniel Yankovitch for the Public Agenda Foundation of New York City, published in October 1984, it was revealed that 81 percent of Americans do not know that it is official U.S. policy to keep open the possibility of "first use" of nuclear weapons; indeed, 69 percent denied that it is U.S. policy to use nuclear weapons in the case of a non-nuclear Soviet attack on Western Europe. When one's political leaders provide no adequate clarity on crucial issues, the churches have a necessary responsibility and a great opportunity. Everts and Hogebrink see this as helping build "bridges between the center and the periphery," that is, "between those supporting the peace movement and its ideas and the supporters of 'peace through strength'." (Everts and Hogebrink, p. 79)

This may be seen as part of a process of reconciliation, which is the category Everts and Hogebrink lift up. They agree with W.A. Williams that real change in democracies (short of revolution) depends "on the extent to which calm and confident conservatives can see and bring themselves to act upon the validity of a radical analysis." (Everts and Hogebrink, p. 82) The churches should not "abandon their fundamental rejection of the system of deterrence or their demands for disarmament," but they should combine them with "a serious effort to restore communication and dialogue for a new consensus to arise." (Everts and Hogebrink, p. 82) Their discussion of the political principles of civility and compromise are similar to the suggestions for "public religion" that Martin Mary recently made for U.S. churches in his *The Public Church*.[5] Moreover, their psychological insight into the way attitudinal conservatism is a useful protection against the feelings of powerlessness of many citizens indicates the importance of not allowing the feeling to grow among church members that even political decisions made in the churches are decided "over their heads" by church leaders. (Everts and Hogebrink, p. 83) Their insights here may be extended by the wisdom of psychotherapists increasingly concerned for peace and disarmament as they address the problem of "reclaiming the power to act" for many citizens in a nuclear age.[6]

Dutch wisdom concerning processes of reconciliation is matched by Eastern European colleagues who stress the importance of genuine dialogue. We may or may not agree with Professor Symonides that such newly emergent structures as

PRON in Poland provide the context for such authentic dialogue, since PRON so obviously is a government-devised substitute for Solidarity (Symonides, p. 214f.); but no one can disagree with Pope John Paul II's teaching in Poland that "dialogue on a national plane" is the sole effective method for maintaining internal as well as international peace. (Kondziela, p. 193) Nor can we ignore in our society and in our communions the commitment to "intra-society trust building" that guides the efforts of our East German colleagues. (Lewek, pp. 126–128) The theological insight in the report of their Conference of Evangelical Church Leaders in 1980 may well guide us too as we continue to learn from the Spirit of Christ in collaboration with all of our European colleagues:

> The trust that comes from Jesus Christ is not an unworldly, beatific trust. It knows the risk and pain of shattered trust. It is sober work in the midst of the conflicts, suspicions and anxieties of our time. (Lewek, pp. 126, 127)

Our churches, informed by the Spirit of such trust, must quickly and increasingly become spiritual communities in which the most difficult political decisions of our era may be and must be debated and decided in the spirit of reconciliation. Many of our congregations, however, experience grave difficulty in dealing with any conflict in the communities of grace we expect and need our congregations to be. The tensions experienced in our increasingly urban, industrial, troubled society are already too much for too many, who enter the church for the personal tranquility that will enable them to bear these tensions, and want no more.

Many of our congregations, therefore, do not realize a sufficient grace to take the tensions into themselves that result from trying to change our society and world of conflict toward policies of peace and disarmament. We then create in our life together what Paul Ricoeur has called "an ideological screen . . . of conciliation at any price."[7] The Christian faith's call to peace is used to reject the conflict-producing dynamics that the struggle for peace in a world of conflict requires.

Congregational life, when formed behind this "ideological screen," focuses only upon the personal and familial. All congregational ministries are directed toward creating personal and familial islands of peace because it is hoped that conflict is not endemic and inevitable in these spheres. Because the political process is judged to be inevitably conflict-producing, political ministries are banned from the congregation.

Sometimes, in this connection, the traditional separation of church and state in U.S. democracy is misinterpreted as a constitutional wall prohibiting our churches from exercising political influence. The truth, rather, is that our democratic foreparents separated church from state so as to guarantee that governmental power could never prohibit or inhibit any church from morally influencing the electorate on issues crucial to our common life.

Wherever this ideological screen rationalizes any congregtion's escape from the tensions of the political process it must be torn away. Concerns for personal-familial peace and sociopolitical peace must be joined with equal intensity. Personal and familial anxieties that increasingly distort our lives cannot be abstracted from the political process that structures, and threatens to de-structure, our nation and world.

We shall never deal adequately in our congregations with the violence we increasingly do ourselves and each other if we continue to ignore the massive violence that envelops our souls in a nuclear age that only maintains what we sometimes dare to call "peace" by threatening the annihilation of everyone and everything we love. Johann Baptist Metz, the German Roman Catholic theologian, has defined the tragic spiritual consequence growing among our people because of the churches' failure to address our violent political context:

> Everyone can see the signs of this looming social apocalypse: the atomic threat, the arms race madness, the destruction of the environment, terrorism, the global struggle of exploitation, or North-South conflict with its attendant danger of a world-wide social war. And yet the catastrophe remains mostly an awareness in the mind, not in the heart. It generates depression but not grief, apathy but not resistance. People seem to be becoming more and more the voyeurs of their own downfall.[8]

Churches in both Eastern and Western societies are learning to minister spiritually to a people caught in the depression and apathy of social and political voyeurism by enabling them to help shape national policies toward peace. They have learned that authentic enabling ministry is achieved only in the context of gracious community where assured personal acceptance permits the difficult work of morally evaluating national policies and shaping the political consensus that can change them.

NOTES

1. One may point especially to the analysis of Prof. Huber, pp. 90, 91.
2. This is the point of speeches delivered to the General Assembly of the Lutheran World Federation meeting in Budapest on July 25, 1984 by West German Prof. Carl Friedrich von Weizäcker and Hungarian Prof. Mihaly Simai, reported in the *LWF Infromation Bulletin*, 30/84, p. 8–9. Prof. Kondziela takes the same position in his essay in this study on p. 188. Cf. also Christa Lewek, p. 125.
3. Mimeographed "Triennium Final Report," submitted by Joyce Yu, coordinator of the National Week for Peace with Justice, NCCC-USA, August 30, 1984.
4. Quoted by Paul Boyer in "From Action to Apathy: America and the Nuclear Issue," *Bulletin of the Atomic Scientists*, Aug.-Sept. 1984, p. 19. It is of interest to note how even Mr. McNamara has now changed his mind. When asked twenty years later how he accounted for the tremendous nuclear buildup by the U.S. and the USSR, his response was, "Because the potential victims have not been brought into the debate yet, and it's about time we brought them in. I mean the average person." *The Washington Post*, acc. *The Christian Century*, Oct. 13, 1982, p. 1016.
5. Martin Marty, *The Public Church: Mainline, Evangelical, Catholic*, N.Y.: Crossroads, 1981. Cf. my review essay, "Marty, Muggeridge, and Metz on Public Theology," *Quarterly Review*, Summer 1982, pp. 99–107.
6. See the essay under this title by Elissa Malamed in *Therapy Now*, Summer 1984, p. 8–9 and 36–37. The entire issue carries helpful psychological insights on "living in the nuclear age."
7. Paul Ricoeur, "El conflicto: signo de contradiccion y de unidad?" *Criterio*, Buenos Aires: May 24, 1973, No. 1668, pp. 253–4.
8. Johann Baptist Metz, *The Emergent Church*, New York: Crossroads, 1981, p. 9.

APPENDIX

STATEMENT ON PEACE AND JUSTICE

Adopted by the Sixth Assembly of the World Council of Churches,
Vancouver, Canada, July 24–August 10, 1983

1. Humanity is now living in the dark shadow of an arms race more intense, and of systems of injustice more widespread, more dangerous and more costly than the world has ever known. Never before has the human race been as close as it is now to total self-destruction. Never before have so many lived in the grip of deprivation and oppression.

2. Under that shadow we have gathered here at the Sixth Assembly of the World Council of Churches (Vancouver, 1983) to proclaim our common faith in Jesus Christ, the Life of the World, and to say to the world:

—fear not, for Christ has overcome the forces of evil; in Him are all things made new;
—fear not; for the love of God, rise up for justice and for peace;
—trust in the power of Christ who reigns over all; give witness to Him in word and in deed, regardless of the cost.

Growing threats to justice and peace

3. Still we are moved to repentence as we consider with alarm the rapidity with which the threats to justice and survival have grown since we last met. The frantic race towards nuclear conflagration has accelerated sharply. In an incredibly short period of history, we have moved from the horrors of Hiroshima and Nagasaki, and the threat that they might be repeated elsewhere, to the likelihood, unless we act now, that life on the whole planet could be devastated. A moment of madness, a miscalculated strategic adventure, a chance combination of computer errors, a misperception of the other's intention, an honest mistake—anyone could now set off a nuclear holocaust.

4. As we have been reminded dramatically during this Assembly, nuclear weapons claim victims even in the absence of war, through the lasting effects of nuclear bombings, weapons testing and the dumping of nuclear wastes.

5. For many millions, however, the most immediate threat to survival is not posed by nuclear weapons. Local, national and international conflicts rage around the world. The intersection of East-West and North-South conflicts results in massive injustice, systematic violation of human rights, oppression, homelessness, starvation and death for masses of people. Millions have been rendered stateless, expelled from their homes as refugees or exiles.

6. The World Council of Churches has consistently drawn the attention of the churches to the economic threats to peace. Even without war, thousands perish daily in nations both rich and poor because of hunger and starvation. Human misery and suffering as a result of various forms of injustice have reached levels unprecedented in modern times. There is a resurgence of racism, often in itself a cause of war. Peoples continue to be driven, as a last resort, to take up arms to defend themselves against systemic violence, or to claim their rights to self-determination or independence.

7. While the equivalent of nearly two billion dollars (U.S.) is being expended globally each day for armaments, the world economy is engulfed in a prolonged and deepening crisis which threatens every country and international security. The spectre of trade warfare, competitive devaluation and financial collapse is omnipresent. This crisis has contributed to even greater injustice for the developing countries, denying millions of basic necessities for life. The failure of UNCTAD VI has dashed hopes for meaningful North–South dialogue. While many factors are involved, the link between the arms race and economic development, the effects of rising defense budgets and accelerated reliance on arms production in the industrialised nations, and the ensuing strain on the international system as a whole pose special threats to peace and justice.

No peace without justice

8. The peoples of the world stand in need of peace and justice. Peace is not just the absence of war. Peace cannot be built on foundations of injustice. Peace requires a new international order based on justice for and within all the nations, and respect for the God-given humanity and dignity of every person. Peace is, as the prophet Isaiah has taught us, the effect of righteousness.

9. *The churches today are called to confess anew their faith, and to repent for the times when Christians have remained silent in the face of injustice or threats to peace. The biblical vision of peace with justice for all, of wholeness, of unity for all God's people is not one of several options for the followers of Christ. It is an imperative in our time.*

10. The ecumenical approach to peace and justice is based on the belief that without justice for all everywhere we shall never have peace anywhere. From its inception, peace with justice has been a central concern of the ecumenical movement. The World Council of Churches was conceived amid the rumblings of looming world wars. Ever since it was formed it has condemned war and engaged almost constantly in efforts to prevent war, to aid the victims of war and to keep war from breaking out anew. It has exposed the injustices that lead to conflict, affirmed its solidarity with groups and movements struggling for justice and peace, and sought to establish channels of communication leading to the peaceful resolution of conflicts. It has repeatedly called the attention of the churches and

Appendix: Statement on Peace and Justice 241

through them the governments and the general public to the threats to peace, the threats to survival, and the deepening crisis. *But we face an even more critical situation now. More than ever before, it is imperative that Christians and churches join their struggles for peace and justice.*

Rampant militarism

11. Through the Council's work on militarism since the Fifth Assembly (Nairobi, 1975), we have come to understand more fully the dire consequences for justice of the increasing reliance of the nations on armed force as the cornerstone of their foreign—and often domestic—policies. Priorities have been dangerously distorted. Attention has been drawn away from the fundamental rights and needs of poor nations and of the poor within the rich nations. The number of military regimes has grown, contributing further to a largely male-dominated process of global militarisation. Justice is often sacrificed on the altar of narrowly perceived national security interests. Racial, ethnic, cultural, religious and ideological conflicts are exacerbated, corruption is rife, a spirit of fear and suspicion is fostered through the increasing portrayal of others as the enemy: all this further contributes to disunity, human suffering and increased threats to peace.

12. We strongly reiterate the Central Committee's appeals to the churches to:

   a. challenge military and militaristic policies that lead to disastrous distortions of foreign policy sapping the capacity of the nations of the world to deal with pressing economic and social problems which have become a paramount political issue of our times;
   b. counter the trend to characterise those of other nations and ideologies as the "enemy" through the promotion of hatred and prejudice;
   c. assist in demythologising current doctrines of national security and elaborate new concepts of security based on justice and the rights of the peoples;
   d. grapple with the important theological issues posed by new developments related to war and peace and examine the challenges posed to traditional positions;
   e. pay serious attention to the rights of conscientious objectors;
   f. continue . . . to call attention to the root causes of war, mainly to economic injustice, oppression and exploitation and to the consequences of increasing tension including further restrictions of human rights.

Justice and Security

13. The blatant misuse of the concept of national security to justify repression, foreign intervention and spiralling arms budgets is of profound concern. No nation can pretend to be secure so long as others' legitimate rights to sovereignty and security are neglected or denied. Security can

therefore be achieved only as a common enterprise of nations but security is also inseparable from justice. A concept of "common security" of nations must be reinforced by a concept of "people's security". True security for the people demands respect for human rights, including the right to self-determination, as well as social and economic justice for all within every nation, and a political framework that would ensure it.

Peaceful resolution of conflicts

14. In this connection, the growing refusal of many governments to use the opportunities afforded by the United Nations to preserve international peace and security and for the peaceful resolution of conflicts, or to heed its resolutions is deeply troubling. We call upon the governments to reaffirm their commitment to the United Nations Charter, to submit interstate conflicts to the Security Council at an early stage when resolution may still be possible short of the use of massive armed force, and to cooperate with it in the pursuit of peaceful solutions. *We draw special attention to the United Nations "International Year of Peace" (1986) and the "World Disarmament Campaign", urging the churches to use them as important opportunities for the strengthening of international security and the promotion of disarmament, peace and justice.*

Nuclear weapons and disarmament

15. It is now a full decade since there has been any substantial, subsequently ratified measure of arms control. Since our last Assembly, global military expenditures have tripled. This past year has marked a new peak of confrontation between NATO and the Warsaw Treaty Organization. There is the real prospect, if the current negotiations in Geneva between the USA and the USSR fail to prevent it, that the world stockpile of nuclear weapons may increase dramatically in the next decade. The growing sophistication, accuracy and mobility of new generations of weapons now ready for deployment or currently being designed make them more dangerous and destabilising than ever before. The failure of arms control among nuclear weapon states has made the non-proliferation treaty, in practice, an instrument of invidious discrimination, inciting the spread of nuclear weapons, and compounding the prospects for nuclear war in several areas of regional tension in the southern hemisphere. Until the superpowers move decisively toward nuclear disarmament, efforts to contain nuclear proliferation are bound to fail.

16. *We call upon the churches, especially those in Europe, both East and West, and in North America, to redouble their efforts to convince their governments to reach a negotiated settlement and to turn away now, before it is too late, from plans to deploy additional or new nuclear weapons in Europe, and to begin immediately to reduce and then eliminate altogether present nuclear forces.*

17. *We urge the churches, as well, to intensify their efforts to stop the rapidly growing deployment of nuclear weapons and support systems in the Indian and*

Appendix: Statement on Peace and Justice 243

Pacific Oceans, and to press their governments to withdraw from or refuse to base or service ships or airplanes bearing nuclear weapons in those regions.

18. The risk of nuclear war is compounded by the rapidly escalating reliance on conventional weapons. Stockpiles of non-nuclear weapons of mass destruction and indiscriminate effect are growing almost uncontrolled. The volume of highly profitable trade in conventional weapons has nearly doubled in the past five years, a very large part of it in the direction of the developing nations and regions where armed conflict already defies containment. The destructive power of these weapons steadily increases, blurring the distinction between conventional and nuclear warfare; and many nuclear disarmament strategies call for major increases in conventional arms production and deployment.

19. Since the Nairobi Assembly, a number of consultations and conferences have been held by the WCC, providing churches with opportunities to deepen their understanding of these issues. From them have come valuable reports and recommendations to the churches for concrete action. The most recent was the Public Hearing on Nuclear Weapons and Disarmament (Amsterdam, 1981). The published report contains careful, thoroughgoing analyses and spells out urgent tasks for the churches. We urge the churches once again to study attentively these reports and to pursue their recommendations.

20. The Central Committee urged the churches to pay special attention to and take clear positions on a number of points developed in the report of the Amsterdam Hearing. We reiterate that appeal with respect to the following:

   a. a nuclear war can under no circumstances, in no region and by no social system be just or justifiable, given the fact that the magnitude of devastation caused by it will be far out of proportion to any conceivable benefit or advantage to be derived from it;
   b. nuclear war is unlikely to remain limited, and therefore any contemplation of "limited" use of nuclear weapons should be discouraged as dangerous from the outset;
   c. all nations now possessing nuclear weapons or capable of doing so in the foreseeable future should unequivocally renounce policies of "first use", as an immediate step towards building confidence;
   d. the concept of deterrence, the credibility of which depends on the possible use of nuclear weapons, is to be rejected as morally unacceptable and as incapable of safeguarding peace and security in the long-term;
   e. the production and deployment of nuclear weapons, as well as their use, constitute a crime against humanity, and therefore there should be a complete halt in the production of nuclear weapons and in weapons research and development in all nations, to be expeditiously enforced through a treaty; such a position supports the struggle to cause one's own nation to commit itself never to own or use nuclear weapons, despite the period of nuclear vulnerability, and to en-

courage and stand in solidarity with Christians and others who refuse to cooperate with or accept employment in any projects related to nuclear weapons and nuclear warfare;
f. all nations should agree to and ratify a comprehensive test ban treaty as a necessary step to stopping the further development of nuclear weapons technology;
g. all means leading to disarmament, both nuclear and conventional, should be welcomed as complementary and mutually reinforcing: multilateral conferences leading to effective decisions, bilateral negotiations pursued with daring and determination and unilateral initiatives leading to the relaxation of tensions and building of mutual confidence among nations and peoples.

21. In addition, we urge the churches to press their governments to abstain from any further research, production or deployment of weapons in space; and to prohibit the development and production of all weapons of mass destruction or indiscriminate effect, including chemical and biological means.

Challenge to the churches

22. In our efforts since the last Assembly to accomplish the purpose of the World Council of Churches "to express the common concern of the churches in the service of human need, the breaking down of barriers between people, and the promotion of one human family in justice and peace", we have been encouraged and strengthened by the movement of the Holy Spirit among us, leading the churches to undertake new initiatives. In this process of conversion the insights and the leadership of women and youth have often been decisive. But our common faith and the times now demand much more of us as stewards of God's Creation.

23. Christians cannot view the dangers of this moment as inherent in the nature of things. Nor can we give ourselves over to despair. As believers in One Lord and Saviour, Jesus Christ, the Prince of Peace, we are stewards of God's hope for the future of creation. We know God's love and confess a Lord of history in whom we have the promise of the fullness of life. God's mercy is everlasting, and the Holy Spirit is moving among us, kindling the love which drives out fear, renewing our vision of peace, stirring our imaginations, leading us through the wilderness, freeing us and uniting us. The peoples of the world are coming to their feet in growing numbers, demanding justice, crying out for peace. These are present signs of hope.

24. We have recognized that our approaches to justice and peace often differ, as do the starting points for discussion among the churches, due to the wide diversity of our histories, traditions and the contexts in which we live and witness. *We call upon the churches now to:*
   a. *intensify their efforts to develop a common witness in a divided world, confronting with renewed vigor the threats to peace and survival and engaging in struggles for justice and human dignity;*

Appendix: Statement on Peace and Justice

    b. *become a living witness to peace and justice through prayer, worship and concrete involvement;*
    c. *take steps toward unity through providing more frequent opportunities for sharing in and among the churches in order to learn more about and understand better each other's perspectives, defying every attempt to divide or separate us;* and
    d. *develop more innovative approaches to programmes of education for peace and justice.*

25. According to the 1980 Geneva Convention, the use of certain weapons of indiscriminate effect is forbidden under international law. We believe nuclear weapons must be considered within that category. We join in the conviction drawn by the Panel of the WCC Public Hearing on Nuclear Weapons and disarmament after it had examined the testimony of a broad range of expert witnesses:
"*We believe that the time has come when the churches must unequivocally declare that the production and deployment as well as the use of nuclear weapons are a crime against humanity and that such activities must be condemned on ethical and theological grounds.* The nuclear weapons issue is, in its import and threat to humanity, a question of Christian discipline and faithfulness to the Gospel. We recognize that nuclear weapons will not disappear because of such an affirmation by the churches. But it will involve the churches and their members in a fundamental examination of their own implicit or explicit support of policies which, implicitly explicitly, are based on the possession and use of these weapons."
We urge the churches to press their governments, especially in those countries which have nuclear weapons capabilities, to elaborate and ratify an international legal instrument which would outlaw as a crime against humanity the possession as well as the use of nuclear arms. We ask the churches as well to urge their governments to acknowledge the right of conscientious objection to military service and to provide opportunities for non-violent alternative service.

26. On the same basis, and in the spirit of the Fifth Assembly's appeal to the churches "to emphasize their readiness to live without the protection of armaments", *we believe that Christians should give witness to their unwillingness to participate in any conflict involving weapons of mass destruction or indiscriminate effect.*

27. It is with a deep sense of pastoral responsibility that we make these affirmations. To live up to them will be no simple matter for any Christian or church, but we recognize that the consequences of taking such positions will be far more serious for some than for others. We state these convictions not as condemnation or in judgement of others, but confessing our own weakness, *calling on the churches and Christians to support one another in love as in these ways we seek together to be faithful to our common calling to proclaim and serve in our one Lord, Jesus Christ, the Prince of Peace, the Life of the World.*

their members in a fundamental examination of their own implicit or explicit support of policies which, implicitly explicitly, are based on the possession and use of these weapons."

We urge the churches to press their governments, especially in those countries which have nuclear weapons capabilities, to elaborate and ratify an international legal instrument which would outlaw as a crime against humanity the possession as well as the use of nuclear arms. We ask the churches as well to urge their governments to acknowledge the right of conscientious objection to military service and to provide opportunities for non-violent alternative service.

26. On the same basis, and in the spirit of the Fifth Assembly's appeal to the churches "to emphasize their readiness to live without the protection of armaments", *we believe that Christians should give witness to their unwillingness to participate in any conflict involving weapons of mass destruction or indiscriminate effect.*

27. It is with a deep sense of pastoral responsibility that we make these affirmations. To live up to them will be no simple matter for any Christian or church, but we recognize that the consequences of taking such positions will be far more serious for some than for others. We state these convictions not as condemnation or in judgement of others, but confessing our own weakness, *calling on the churches and Christians to support one another in love as in these ways we seek together to be faithful to our common calling to proclaim and serve in our one Lord, Jesus Christ, the Prince of Peace, the Life of the World.*